Introduction to Computer Science

Introduction to Computer Science

P. M. Banks
J. R. Doupnik

Department of Applied Physics and Information Science
University of California, San Diego

 John Wiley & Sons, Inc.
New York • London • Sydney • Toronto

Library of Congress Cataloging in Publication Data:

Banks, Peter M
  Introduction to computer science.

  Includes bibliographies and index.
  1. Electronic digital computers—Programming.
    I. Doupnik, J. R., 1938- joint author. II. Title.

QA76.6.B353   001.6′42   75-20407
ISBN 0-471-04710-4

Printed in the United States of America

10 9 8 7 6 5 4 3 2 1

Preface

This book is directed towards first and second year college and university students of general background who are entering a first course in computers, computing, and computer science. For most students, and especially those in the Humanities, such a course represents an abrupt change in the pattern of their earlier studies, demanding a rapid integration of new ideas and techniques. Nevertheless, these students are keenly interested in computers as possible tools and as legitimate objects of social concern.

Our experience indicates that considerable care must be taken in choosing the curriculum of the introductory course. Students are strongly motivated by the "hands-on" approach of computer programming, often so much so that they neglect theoretical ideas relating to the development of computer science. One successful approach, adopted in this book, is to initially emphasize the problem-solving character of computers providing, through flowcharts and a flowchart language, a logical framework for reducing complex problems to algorithmic form. Later, as the students gain skill in a particular computing language taught in parallel with this material, more abstract concepts concerning computer organization and operation can be introduced.

Within the text, considerable emphasis has been placed upon the development of problem-solving skills. The problems at the end of each chapter are appropriate for programming purposes and have been chosen to expand students' appreciation of the use of computers as tools to extend human capabilities of analysis. To a large extent, the problems are nonmathematical in character, relying as much as possible upon simple computations mixed with various levels of decision making.

In the initial chapter the historical development of computers and computing devices is traced in some detail. Such material represents our effort to provide humanities students with an abbreviated view of the way in which concepts of numbers and computation have developed. Although some may regard computer science as a discipline without historical perspective, the development of computers and their related internal organization provides an interesting view of the mutual dependence of developing technology and the philosophy of computation.

In the chapters immediately following the development of flowcharts and problem solving skills, material relating to the internal operation of computers is given, culminating in discussions of programs expressed in simple assembly language. Execution of assembly language problems on a computer is difficult at this level of development, so most problems were solved on paper. In teaching this material, it has been found useful to introduce *CARDIAC*, a *card*board *i*llustrative *a*id to *c*omputation developed by the Bell Telephone Laboratories.[1] CARDIAC is simple in operation, yet allows students to practice many of the basic aspects of stored-instruction programs.

In the final two chapters, binary arithmetic and Boolean algebra are introduced and applied to the design of logic networks. In our own courses, these topics have met with considerable enthusiasm from students lacking previous mathematical training.

The order of presentation of topics in this book follows that of an introductory one quarter (10 week) course given at the University of California, San Deigo. Lectures covering the first two chapters were given during the first week. During the subsequent 5 to 6 weeks the topics of Chapters Three and Four were presented in parallel with instruction in a specific programming language (ALGOL or FORTRAN in our case). During the final three to four weeks, the students continued to develop their programming skills through a variety of homework assignments, while emphasis in the main lectures shifted to topics taken from Chapters Five through Ten. At the end of this course, students could continue to expand their interests in digital computers through a subsequent 10 week course devoted to system programming with application to computer software and information-handling problems in the Humanities. A final 10 week course, aimed at students with some mathemati-

---

[1] D. Hagelbarger and S. Fingerman, *CARDIAC*, A cardboard illustrative aid to computation, Bell System Educational Aid, Bell Telephone Laboratories, 1970.

cal training, gave an introduction to numerical algorithms, again with emphasis upon computer usage.

The level of the material presented here is appropriate for Humanities students in their first 2 years of college or university. More technically inclined students at 2 or 4 year colleges can be expected to make extensive use of the more mathematically oriented topics relating to Boolean algebra and the design of logic circuits. Although it has not been possible to eliminate all mathematical concepts, we have attempted to emphasize the non-numerical aspects of digital computers, keeping the level of instruction within reach of students possessing a normal high school mathematics background. Thus, simple computations and calculations remain as the conceptual mainstay of instruction in the basic computer languages and the presentation of this text.

We would like to acknowledge the assistance given us by the staff of the Department of Applied Physics and Information Science and express our thanks for valuable criticism from our students and various instructors, especially Dr. T. H. Hankins.

P. M. BANKS
J. R. DOUPNIK
La Jolla, California

Contents

six

How a Computer Stores Information   199

seven

Computer Instructions   231

eight

Putting Instructions to Work 263

nine

Binary Arithmetic for Computers 293

ten

Boolean Algebra 313

Appendices 347

Index 357

Introduction to Computer Science

one

Numbers, Calculations, and Modern Computers

1

COUNTING AND CALCULATIONS

Numerals, numbers, and arithmetic.

Widespread knowledge of simple calculation makes it easy for us to forget that common use of Arabic numerals and memorized steps of addition, subtraction, multiplication, and division only began in the Middle Ages. Prior to the sixteenth century, numbers in the Western civilizations were written using Roman, Hebrew, Greek, or similar numerals in ways quite different from today's system. (See Figure 1.1.) These older forms of number expression generally lacked the ease of modern written computations and it is not surprising that alternative methods of calculation were developed. These methods, now mostly forgotten in our technology of slide rules, calculators, and digital computers, were based on sophisticated forms of finger counting and mechanical aids such as the ancient counting table and the abacus.

This text is concerned with the ideas surrounding modern digital computers. These machines, combining advanced electronic technology with an internal structure based on the principles of mathematical logic, are a singular invention of our age. Nevertheless, the use of mechanical aids for solving computational problems is not a development unique to the twentieth century. Long before mankind guessed at the laws of electricity or developed its present skill in building machines, repeated attempts were made to ease the tiresome burden of computations arising from the exchange of monies, trading of goods and the complexities of government finance and record keeping. As we shall see, these attempts were at first satisfied by the use of hand and finger computations, followed later by the development of mechanical computing aids in the form of the early Greek and Roman counting boards. From these beginnings a chain of successive computational tools can be traced through the later forms of the abacus; the seventeenth century inventions of calculating rods and the slide rule; the later ingenious mechanical computing machines of Pascal, Leibniz and others; the analytical engines of Babbage; and on to the use of electronic devices in the 1930s.

FIGURE 1.1. Multiplication with old Roman numerals.

The modern digital computer has emerged from these extensive foundations as a synthesis of mechanical, mathematical, and electrical inventions. It is now generally recognized that a computer is a machine which not only works with numbers but, even more importantly, acts as a device which can store and process nonnumerical information. Examples of computer uses are found in language translation programs, airline reservation systems, air traffic control networks, newspaper composition, medical diagnosis and control, and a myriad of other applications.

It is in the area of data processing and decision making that computers most directly affect us. The complexities of our technical civilization continually demand choices among alternatives and accountings based upon vast amounts of information which, in turn, requires special storage and rapid processing. Within this context the term *digital computer* is misleading, since the older ideas of computation and number processing have been outgrown and modern general computers are designed to deal equally well with numerical and nonnumerical data.

To gain a better perspective of the roles played by digital computers, it is useful to first emphasize their numerical character while examining the ways counting and simple calculations were done in the past. Such an approach leads in a natural manner through the development of scientific computation into the much broader areas of electronic data processing and the way computers are presently used to manipulate general forms of information.

As we know, our modern concepts of numerals, numbers, and computations were not created at their present level of sophistication, but rather matured slowly during several thousands of years in many different civilizations before emerging as a remarkably outstanding achievement of human intellect. In tracing the development of number symbols and the way numbers were constructed in the past, there occurs an inevitable intertwining of the methods of number expression with the basic procedures of arithmetic calculation. For the present, it is sufficient to focus our attention first upon the way simple calculations were made before the age of the modern digital computer. The parallel discussion of the development of numbers and number expressions will be deferred until Chapter five when a more complex treatment of computer data storage can be given.

FINGER COUNTING

While the number symbols of most ancient civilizations are known from various preserved writings, the different ways these people actually made their calculations remain hidden. Even in the case of Egypt during the age of the Pharoahs, the large number of papyri dealing with agriculture, mathematics, and government give almost no information about their methods of practical arithmetic. However, through simple experiment it can be shown that, with the exception of the Babylonians at the time of Hammurabi (1800 B.C.), the number symbols of the early civilizations, including those of the Egyptians, Greeks, and Romans, made calculations involving multiplication and division extremely impractical.† Nevertheless, the ordinary aspects of life even in these early eras demanded a basic level of arithmetic competence. How then were the essential calculations of these civilizations actually done?

From many different pieces of evidence it is reasonably certain that computational problems in the early Mediterranean and Mesopotamian civilizations were probably solved through recourse to counting methods involving both the use of fingers (See Figure 1.2.) and specially ruled counting boards with movable markers. These devices were not simply ways of keeping track of

†An outstanding example of the difficulty of Egyptian arithmetic is given by the Rhind papyrus. For a complete description see J. R. Newman, "The Rhind Papyrus," *The World of Mathematics,* ed. J. R. Newman (New York: Simon & Schuster, 1956), p. 170.

FIGURE 1.2. The number 800 shown on the fingers. This illustration is taken from the twelfth century copy of Bede's eighth century treatise on finger counting (from D.E. Smith, *History of Mathematics*, 1928).

numbers, but rather provided a medium for actually making numerical calculations.

The role of finger counting in early arithmetic is particularly difficult to
assess owing to the lack of any extensive historical description. Apparently
this method of number representation was developed in classical antiquity
and served as a principal means of ordinary computation until the Middle
Ages. In fact, the basic idea of finger counting is still commonly used by
Indian and Arab traders of the Middle East.

The positions of the fingers used to represent numerals in medieval times
have been preserved for us through the writings of the eighth century English
Benedictine monastic, the Venerable Bede. As shown in Figure 1.3, numbers
were formed through the grouping of fingers bent entirely over *(digitii)* or
bent at the joint *(articuli)*. The relationship between the term *digit* and the
first nine numerals of the counting series (1 to 9) originated from finger counting. We should also note that the formation of numbers in finger counting
followed the positional or *place-value* system in which the relative position of
the digits is vital; for example, 15 differs from 51. (See Figure 1.3.) Starting
with the left hand, the first rank of units was formed with three fingers (little,
ring, and middle); the tens rank was formed with the index finger and thumb;
and the right hand contained the hundreds rank (thumb and index finger) and
the thousands rank. Thus, a form of our modern place-value system was in
common use long before the adoption of Arabic numerals or the incorporation
of such ideas into the written numbers of the Greek or Roman Eras. When a
number is formed on the fingers and shown to another person using this
system, the order of the ranks—units, tens, hundreds, and so forth—is precisely right to left (i.e., the same ordering used in our present place-value
notation).

Computations were also done on the hands through clever steps which
permitted addition, subtraction, and multiplication to be accomplished with
some ease. Two interesting quotations from Leonardo of Pisa (1180—1250
A.D.), known to the world of mathematics as Fibonacci, give an idea of the
importance of numbers formed by fingers:

> If these numerals of the Indians (the Arabic numerals) and their place-value nota-
> tion are to be thoroughly mastered through constant practice, it behooves those who
> would become adept and expert in the art of computation to learn to count on the
> fingers, which masters the computation according to the old manner once found to
> be invaluable.

and

> . . . multiplication with the fingers must be practiced constantly, so that the mind
> like the hands becomes more adept at adding and multiplying various numbers.‡

‡Quoted by K. Menninger, *Number Words and Number Symbols* (Cambridge: MIT Press, 1969).

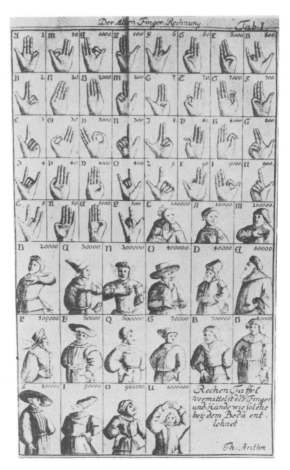

FIGURE 1.3. An illustration of the positions for finger counting, taken from Jacob Leupold' *Theatrum Arithmetico-Geometricum*, published 1727.

The rules governing computations using the finger numbers are not known today, but D. E. Smith, in *The History of Mathematics*, (Dover Publications), has outlined various methods which may have been used. (See Figure 1.4.)

COUNTING BOARDS

The use of hands was adequate for simple arithmetic, but obvious difficulties existed both for the representation of large numbers and the dexterity needed to do complicated calculations. These problems were overcome two

FIGURE 1.4. Two Roman counters showing the numbers VIIII and VIII formed with the hand. These counters probably date from the first century AD.

to three thousand years ago through the development of special counting boards in which movable markers could be arranged to represent numbers. (See Figure 1.5.) While the origin of counting boards is hidden in the past, there is some evidence that both finger counting and counting boards were used as early as 1000 B.C. in the Babylonian and Egyptian civilizations. As practical aids to computation, counting boards continued in use through the decline of the Roman Empire. Following a period of disuse in medieval times, counting boards reappeared as the ubiquitous reckoning boards of merchants, traders, and government officials throughout Europe in the Middle Ages. Their popularity declined in Western Civilization only with the adoption in the 1500s of written computations made with Arabic numerals and place-value notation.

The face of a typical counting board is shown in Figure 1.5. Each ruled column represents a separate rank for the number of units, tens, hundreds, and so forth. A number such as 15,408 is represented on the board by placing the appropriate number of counters in the proper columns. Addition and subtraction of numbers is easily done through movement of the markers onto or away from the board. For multiplication and division more advanced

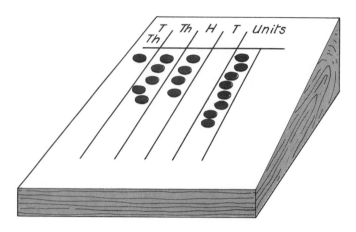

FIGURE 1.5. The face of a counting board showing the number 15,408

FIGURE 1.6. This reproduction shows a competition between advocates of hand and counter arithmetic. (The Bettman Archive.)

methods were used which involved essentially the same steps we use today in making written computations. (See Figure 1.6.)

The counting boards of the early Greeks were frequently built as tables with inscribed rulings on the flat upper surface. (See Figure 1.7.) Although different methods of forming the rank values of the columns are found at various places and times (ranks of five, fifty, and five hundred were often added to reduce the number of counters needed to represent a number), in one form or another counting boards were widely used for making calculations through the Middle Ages and references to their use are often found in the art and writings of these periods. The scholar Karl Menninger quotes the will of an English dyer who, in 1493, wrote:

> Also I bequethe to Kateryn my wyff my countour standing in my parlour, with this condition, that she bye another for my daughter Anneys . . .

Menninger has also pointed out that another counting table can be found in the famous Greek ceremonial Darius Vase of the fourth century B.C. (See Figure 1.8.) In part of the decorative drawings on this vase is a Persian treasurer counting tribute offered by conquered tribes. While the ruled columns of the board are missing, the Boetian (a province of modern Greece) number symbols at the top represent place-values with counters giving the number 1731 4/6.†

The use of counting boards and finger counting presents one aspect of an interesting problem of intellectual consistency. Before 1500 A.D. written numbers were usually expressed with Roman numerals in which value is generally given by the grouping and counting of symbols rather than by their position relative to each other (we could call this face-value rather than place-value). Thus, the number 1973 was written as (1)DCCCCLXXIII with

†A more complete description of this vase is given by K. Menninger, *Number Words and Number Symbols* (Cambridge: MIT Press, 1969).

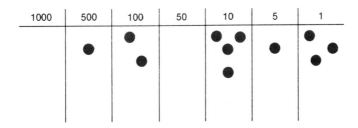

| 1000 | 500 | 100 | 50 | 10 | 5 | 1 |

FIGURE 1.7. A counting board with intermediate ranks used to reduce the number of counters.

FIGURE 1.8. The Darius Vase (A), dating from the fourth century BC, and an enlargement (B) of the lower section which shows a calculator tallying tribune using a counting table with markers.

10

the symbols (1) = M= 1000, D = 500, C = 100, L = 50, X = 10, V = 5 and I = 1. For practical computations, however, we have seen that the much more sophisticated notions of place-value numbers were used and numbers were represented, either on the hands or the counting board, with a decimal (power of ten) rank system. This contradiction between number writing and number calculating continued in the western world for more than 2500 years. The contradiction gradually vanished as the Hindu-Arabic system of numerals and number representation became more widely known in the centuries following its introduction into Europe at the end of the Middle Ages.

THE ABACUS

The Roman counting table remained in use for many centuries and probably inspired development of the more portable *abacus*. (During the Middle Ages, the counting table itself was called an abacus.) In its original form the Roman hand abacus was constructed as a brass tablet with eight grooves, along which were placed groups of movable spheres. Place-value notation was used so that each groove represented a decimal rank. To reduce the number of spheres, collections of five spheres in a given rank were indicated by moving a single separate sphere upward into a special space above the rank, as shown in Figure 1.9.

Such a simple calculating device was ideally suited for simple problems of addition and subtraction. Its influence upon the western European civilization was never great, but its introduction into China during the twelfth century may have led to the development of the *suan pan* in which the spheres in grooves became beads on wires and various minor changes in number representation were made. The *suan pan* later became popular as the *soroban* (See Figure 1.10.) in Japan after the sixteenth century and, again in Russia, as the *Scet*. Surprisingly, it is difficult to overemphasize the importance of these different forms of the abacus as computing tools in eastern countries. Modern markets, offices, banks, and hotels all use the abacus as a principal instrument of computation, relying upon skilled operators who are able to do all arithmetic operations with unbelievable speed.

THE TRIUMPH OF THE ALGORITHMICISTS

ARITHMETIC is where you have to multiply, and carry the multiplication table around in your head and hope you don't lose it.

CARL SANDBURG

Our present system of written numerals appears to have evolved from Indian Brahmi numerals dating to 200 B.C. Place-value notation was already in

FIGURE 1.9. A Roman hand abacus.

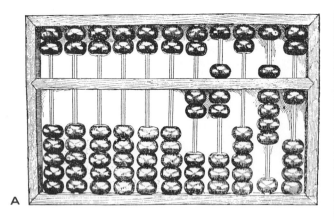

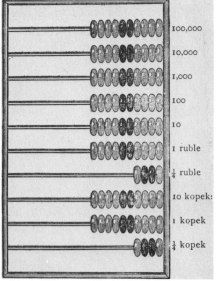

FIGURE 1.10. (A) Modern Chinese abacus. (The Bettman Archive.) (B) A Russian abacus. (The Bettman Archive.)

FIGURE 1.10. (C) A Japanese soroban.

use by 1800 B.C. in Mesopotamia, but whether this exerted influence upon later development in India is not known. By 600 A.D. the precursor of our modern number system was in limited use in parts of India. The Islamic mathematicians and astronomers of the seventh and eighth centuries were the first to benefit from the new system. The rapid extension of the Islamic civilization to the edges of the Mediterranean introduced Arabic numerals and place-value numbers to the western civilization. Probably the single most important event in this transfer was a small arithmetic text written in the ninth century by the mathematician Abu Jafar Muhammad ibn Musa al-Khwarizmi (Mohammad, the father of Jafar and the son of Musa, the Khwarizmian). This text and a second established the name of algebra. *Hisab aljabr w'almugabala (The Book of Restoration and Equalization)* had a profound influence in the West. With the book's arrival in Europe during the twelfth century, a new system of numbers and method of calculation was introduced at a time when there was a resurgence in intellectual activity. Al-Khwarizmi, known as Algorismus in Latin manuscripts, provided a detailed exposition on the new numerals, which was eventually transcribed into forms for practical teaching throughout Europe.

Widespread use of the Arabic system was encouraged in the early 1500s by the invention of printing and the publication of several popular arithmetic texts in Germany, France, and England. (See Figure 1.11.) Even with this impetus, however, the transition from the old system of Roman numerals and reckoning tables to the new numbers and memorized steps of Algorismus was neither rapid nor uniform. The prints reproduced in the Figures 1.12 and 13 dramatize the sixteenth century arguments and competitions between the algorithmicists (written computationalists) and the abacists. Eventually, however, the advantages of the new number system became known and new generations coped more successfully with the problems of practical finance, trading, and other interests of a rapidly developing civilization.

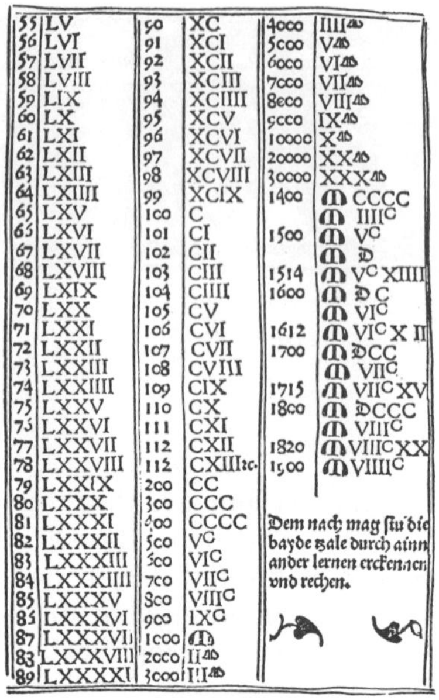

55	LV	90	XC	4000	IIII^{M}
56	LVI	91	XCI	5000	V^{M}
57	LVII	92	XCII	6000	VI^{M}
58	LVIII	93	XCIII	7000	VII^{M}
59	LIX	94	XCIIII	8000	VIII^{M}
60	LX	95	XCV	9000	IX^{M}
61	LXI	96	XCVI	10000	X^{M}
62	LXII	97	XCVII	20000	XX^{M}
63	LXIII	98	XCVIII	30000	XXX^{M}
64	LXIIII	99	XCIX	1400	M CCCC
65	LXV	100	C		M IIII^{C}
66	LXVI	101	CI	1500	M V^{C}
67	LXVII	102	CII		M D
68	LXVIII	103	CIII	1514	M V^{C} XIIII
69	LXIX	104	CIIII	1600	M D C
70	LXX	105	CV		M VI^{C}
71	LXXI	106	CVI	1612	M VI^{C} X II
72	LXXII	107	CVII	1700	M DCC
73	LXXIII	108	CVIII		M VII^{C}
74	LXXIIII	109	CIX	1715	M VII^{C} XV
75	LXXV	110	CX	1800	M DCCC
76	LXXVI	111	CXI		M VIII^{C}
77	LXXVII	112	CXII	1820	M VIII^{C} XX
78	LXXVIII	113	CXIII ꝛc.	1900	M VIIII^{C}
79	LXXIX	200	CC		
80	LXXX	300	CCC		
81	LXXXI	400	CCCC	Dem nach mag ſtu die	
82	LXXXII	500	V^{C}	bayde zale durch ainn	
83	LXXXIII	600	VI^{C}	ander lernen erkennen	
84	LXXXIIII	700	VII^{C}	vnd rechen.	
85	LXXXV	800	VIII^{C}		
86	LXXXVI	900	IX^{C}		
87	LXXXVII	1000	M		
88	LXXXVIII	2000	II^{M}		
89	LXXXXI	3000	III^{M}		

FIGURE 1.11. A page from Köbel's *Rechenbiechlin* (1514), which was intended to instruct students in the use of arabic numbers.

NEW TOOLS

The increasing influence of the algorithmicists in the early 1500s led to a rapid spread in the use of Arabic numerals and place-value numbers. It also provided new tools for the study of mathematics at a time when science and technology were rapidly developing. The invention of logarithms by John Napier in the late 1500s, for example, could only have developed from the immensely practical place-value number system. Tables of logarithms facilitated astronomical and other arithmetical calculations in ways scarcely imaginable without the new numbers. And logarithms, with their obvious advantages in multiplying, dividing, and finding roots of numbers, gave a basis for the invention of a new computational tool, the multiplying rod, by Edmond Gunter in 1625. Since logarithms permitted products and quotients to be found through addition and subtraction, Gunter inscribed logarithmic divisions on movable wooden sticks and created a primitive form of the slide rule. Today such a mechanical aid is called an *analog* device, because it represents numbers through a physical correspondence—in this case the sum or difference of two lengths along the wood sticks.

FIGURE 1.12. A woodblock showing calculators in competition with a counting board and written numerals. Pythagoras is to the right of the female figure of Arithmetic. On the left sits Boëthius with computations in Indian numerals. From the *Margarita Philosophica* of Reisch, 1503.

15

FIGURE 1.13. The method of counting on the lines is shown by this woodblock print taken from the title page of Köbel's *Rechenbiechlin* (1514).

A more ingenious multiplying tool was invented by Napier in the early seventeenth century using the Italian idea of diagonal lattice multiplication. As shown below, in diagonal lattice notation the product of one number such as 8432, by another such as 7 can be obtained by multiplying each digit of 8432 by 7 (i.e. $8432 \times 7 = 14 + 210 + 2800 + 56{,}000$).

$$
\begin{array}{r}
8432 \\
\times\,7 \\
\hline
14 \\
21 \\
28 \\
56 \\
\hline
59{,}024
\end{array}
$$

In the lattice method (see Figure 1.14), each of the two-digit products (ignoring the final zeros) are written in diagonally divided squares with the ten's digit put in the upper left part and the unit's digit in the lower right part.

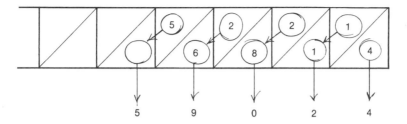

FIGURE 1.14. The lattice method of summing the products of a multiplication. Each partial product is placed in a separate box divided into two parts. The final product is found by summing downwards to the left along the diagonals.

Starting from the right, if we now sum downwards along the diagonals, (being sure to move in the correct direction) we automatically make the rank to rank carries of multiplication and obtain the final product, 59,024.

Napier took this idea to create mechanical "calculating rods". As shown in Figure 1.15, this device was composed of wooden rods which were subdivided into squares and diagonal lines. Each rod was inscribed with the multiples of a particular digit: 3, 6, 9 . . . 36 for 3; 9, 18, 27 . . . 81 for 9; and so on. To make a multiplication such as 4321 × 123, the rods for 4, 3, 2, and 1 would be gathered in order and the partial products 4321 × 3, 4321 × 20, and 4321 × 100 could be immediately obtained by summing along the diagonals in the row given by the proper digit of the second factor (indicated with Roman numerals to avoid confusion). (See Figure 1.16). This tool for calculating, while still requiring the aid of humans for motive power and organization, was a first, rather small, step towards the fully-automatic mechanical calculation achieved a few years later.

Soon after the Napier's invention of calculating rods (also known as Napier's bones) in 1614, more advanced mechanical calculators were built synthesizing the developing technologies of watchmaking, metallurgy, and engineering. The details of these devices varied, but all used both linear and angular motions of moving rods and geared wheels with attached numbers to make computations. An example of these converging technologies was the Pascaline calculator of Pascal (see Figure 1.17), built in 1643 to demonstrate the way cogged wheels could be interconnected to carry out simple arithmetic. In the Pascaline, addition was achieved through successive rotations of nine-step cogged wheels which, in the tenth rotation, would activate a carry lever capable of rotating the next higher decimal wheel by one notch.

Another more sophisticated machine capable of performing all four arithmetic operations was designed and built in 1694 by the German

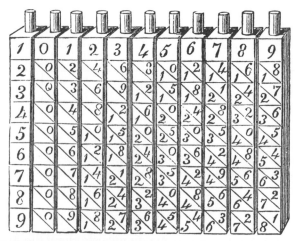

FIGURE 1.15 Napier's calculating rods. (The Bettman Archive.)

philosopher-politician-mathematician, Gottfried von Leibnitz. (See Figure 1.18.) Constructed to a new design which was based upon a principle of stepped-wheels, this new calculator was not dependable in operation and it remained as a technical curiosity of no practical importance.

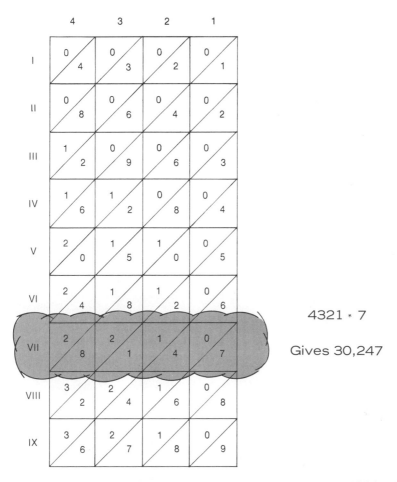

FIGURE 1.16. Assembly of Napier's calculating rods to evaluate 4321 × 7.

As it turned out, more than 120 years were to pass before Charles Thomas, a French insurance executive, was able to synthesize the engineering developments of his age to perfect the internal design of an accurate, computing machine. The Arithometer, first available in 1820, was the first commercial calculator widely used for business accounting. Unfortunately, its mechanism was complicated by large numbers of cog wheels and springs which were difficult to keep in adjustment. Nevertheless, the Arithometer was a practical success and different models of this device are still in use in France.

Further progress toward a dependable mechanical calculator was made in the last half of the nineteenth century through the mechanical abilities of the American inventors George Grant, Dorr Felt, and William Burroughs. Grant

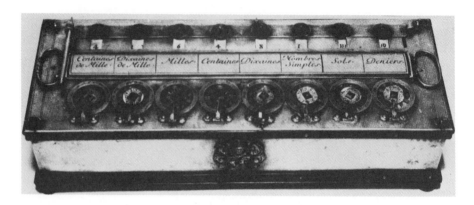

FIGURE 1.17. View of the Pascaline mechanical calculating engine created by Blaise Pascal in 1643.

FIGURE 1.18. The internal mechanism of the Leibniz calculating machine constructed in 1694. Digit values were indicated by the dials.

was an expert on the technical problems of gears. Convolute, spiral, spur, cycloidal, pin-tooth and worm gears are but a few of the basic types he studied and applied to the improvement of Thomas' Arithometer. Still, it was Dorr Felt who was able to look beyond the narrow world of gears to apply the ideas of ratchets and key–driven wheels. Through these additions, Felt developed in 1885 the technical design of the modern mechanical calculator. The first commercial models, produced the next year, were called Comptometers (See Figure 1.19)—business machines which remained unsurpassed in the calculator market for 20 years.

With the widespread availability of mechanical calculators, the toil of arithmetic operations was immediately reduced. It quickly became apparent, however, that most businesses and banks needed not just the results of arithmetic, but also permanent printed records of the actual computations. An attempt to provide such records was made by Felt in the 1880s with a complicated combination of calculator (the Comptometer) and printer. As time passed it was found that while the Comptometer was a successful calculating machine, it did not provide the simplicity needed for a permanent recording calculating system.

William S. Burroughs began his adult life as an accountant in a small bank in New York. Owing to failing eyesight brought about by the strain of bookkeeping, Burroughs left the bank after 5 years to become a mechanic in a machine shop. Motivated by his banking experience, he, too, began to design a simple recording adding machine. After several years marked by extensive practical difficulties, Burroughs completed his designs and found financial support to construct a calculator that could do accurate decimal addition and record the final answer on paper.

FIGURE 1.19. The Comptometer, the first key-driven calculating machine.

In 1886 an improved version of this printer-calculator was able to record numbers as they were entered into the machine, gave intermediate subtotals as the additions were made, and printed the final total. To market the printer–calculator, in 1886 Burroughs created the American Arithometer Company. Success quickly compounded success as business persons, bankers and accountants learned to depend upon mechanical computations. In 1905 the American Arithometer Company became the Burroughs Adding Machine Company, the forerunner of the Burroughs Corporation, one of the largest American corporations manufacturing digital computers and electronic data processing equipment today.

Mechanical printing calculators are still in common use today in homes and small businesses. In internal design, however, the basic ideas have not changed greatly from those developed by Felt and Burroughs in the 1880s. Electrical calculators first became possible in the 1920s when it was apparent that simple electrical devices could replace complex mechanical assemblies of gears, rods and wheels. The early electrical designs used relays (which are simple switches controlled by electromagnets) to represent digits of numbers. By making the proper connections between different relays, it was possible to do rapid and accurate arithmetic calculations. As technology advanced, relays were discarded in favor of vacuum tubes, then solid state transistors, and finally integrated circuits. Shown in Figure 1.20 the electronic hand calculator is a product of these revolutionary advances.

Looking into the past, we can see a remarkable progress in the development of computational tools. In less than 500 years civilization has progressed from rudimentary ideas about numbers to pocket-sized electronic devices which can do ordinary arithmetic, compute logarithms, take roots of numbers, evaluate trigonometric functions, and perform any number of other sophisticated operations in a fraction of a second.

With such progress it is fair to ask the question: Has the ultimate goal of the search for computational aid been achieved?

BUT WHAT ABOUT COMPUTERS?

Up to this point we have traced the development of numbers and computational aids but very little has been said about digital computers. This neglect was purposeful and intended to emphasize this point: While there has been progressive development of mechanical and electrical computation aids, the modern digital computer is a unique creation of our time that incorporates basic organizational concepts developed only in the past half century.

Prior to the twentieth century, fingers, the reckoning board, the abacus, the slide rule, and the later mechanical and electrical calculating devices were

FIGURE 1.20. Hewlett-Packard's HP-45 battery-powered scientific calculator. (Courtesy of Hewlett-Packard Corporation).

regarded as tools available to help make arithmetic computations. Thus, for example, bankers computed loan rates and interest, government officials computed budgets, and traders computed sales and purchases. Although these operations are superficially dissimilar, it is important to note a common theme: Data of one form or another is given to a person who, having learned a certain set of procedures, manipulates the data, perhaps using a calculating device, to arrive at the final results. In such an arrangement the calculating device, no matter how sophisticated, is clearly just a tool for computations. The major decisions relating to the way a solution can be found, the specific actions needed to carry out the calculations, and the interpretation of the results were all a product of human ingenuity and labor.

A more graphic view of the organization of problem solving is given by the astronomical researches of Johann Kepler in the early seventeenth century. Kepler's ambition was to find the mathematical laws that governed the motions of the planets. To do this, he spent many years attempting to predict the future locations of planets by taking measurements of their present locations and assuming that their trajectories could be described by closed geometrical curves. (See Figure 1.21.) While the planetary observations were provided by Tycho Brahé from his observatories in Denmark and Prague, the tedious computations of prediction were made by hand by Kepler and his assistants.

To carry out his astronomical studies, Kepler needed an organizational structure involving four key elements. The first element involved the collection and organization of Brahé's precise astronomical data (i.e. data presentation). Second, to analyze these data Kepler needed to prepare a set of *computational instructions* that described in full detail the sequence of arithmetic calculations needed to predict the motion of the planets. Third, a *computational organization* (See Figure 1.22) was created so that these instructions could be used by Kepler and his assistants to guide the laborious computations leading to predictions of the future locations of the planets (Mars was favorable owing to its relatively rapid motions and a large data base). Finally, the results of the arithmetic computations yielded predictions which could be compared with the observations made at later times to assess whether the assumed geometrical curve matched the actual planetary path.

The organizational structure used by Kepler provides a useful comparison for describing the development of the digital computer. In the Kepler scheme,

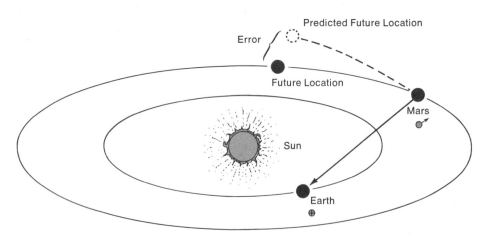

FIGURE 1.21. Predicting the location of Mars as seen from the Earth.

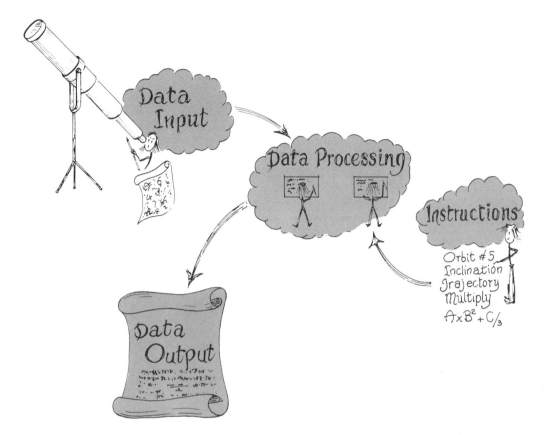

FIGURE 1.22. Illustrating the astronomy calculations of Johann Kepler in the seventeenth century.

the major functional elements were limited to data gathering (data input), data processing following a list of instructions (program, memory, and processing) and interpretation of the results (output). Mechanization was available only for carrying out a few specific numerical operations.

The first step towards the modern computer was taken by Charles Babbage, a nineteenth century English gentleman who conceived the notion that it was possible to build a mechanical calculator to carry out a series of numerical operations according to a predetermined plan (i.e. he contemplated a system of fully–automatic computation). In essence, Babbage attempted to combine the task of separate arithmetic calculations with a computational plan outlining the arithmetic steps needed to reach the final result. In his scheme the goal was to achieve automatic computation by following a set of instructions that specified which arithmetic operations were needed and in what order for a given set of initial numbers.

Through years of effort, Babbage was able to show some success with a Difference Engine that was designed to assist the generation of astronomical and other mathematical tables. In operation, an initial series of numbers was set on mechanical dials. The internal mechanism was built to do repeated internal subtractions and multiplications such that after the operations were completed, a new set of numbers were generated through completely automatic processing of the original numbers. (See Figure 1.23.)

Unfortunately, Babbage's conception was in advance of the engineering skills of the early 1800s and the Difference Engine, along with a later planned Analytical Engine, remained incomplete. Nevertheless, the work of Babbage and his patron, Lady Lovelace, showed that it was possible to design a mechanical apparatus which could perform a series of complicated sequential arithmetic steps. Today we might consider such an idea trivial. Yet, it was the first step towards the idea of automatic computation and the complex digital computers used today.

Further developments with mechanical machines continued slowly in the late 1800s and early 1900s and eventually led to the class of electro-mechanical analog computers which we will discuss later. The search for truly automatic computation machines remained static, however, until the 1930s when the Automatic Sequence Controlled Calculator (ASCC) was built at Harvard University to Howard Aiken's designs with the support of the IBM Corporation. The ASCC (See Figure 1.24), also called the Mark I computer, used both electric relays and mechanical gears, clutches, and rods. Numbers were stored by ASCC using decimal wheels. The wheel's rotations were sense by electrical contacts. Internal relays and motors were provided for the electrical and mechanical changes needed to carry out arithmetic operations.

In addition to the ASCC's advanced technology, the machine provided a unique feature that raised it above the class of ordinary calculators: The order of calculations was determined by external instructions given sequentially to the computer on punched paper tape or punched cards. Thus, with this machine external programs could be written to make long series of automatic, sequential computations. Babbage's original goal had been met and even surpassed. Yet, there were certain problems. While the combination of electrical and mechanical parts proved reliable (the ASCC generated accurate mathematical tables for more than 10 years and was the basis of a later IBM printing calculator), it was slow, being able to add or subtract 23 digit numbers in about half a second, multiply them in less than 5 seconds, and divide them in 10 seconds. A further difficulty lay in the instruction list which, because the list had to specify the settings of all internal switches, relays and other parts, was exceedingly time-consuming to create.

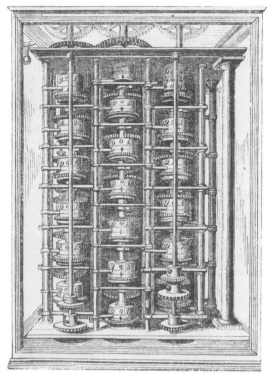

A   B

FIGURE 1.23. Two views of a part of Charles Babbage's difference engine, a machine designed to carry out automatic computations following a specific set of operations. Technical and financial difficulties prevented completion of the engine. (The Bettman Archive.)

FIGURE 1.24. The Automatic Sequence Controlled Calculator (ASCC) was built by IBM at Harvard University during the 1930s. (Courtesy IBM.)

The needs of nations at war provided the impetus for the first electronic computer which was built at the University of Pennsylvania. The Electronic and Numerical Integrator and Calculator (ENIAC), built to the designs of John Mauchly and J. Presper Eckert during the second World War, discarded mechanical parts in favor of electronic vacuum tubes. As with the ASCC, the list of instructions needed to guide the internal operations was stored outside the machine using punched paper cards. Due to its electronic structure, the ENIAC computation speed was substantially faster: Multiplication could be done in less than 3 thousandths of a second, addition of a pair of five digit numbers took 20 millionths of a second. Clearly, new standards for automatic computation had been achieved. The ENIAC, however, was a relatively inflexible machine of the same species as the ASCC and was used mainly for computations of army artillery tables. ENIAC's real accomplishment was the demonstration that fully-automatic computation was indeed possible.

In the course of building ENIAC, Mauchly and Eckert came in contact with John Von Neumann, a young Hungarian mathematician who was working on computations related to the development of the atomic bomb. Von Neumann quickly realized the importance of automatic computation and soon contributed a number of ideas that created the basis for the modern digital computer.

Von Neumann's most important idea involved the program governing the operation of the computer. In the ASCC and ENIAC this list of instructions was given to the computer in a step-by-step fashion as each instruction was needed within the computer. Von Neumann suggested that future machines be built with a memory unit contained inside the computer so that both instructions and data could be simultaneously stored in adjacent memory cells or storage areas. This arrangement had two advantages. First, the new computers would have more rapid access to the instruction list. Second, the computer could now perform operations upon its own instructions. This latter feature opened the possibility of jumping back and forth or even skipping instructions, depending upon tests and branches placed in the program.

A second revolutionary step in the advancement of computers lay in the form of the instructions given to the computer. Previously, it was necessary to prepare a meticulously accurate instruction plan specifying how each electrical part should operate during the program. As the automatic computers grew in complexity, so did the programs. In the new computers the difficulty of creating instruction lists was removed through the introduction of new computer programs called *compilers*. These special programs were designed to translate simple, human-oriented computer languages like FORTRAN, BASIC or ALGOL into the far more complex and detailed internal language of the computer.

Finally, number systems other than decimal were adopted for the computer's internal operations. Using the results of Claude Shannon, a young mathematician who studied at MIT and worked at the Bell Telephone Laboratories, it was possible to show a close relationship between electronic switching circuits and the algebra of logic: True or False values became analogous to the open or closed states of electrical switches. Shannon coined the term *bit* (binary digit) and described it as the choice between yes or no, plus or minus, or true or false. The bit is the basic information needed to remove uncertainty between two alternatives.

The new ideas described above were exploited by Mauchly, Eckert and Von Neumann in a new machine, the Electronic Discrete Variable Automatic Computer (EDVAC), which was based upon internal programming and the binary number system. Although slow and cumbersome by today's standards, EDVAC was the first of the modern automatic digital computers. It was also the first machine which could be used for a nonarithmetic purpose. In 1945 Von Neumann wrote a program that was designed to rearrange a list of numbers into numerical order. His object was to show that computers could be used for tasks other than those of a purely computational nature. Since alphabetic formation is easily represented through number codes, Von Neumann opened the way to the modern ideas of general data processing and the truly enormous power of digital computers.

During the construction of EDVAC, Mauchly and Eckert decided to form a small company which, in course of time, was purchased by Remington–Rand Corporation. Further development along the EDVAC designs soon led to the first commercial computer in 1951: The Universal Automatic Computer (UNIVAC I). The UNIVAC I was used by the U.S. Census Bureau to analyze data obtained in the 1950 census and was popularized in the 1952 Presidential campaign when UNIVAC I was used to correctly predict General Eisenhower's election.

From the foregoing it should not be thought that the development of new automatic computers was restricted to the United States. In England, Alan M. Turing had, in 1937, created a means for formal analysis of computers through the use of mathematics. Turing's early reputation was based upon his creation of the Turing Machine—a simple, idealized model of a universal computer which showed that it was possible to construct a single, all-purpose computer that could be programmed to solve any deterministic (definite steps) problem. By 1946 Turing was involved in the design of ACE, an Automatic Calculating Engine which, when built in 1950, was somewhat in advance of ENIAC. Before ACE was completed, however, Turing had turned to the new field of cybernetics which is concerned with automatic control and communication in animals and machines. Drawing parallels between the operation of the brain and that of a computer, Turing turned his energies into MADAM, the Manchester Automatic Digital machine. Although there were many practical difficulties, ACE and MADAM formed the basis for the future development of the English computing industry and led to the SEC (Simple Electronic Computer) and the APEC (All-Purpose Electronic Computer).

Since the appearance of UNIVAC I and its English equivalents, hundreds of new computer designs have been introduced and succeeding generations have appeared with dramatic improvements in size and computing power as a result of the progress of electronic technology from vacuum tubes to modern solid state devices.

Today, more than 250,000 general purpose digital computers are in use throughout the world. While such a large number of operating computing systems provides proof of their usefulness, it is important to realize that these machines are the modern version of the ancient need to solve problems. As such, computers are only tools as were the hands of our ancestors. But in the ages between the use of hands and the use of computers, the fundamental approach of problem solving has changed. The simple problems of arithmetic are now just a minor part of the work done by a computer. Today, the far greater complexities of data organization and information processing are the tasks which preoccupy us and it is with these problems in mind that we turn to the computer.

REFERENCES TO FURTHER READINGS

BELL, D. G. and NEWELL, A.
  Computer Structures: Readings and Examples. New York: McGraw Hill, 1971.
  Gives an interesting discussion of the development of computer architecture. Advanced level.

BERKELEY, E. C.
  Giant Brains: Or Machines That Think. New York: John Wiley & Sons, 1961.
  Discusses the early history of computing machines.

HAWKES, N.
  The Computer Revolution. New York: E. P. Dutton, 1972.
  A fascinating introduction to the uses of computers.

MENNINGER, K.
  Number Words and Number Symbols. Cambridge: MIT Press, 1969.
  The outstanding source of information about numbers and number systems. Highly recommended to all persons interested in the incredible history of our contemporary numbers.

MORRISON, P. and MORRISON, E.
  Charles Babbage and His Calculating Engines. New York, 1961.
  An interesting account of a complex and inventive life.

NEWMAN, J. R.
  The World of Mathematics. New York: Simon & Schuster, 1956.
  A collection of interesting articles describing ancient arithmetic, number systems
  and the history of mathematical symbols can be found scattered through the four
  volumes of this interesting text.

PYLYSHYN, Z. W.
  Perspectives on the Computer Revolution. New Jersey: Prentice-Hall, 1970.
  Contains a collection of essays by outstanding contributors to the field of computer
  science.

ROSENBERG, J. M.
  The Computer Prophets. London: The Macmillan Company, 1969.
  Contains accounts of the lives of the inventors and companies that helped develop
  computers.

SMITH, D. E.
  The History of Mathematics. New York: Dover Publications, 1958.
  A standard text in two volumes covering the history of mathematics.

EXERCISES

1. Find the sum of 1743 + 649 using Roman numerals. Explain why it is easier to do addition and subtraction in this system than in our own. Is this true of multiplication and division? Why?

2. Make a simple counting table and evaluate the following: 351 + 63; 9049 − 123; 17 × 4; 13 ÷ 3. What rules were necessary to do multiplication and division?

3. Using the diagonal lattice method, multiply 89 × 9. How does the evaluation of this product go beyond the description given in the text?

4. Construct a set of Napier's bones to evaluate the product of 562 × 21.

5. Can Napier's bones be used for addition or subtraction?

6. In what way is the lady on the knight's left side repeating the obvious? (see Figure 1.25)

7. What is the basic distinction between Babbage's Difference Engine and Leibniz's calculator?

8. How does a computer differ from a calculator?

9. Why is the ASCC similar to the Difference Engine?

A KNIGHT AND TWO LADIES

FIGURE 1.25. A Knight and Two Ladies: taken from the Manessa Ms., c 1320—Universitatsbibliothek, Heidelberg, Hiltbolt von Schwangäu.

10. Explain why it is essential for a modern computer to have its instruction list stored within the computer memory.
11. How can numbers be used to represent the letters of the alphabet?
12. Why is EDVAC regarded as the prototype of the modern digital computer?

What is a Digital Computer?

THE ORGANIZED MACHINE

Modern digital computers range in size from mini-sized desk units to the large multi-unit systems found in national computer centers. Physical size is not a true guide to a computer's capability, because advances in solid state electrical technology permit electronic devices to be packed into incredibly small spaces. With this compactness has come diversity of purpose and many smaller computers are now designed and programmed to work efficiently only with particular types of problems such as data gatherers in laboratories, satellites to larger computers, or for business applications. (See Figure 2.1.)

Although there are obvious differences in appearance and specialization, most digital computers are designed with a common organizational structure and use only a limited number of fundamental internal operations. In terms of internal functions, a computer is a collection of simple counters, adders, switches, and memory storage cells. These individual parts, when organized under the direction of a central controller, can be used to store and process numerical and alphabetic information following specific steps listed in a computer program.

To see how a computer works, let us create a prototype that uses simple devices to stimulate the various internal functions of a computer. Let us suppose that a person is given a desk calculator which permits him to add, subtract, multiply, divide, and compare two numbers. A ruled paper pad with numbered lines is also provided so that instructions and the values associated with the various computations can be recorded. With such simple items, a prototype computer is equipped to solve numerical and nonnumerical problems in ways which are similar to those used by true digital computers.

To solve a particular problem, our prototype computer must be given a specific set of instructions which list in correct order the various steps needed in the computation. These instructions give the computer controller the following information:

1. Where to find data.
2. How the data are to be processed.
3. Where the results are to be placed.

To avoid any possibility of error, these instructions, even if trivial, are written in full detail in their order of execution on our paper pad "memory".

To carry this example further, suppose that we wish to evaluate the expression (X + Y) for arbitrary values of X and Y. A list of instructions has been developed in Figure 2.2 to provide for the evaluation of this expression. For

FIGURE 2.1. The highly versatile PDP 8/E minicomputer created by the Digital Equipment Corporation. (Courtesy of Digital Equipment Corporation.)

clarity, the instructions have been stored on consecutive lines of the memory, each of which has been given a separate identification number or *address* to allow for references between the different instructions. As shown, the first seven locations of the computer memory are used for storing program instruction addresses 1 through 7. The last three storage locations, addresses 8 through 10, are reserved for storing numbers used in or resulting from the calculation.

Examination of the instruction list shows that the first instruction, which is stored in location 1 of the memory, requests that a value corresponding to the quantity X be stored in location 8. Likewise, the instruction stored in location

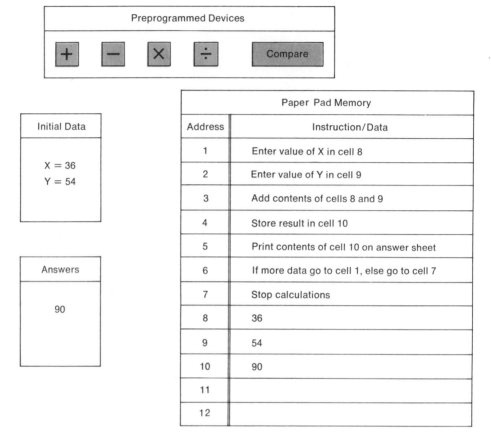

FIGURE 2.2. A proto-type computer which uses pre–programmed arithmetic units to carry out a set of instructions listed on a paper pad memory. The instruction set shown evaluates the expression (X + Y) for the various values of X and Y.

2 brings a value for Y into location 9. It is important to note that the actual values of X and Y to be used in the computations are not specified by the instructions and are quite arbitrary. These numbers are provided after the program has been developed and stored in the paper pad memory, that is, in the *execution phase* of the program.

In operation, the prototype computer begins by executing the instruction given by address 1. When this instruction is completed, the second instruction is executed, and so forth. The present instruction set is particularly interesting because it has a provision for repetition. The instruction stored at address 6 can, in the proper circumstances, cause the computer controller to return to the instruction stored at address 1. However, when the supply of values for X and Y is exhausted, the instruction at location 7 will be executed and the calculations stop.

The organization and function of the various units in this simple model closely parallel those of a real digital computer. (See Figure 2.3.) The ruled paper with instructions, data, and addresses corresponds to the *memory* unit of a digital computer, while the arithmetic desk calculator is similar to the arithmetic devices of a computer's *central processing unit*. In our simple model, the human operator has assumed two roles. First, he provides a central direction to keep track of instructions and arrange for their execution. In this capacity the human coordinator acts in a manner similar to the *central control unit* of a computer. Second, the human provides a means for transferring data into and out of the program. This function corresponds to the actions taken by the *input* and *output* units of a computer.

To make the parallels described above more concrete, the four basic units of a digital computer can be visualized in block form. (See Figure 2.4.) The units have certain specialized functions which, when taken together, comprise the overall computer system. As we have already seen, the data input and output units provide the computer with communication links to the external world. Incoming data, new programs, and outgoing data must pass through these units as part of the transfer to and from the computer memory.

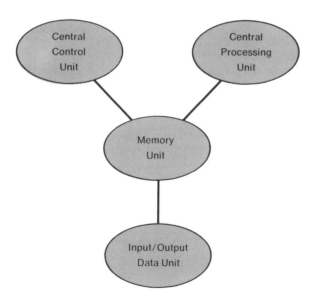

FIGURE 2.3. Organizational structure of a digital computer.

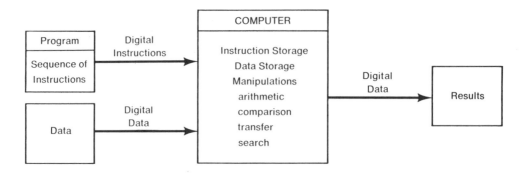

FIGURE 2.4. Functions of a digital computer.

The memory unit itself serves as a repository for program instruction lists and external and internal data.

When calculations are to be made, data are copied from the memory unit and taken to the central processing unit where various calculating devices are applied under the direction of the central control unit. Following modification of the data in the central processing unit, the central control can arrange to have the results returned to the memory, placed in the input/output unit or even reprocessed. In practice, the central control unit not only guides the central processing unit, but it also provides overall coordination for the entire computer system.

A real digital computer has several advantages over its prototype. Since the reaction time of humans is measured in tenths of a second, the execution of instructions in the prototype computer would be slow. Further, humans have a tendency to make errors, especially when they are fatigued or bored by excessive computation. Electrical devices, in contrast, are rapid and intrinsically predictable. The simple acts of adding, counting, comparing, and storing data using solid state electronic devices are measured in time periods of a millionth of a second or less. Such speeds are incredibly fast and allow machines to do millions or billions of individual operations in relatively short periods of time.† Although properly organized, highly motivated humans could duplicate any computer calculation using the simple devices of the prototype computer, practical consideration of the time spent to obtain accurate results precludes any man versus machine computational competition for all except the simplest problems.

It is generally recognized that there are six primary attributes of computers which have been of basic importance to their acceptance as useful devices.

†In one millionth of a second a pulse of light can only move a distance of 300 meters or about 328 yards.

These are:

1. Speed. With internal operation times measured in time scales of less than one millionth of a second (a microsecond), large data processing tasks can be accomplished in relatively short periods.

2. Reliability. Errors in an electrical part of a computer as frequent as once every 100 million operations would be intolerable in a modern high-speed computer. Present computers are designed to be virtually error-free over long periods of time through the use of redundant circuits and error detection devices.

3. Automatic Computing. The programs procede without human control. The steps are built into the program.

4. Memory. Permits instructions and data to be stored and operated upon with microsecond speeds.

5. Conditional Control. The order in which instructions are executed in programs can be sequenced according to data values obtained in the course of execution. Such conditional control permits the computer to make decisions.

6. Nonnumerical Processing. Information other than numbers can be stored and manipulated in the computer.

THE LANGUAGE OF THE COMPUTER

To make the movement of my machine's operation the more simple, it had to be composed of a movement the more complex.

BLAISE PASCAL

Pascal's observation referred to frustrations associated with his designs for the digit wheels of the Pascaline adding machine. (See Figure 2.5.) Similar comments apply to the complexity of modern digital computers. Our previous description of the four main functional units of a computer, while useful for understanding the operational organization of computers, ignores the millions of electrical devices which have been carefully arranged to form the internal structure. These individual parts, like the more commonplace wheels, relays, gears, and rods of the early automatic computation machines, are used to process information within the computer. Just as in the older machines, the synchronization of this complex structure requires the use of instructions to control the behavior of all internal parts involved in the computations. Up to the era of UNIVAC I, programming of computers was done by humans using instructions that specified the precise switch settings needed within the internal structure of the machine to make the desired computations. The writing of the complete instruction list, or program, was exceedingly laborious, re-

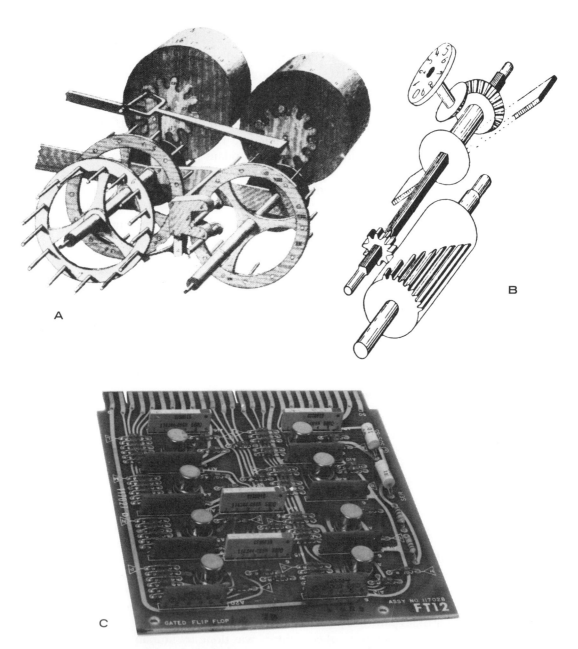

FIGURE 2.5 The growth of computing technology. (A) The ratchet digit-carry mechanism of the Pascaline calculator. (B) The stepped cog wheels of the Leibnitz calculator with digit display device. (C) An integrated circuit logic module used in a recent computer. (Courtesy of Xerox Data Systems.)

quiring attention to the most minute details expressed in terms of the internal structure of the machine. (See Figure 2.6.)

Today's digital computers, with their complex structure, require even more detailed instructions than those given to the older automatic computation machines. The creation of machine language programs for these machines is no longer the task of programmers, but is done by special computer translation programs called *compilers* which convert instructions written in a standard programming language such as BASIC, FORTRAN or ALGOL into the specialized internal language of the machine. (See Figure 2.7.) Such a translation service makes it possible for computation of expressions like "X + Y" to be made without entering into the myriad of internal instructions that guide the transfer, addition, and restorage of the answer within the machine.

In a real sense, compilers permit us to communicate our problems to the computer. Without these translations, computers would lose much of their versatility and usefulness. Of course, since compilers are just computer programs that use the standard language program as input data (and give the machine language instructions as output data), at some time someone had to write specialized instructions directing the operation of the compiler program. However, such drudgery is soon forgotten and the compiler program,

```
S T Q 2 1 6 0 0 0 0 0
R T J 7 5 4 4 6 7 1 7
I N I 5 1 6 0 0 0 0 1
I J P 5 5 3 4 6 7 2 2
E N A 1 0 6 4 6 7 6 2
E N A 1 0 0 0 0 2 1 0
A J P 2 2 1 4 6 7 4 3
I N I 5 1 1 0 0 0 0 0
I N I 5 1 1 7 7 7 6 7
I J P 5 5 2 4 6 7 1 3
E N A 1 0 0 0 0 0 0 0
L D A 1 2 0 4 7 2 7 2
S A U 6 0 0 4 7 2 7 4
E N A 1 0 0 0 0 0 0 0
R X T 0 0 7 5 1 1 5 1
U J P 7 5 0 4 6 7 2 2
L I L 5 3 6 4 7 2 7 3
E N A 1 0 0 0 0 0 0 0
```

FIGURE 2.6. Sample of assembly language instructions from a Burroughs 6700 ALGOL compiler.

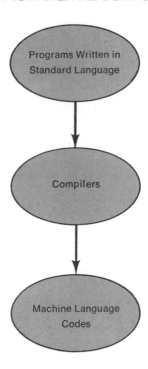

FIGURE 2.7. The translation process from standard computer language into machine language of a particular computer.

once written, provides translation services for all subsequent users of that standard programming language.

For both computers and people, the art of communication is contained in languages. Unfortunately, our own natural language is not sufficiently precise for computers. To overcome this difficulty, standard computer languages have been created to bridge the gap between the vague meanings of natural languages and the rigid requirements of electrical devices. As with human languages, computer languages include four basic elements: An *alphabet*; a *vocabularly*; a *grammar*; and a *syntax*. Normally, computer languages use ordinary alphabetic and numerical characters as part of their alphabet. (See Figure 2.8.) However, new symbols can also be included to represent special operations which are important to a particular language.

The vocabulary of a computer language represents allowed groupings of its alphabetic characters. Similarly, grammars and syntactical structures can be defined to identify classes of words, specify the arrangement of word forms, and to provide definitions of allowed operations.

Presently there exist a number of widely used computer languages (FORTRAN, ALGOL, COBOL, BASIC) which have separate alphabets, grammars, and syntactical structures that can be used to communicate programs to computers. Although the broad proliferation of computer languages might at first appear unnecessary, such a diversity actually reflects a certain economy of operation in which the basic operations underlying a particular language have been chosen to optimize particular types of programs. Similar specialized languages exist, at least in rudimentary form, for knitting, choreography, symbolic logic, and integral or differential calculus.

The letters: ABCDEFGHIJKLMNOPQRSTUVWXYZ
The digits: 0123456789
The blank:
The special characters: $+ - / = [ ] ( ) < > " . , : ; @ \% \$ \& \# *$

FIGURE 2.8. The complete character set for the ALGOL Burroughs 6700 computer language.

Although there are many similarities between the different computer languages, each was created to meet the demands of particular types of problems. Numerical problems of mathematics, science, and engineering, for example, are often expressed in the FORTRAN (FORmula TRANslation) language. BASIC is frequently used as a FORTRAN-like language available at remote access terminals where program statements are given to time-sharing computers using special teletypewriters. ALGOL and PL/1 are more recent languages allowing problems to be expressed more directly in terms of machine operations than possible with BASIC or FORTRAN. Finally, for business applications the expression of problems in COBOL (COmmon BUsiness Oriented Languages) is greatly simplified.

The creation of new computer languages is not conceptually difficult, but does involve close attention to detail in the derivation of complete sets of definitions for the allowed grammar and syntactical structure. Eventually, these definitions are expressed in a compiler that translates the stated actions of the new language into actual machine operations. The writing of a complete compiler program is not a trivial task, but even here computers have been partially trained to help. Certain programs now exist which can aid in the creation of compiler programs.

ALGORITHMS AND PROGRAMS

The standard computer languages permit us to communicate with computers but, like the ancient counting tables or modern high speed arithmetic units, these languages are also only tools. As we saw in Chapter One, there have been repeated advances in the mechanization of simple arithmetic calculation. The significant achievement of the computer, however, has been the mechanization of *problem solving* in its broadest sense. No longer, for example, is the business manager concerned with the arithmetic operations needed to compute a paycheck. Rather, he wants his computer to handle the complete scheme of employee remuneration, taking charge of the calculations involving the number of hours each individual works, the rate of pay, taxes, benefits, deductions, and even the printing and distribution of the checks. Such a generalization of function is often called the *total system concept*.

The extension of our concepts about the role of computers requires that we must give more thought to the actual techniques of problem solving. Indeed, one of the major topics in any introductory computer course revolves around the rational methods needed to solve different types of problems. Although such methods might appear to be intuitively obvious, the solution to most problems must follow from a series of logically consistent steps that outline a progression of actions which, if followed in order, will lead to the final result. Such a series of logical steps is called an *algorithm* in honor of Algorismus (Abu Jafar Muhammad ibn Musa al-Khwarizmi) and his textbook on arithmetic, which presented the use of the Arabic numerals and place-value numbers to the European world.

Although we seldom think about them, algorithms are implicit in many of our ordinary activities in which a sequence of logical steps is needed to produce a result. Recipes, income tax forms, and how-to-make-it instructions are typical algorithms. Such common algorithms may seem obvious to us. But when new problems arise, new algorithms must be found and tested.

Algorithms express the consecutive steps which must be taken to solve problems. To communicate the algorithm to the computer, however, requires that the ordered steps be expressed in a standard computer language. The translation of algorithm to program is the task of the computer programmer who, knowing the alphabet, vocabulary, grammar, and syntax of the computer language, rewrites the algorithm steps as instructions to the computer. Thus, the transition from *algorithm* to *program* involves the adoption of specific rules and expressions of a particular standard language (like FORTRAN or ALGOL). The algorithm gives the general method of solution while the program is its specific, computer–oriented, expression.

The separate steps, or commands, within a computer program are usually called statements. (See Figure 2.9.) Each statement specifies a general action to be taken by the computers (i.e. comparison of quantities, evaluation of an arithmetic expression, and so forth). To actually accomplish a particular action dictated by a statement, the compiler will have to generate many machine language instructions to specify the necessary internal actions in complete detail. The relationships existing between algorithms, programs, compilers, and machine language programs carry the idea of problem solving from the general steps to the particular commands.

Computers are valuable tools in solving both numerical and nonnumerical problems ranging from the real time control of factories to information storage

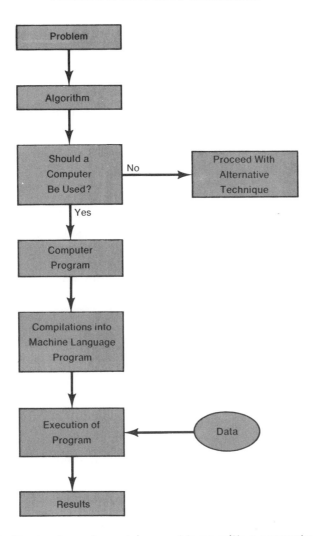

FIGURE 2.9. Basic steps for solving problems with a computer.

and retrieval. Nevertheless, not every problem can justify the time and effort needed to construct a computer program to obtain solutions. As an example, computers can readily store, compare, and collate large amounts of nonnumerical data. To write a program for a computer to alphabetize a single list of five names is clearly a waste of time. On the other hand, a statistical evaluation by human analysis of data collected in a national census is even more wasteful. Only computers are sufficiently rapid and error-free to carry out such a project.

Finally, it does not necessarily follow that direct-statement algorithms (See Figure 2.10) can always be devised to solve particular problems. Some problems are far too complex to permit a simple enumeration of steps which will always lead to the desired solution. The prevention of wars, for example, is apparently beyond our present algorithmic capability, both as a consequence of our ignorance of human behavior and also as a result of the large number of variables that interact to produce war itself.

PROGRAMS: A BIOGRAPHICAL SKETCH

To obtain a better view of the relationships between algorithms, programs, and the operating environment of a computer system, let us follow the progress of a typical computer program from its embryonic stage as an algorithm through its execution and final demise. For the present, suppose a problem's solution is sufficiently demanding to require the use of a computer. The four major steps needed to obtain a satisfactory solution are:

1. The design of an algorithm.
2. The conversion of the algorithm into a standard computer language program.
3. The translation of the program into machine language instructions.
4. Execution of the instructions by the computer.

The first step is often difficult. The algorithm must list all steps needed to achieve a solution, taking into account the possible alternatives that may appear in the course of the analysis. The algorithm must include all aspects of relevant data flow—arithmetic and comparison operations, steps where decisions must be made, indications of data input and output, and so forth.

After the algorithm has been prepared, a computer program must be written using a standard computer language. This process is a human translation effort in which the logical steps of the algorithm are written in terms of the formal structure of a particular language. The result of this translation is a set of sequential statements that reflect the basic steps of the algorithm. These statements, when taken together and examined for errors, form a program telling the computer how and where to obtain its operating data, how it is to process the data, and how it should present the results. (See Figure 2.11.)

At this point the program is ready for the computer. There are two principal ways to give the information contained in the program to the computer system. The first, commonly used when the computer is capable of processing many programs at virtually the same time in a mode of operation called *time–sharing*, involves typing each statement of the program at a typewriter–like

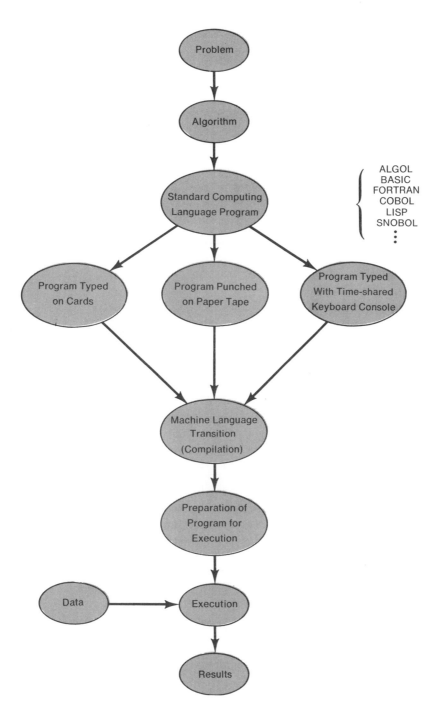

FIGURE 2.10. A flowchart of computer usage.

47

```
BEGIN
INTEGER ARRAY LR[1:20],CARD[1:14];
INTEGER I, J, K, NRR, NRC, NRL, IR, NCH, NW;

DIRECT INTEGER ARRAY IBUF[1:5400];
DIRECT FILE DECKS(KIND = 14 DENSITY = O,TITLE = "PROGS.");


FILE PRINTER(KIND =PRINTER,MAXRECSIZE =22);


FILE READER(KIND =READER);


FORMAT F1 (2014);
FORMAT F2 (13A6,C2);
LABEL RD;
POINTER P,Q,P1,Q1;
EVENT IOFIN;
P: =POINTER(IBUF);
Q: =POINTER(CARD);
NRC: =0;
READ(READER,FI,NRR);
READ(READER,F1,FOR I: =1 STEP 1 UNTIL NRR DO LR[I]);
FOR IR: =1 STEP 1 UNTIL NRR DO BEGIN
    NRL: =LR[IR];
    RD: RESET(IOFIN);
    READ(DECKS,5400,IBUF[*]) [IOFIN];
    NRC: =NRC +1;
    WAIT(IOFIN);
    IF NRL NEQ NRC THEN GO TO RD;
    P1: =P;
    Q1: =Q;
    WRITE(PRINTER[SKIP 1]);
    NW: =IBUF[*].IOWORDS;
    NCH: =6*NW;
    FOR J: =1 STEP 80 UNTIL NCH DO BEGIN
        REPLACE Q1 BY PI:PI FOR 80;
        WRITE(PRINTER,F2,FOR K: =1 STEP 1 UNTIL 14 DO CARD[K]);
END;
END;
END;
```

FIGURE 2.11. A portion of a program written in ALGOL.

48

terminal (see Figure 2.12) connected directly to the computer system. As the program is given to the computer in this way, it is examined and stored within the computer memory until the process of compilation is completed and the list of machine language instructions is prepared for execution. Since the typing of the program is relatively slow, many people can use the computer simultaneously, receiving what seems to be individual attention, as error detectors in the compiler program find mistakes and bring them to the attention of the terminal user.

A second way to give programs to the computer involves the use of punched cardboard cards. In this method, the information given by the program is first converted by a keypunch typing machine into a series of punched holes on the cards (an idea first devised by Herman Hollerith in the 1880s for processing census data). As shown in Figure 2.13, each card is divided into 80 columns and 12 rows. Using the punch codes listed in the Appendix I, each column can represent one alphabetic character, numeral, or operational symbol. By typing the program statements onto the cards, the complete program is given in terms of punched symbols.

FIGURE 2.12. Information display terminats provide data communication links to a variety of computers and other data processing units. Both input and output information are visually displayed according to designs created by the user. (Courtesy of OMRON Corp.)

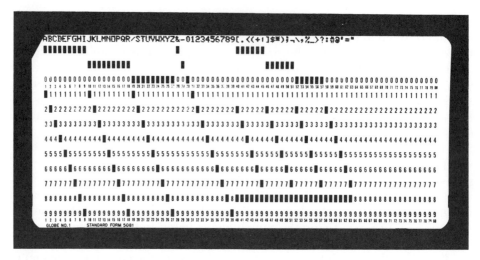

FIGURE 2.13. A computer card punched with alphabetic characters, numerals, punctuation, and arithmetic operators. The punch code for each symbol can be found by looking at the row location of each punched hole in the column immediately below the symbol.

At this point the program is ready for computer processing. The deck of cards containing the program (together with a series of initial cards that indicate the compilation program needed, who is to pay for the program, how long the program should be allowed to run on the computer, and other details) is placed in a card reader. This machine gives a reading of the keypunched information, converting the punched hole codes into electrical pulses. This translation is a purely electrical process that involves no decision capability other than those made by properly wired circuits.

The resulting information, representing the program and accompanying data, is then stored either in the computer's main memory unit or on magnetic tape, a rapid access magnetic disc, or other temporary storage medium. At this point no computer translation of the program has yet occurred.

With the program and data now safely held in a storage area of the computer system, the compiler program is called into action by the computer and begins its initial step of translating the program statements into machine language instructions. The compiler accomplishes one of two related tasks: It can either directly produce a complete machine language translation of the original pogram or it can give an intermediate language (assembly language). If the compiler produces an assembly language version of the program, another internal program, called the assembler, is needed to perform the final translation to machine language. In either case, the machine translation of the original lnguage is accomplished by another previously stored program manipulated by the computer. The very substantial effort and cost of writing a sophisticated compiler program is repaid an enormous number of times by greatly reducing the programming burden on individual computer users.

Following compilation, the program statements are expressed in machine language and the program is ready for loading into the computer memory. When loading occurs, the machine language instructions are placed in consecutive storage locations within the computer memory. Execution of the program then begins at the first instruction and progresses through the instruction list. Each instruction guides the computer through individual operations. When numbers are to be multiplied, for example, the storage addresses of the numbers are given, the operation to be performed is directed, and an address is given where the result is to be stored.

During execution of the program, the computer passes from storage location to storage location, carrying out the individual instructions. Occasionally, this sequential execution of instructions is broken and a branch is made forwards or backwards in the list of instructions. Branches of this type permit the repetition or avoidance of many individual instructions. Branches are both powerful and interesting since they give a program flexibility to handle sophisticated problems without resorting to periodic human guidance during computations. The technique and consequences of branching are explored more fully in later chapters.

Those instructions that require the computer to take external data and store them in assigned storage locations within the computer are particularly important. The external data may be obtained from magnetic tape or other data storage units to which the computer has access. Often, but not always, data stored in this way has its origin in punched cards read into the computer along with the standard language program. An important exception occurs when the computer is being used in a "real time" or interactive mode with a process occuring while the machine is executing the program. In these circumstances, time is of the essence and special instruments report physical measurements that are interpreted by the computer in terms of its stored instruction set. Corrections ordered by the program are then returned to other devices and converted into physical changes.

Since the purpose of using computers lies in obtaining solutions to problems, those instructions which transfer data out of computers are also important. The removal of data from the computer memory is often done by transferring the data to a temporary storage medium (magnetic tape, magnetic discs, and so forth) called a buffer (See Figure 2.14). This intermediate temporary storage area is used to free the main computer from waiting for the relatively slower output display units to complete their jobs. From buffer storage, data can be processed by a number of different units outside the computer that convert the digital symbols into symbols more useful to human communica-

FIGURE 2.14. Digital data are often stored on magnetic tapes or rotating magnetic discs. The casettes shown here are a recent innovation used with minicomputers and other data processing devices. (Courtesy of Maxwell Corp.)

tion. Frequently, results are given in the form of printed text. Alternatively, the data can be punched on cards, be used as an input to a visual display tube, control the printing of characters on photographic film, produce an elaborate inked graph, or simply be written in appropriate form on magnetic tape or punched paper tape.

After a program's execution phase is completed the computer cannot be allowed to stop. Digital computers are expensive to operate and such a halt, even for one second, would mean a loss of hundreds of thousands of machine manipulation cycles. All computers operate under the overall guidance of an *operating system* program which, as the essential heart of the central control program, has the ultimate machine authority in directing the way subsidiary programs are loaded into the computer and processed. The operating system is a *resident* program (it is almost never removed) that gives coordinating instructions to assist the rapid flow of program onto and off of the computer. The operating system, acting at the request of the computer user, and the central control program determine when a compiling program should be called into the computer, when portions of a particular program will be compiled, and when loading and execution of a program will begin. After a particular program is completed, control is returned to the operating system and the computer's work continues. As for the executed program, following transfer of control to the operating system, all storage areas used in program execution are made available for use by other programs and the program no longer exists within the main computer memory.

WHY DIGITAL

Information symbols are an essential part of our society and their uses have become proportionately more important as the degree of sophistication of our society increases. Many information symbols are present in our daily activities, among the most important being the letters of the alphabet A to Z, the digits 0 to 9, punctuation marks, the arithmetic operation indicators (+ , − , × , ÷), road signs, traffic lights, and so forth. These symbols are pivotal in our lives, permitting us to regulate our relations with the world. Unfortunately, the manipulation of these symbols is not trivial and the sheer magnitude of processing and distributing information in the form of tax data, bills, books, airline reservations, and mathematical computations has reached the point at which information processing using human efforts is inadequate. Computers must be used.

It would be convenient if the information symbols used by humans could also be used by computers. The internal structure of computers, however, prevents these symbols from being used directly. Translation of external symbols into an internal representation must be made. In the old automatic computation machines the values of numbers could be represented through the rotation of individual wheels representing the digits of numbers. For digital computers another method has been adopted and the internal representation of numbers and alphabetic data is accomplished through coded patterns of ON/OFF states in simple electrical devices such as switches or magnetic cores.† The switches and cores used in computers, like ordinary lightswitches, have just two settings or *states*: ON and OFF, or written more concisely, 1 and 0. (See Figure 2.15.)

To show how our ordinary symbols can be represented by switches or similar devices having just two states, suppose we are given eight adjacent ON/OFF switches (See Figure 2.16). If we define a particular pattern of zeros and ones to correspond to each alphabetic character, numeral, punctuation mark, and arithmetic operation, we have created a digital representation for external data. The idea of such a coded representation is illustrated in more

†Magnetic cores are small ring-like devices used extensively in computer memories. A more complete discussion is given later.

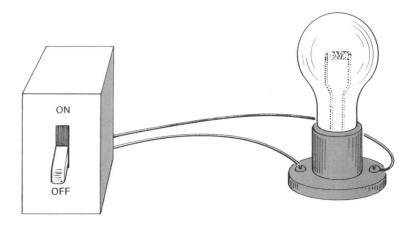

FIGURE 2.15. A simple lightswitch. The lightbulb is used to indicate the state of the switch with the ON represented by the digit 1 and OFF by the digit 0.

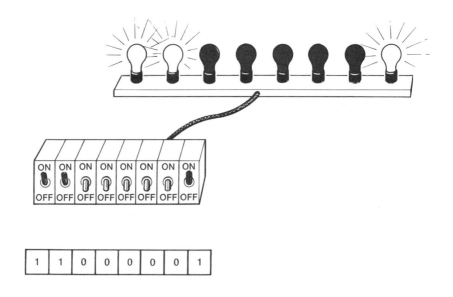

FIGURE 2.16. Representation of the character A by a block of eight switches. The physical arrangement of switches and lights shown in the upper diagram can be given a stylized representation in terms of binary digits (0s and 1s).

detail below using the standard EBCDIC character code listed in the Appendix II. The first two symbols, the letter B and the multiplication symbol, ∗, are expressed as patterns of 0s and 1s stored in the eight adjacent switches. Groups of characters can be represented if we consider blocks of switches with each block containing the code for one external character.

External Symbol	Internal Representation		
B	11000010		
X	01011100		
YOU	11101000	11010110	11100100
A × B	11000001	01011100	11000010

FIGURE 2.17. Representation of external symbols using a code based on eight binary digits. Each block of eight binary digits could be constructed out of switches and lights as shown in Figure 2.16.

To show how words or other groupings can be represented, coded patterns of 0s and 1s have been gathered as adjacent blocks in the Figure 2.17. The code patterns on the right show the way these symbols are stored inside the computer. When such internal switch patterns are used to represent our external information, it is possible to arrange for the symbols to be moved about, compared, and altered by means of electrical devices within the computer. Thus, in digital computers the transition from external written characters to an internally acceptable form of character representation is accomplished through the use of codes based on groups of digits. Further, while the fundamental alphabet of the computer is limited to the two symbols 0 and 1 (reflecting the two physical states of a switch), groups of these internal 0s and 1s can be arranged to represent the more complex alphabetic and numerical symbols of human communication in a manner similar to the way letters are used to make words. Thus, we see the term *digital* in the name digital computer reflects the fact that quantities inside the machine are represented by simple digits.

DIGITAL DEVICES

Not every digital device can be called a digital computer. A computer is a rather special arrangement of individual digital units that can carry out many different operations using an instruction set stored within its memory. As a result, a computer can continually alter the way data is manipulated and stored within itself. At the same time the basic instructions themselves may be modified according to guidelines provided by the computer programmer.

The difference between digital devices and digital computers can be illustrated in terms of a household lightswitch. As shown by Figure 2.15, an ordinary electric switch is a simple digital device having two states—ON and OFF or 1 and 0. When we have a row of switches, as shown previously in Figure 2.16, we can represent external characters as sequences of 0s and 1s. Now, if we were sufficiently clever we could make a simple calculating device by finding a way of connecting two rows of switches together with lightbulbs so that particular operations (such as comparison or arithmetic) could be automatically carried out. The initial numbers needed for such operations could be given to our calculating device, for example, by arranging two rows of switches into patterns of 0s and 1s corresponding to the numbers (see the character code table in Appendix 1). Through the proper internal connections, the switches could control a panel of lightbulbs which would show the answer. Such an arrangement of switches and bulbs is called a digital device. (See Figure 2.18.) By the way it is constructed, this device can only carry out

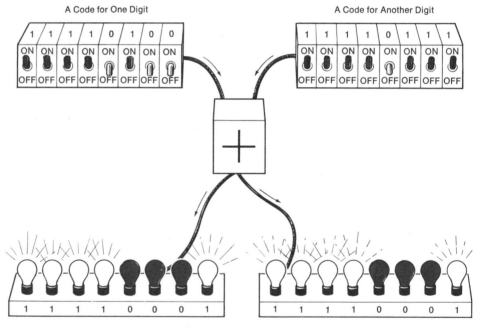

A Code for One Digit | A Code for Another Digit

Codes for the Answer Digits

FIGURE 2.18. A simple pre-programmed device for adding a pair of one digit decimal numbers. Since the largest sum of such numbers is 18, we must provide two blocks of output indicator lights, one for each possible decimal digit of the answer. Using the eight digit code of Appendix I find the digits being currently summed.

the one arithmetic operation for which it was designed. If we wish to have another type operation, the internal connections of the digital device must be altered in an appropriate fashion.

The actions of another very simple digital device are shown in Figure 2.19. When a digit is placed in the device by setting the switch, a new digit is automatically indicated by the lightbulb.

In summary, the specific function of a digital device is determined by the fixed connections between the internal parts. In a digital computer a new degree of freedom is provided by letting many of the internal switch settings be determined by the machine language instructions stored in the computer memory. Thus, as in the old automatic computation machines, the machine language program is nothing more than a list of instructions guiding the setting of switches within an extremely complicated structure. By arranging these settings properly, data is processed, computations are made, and problems are solved.

A SECOND TYPE OF COMPUTER

Digital computers manipulate information symbols that have been coded into digital form. The actual operation of a digital computer is guided through instructions stored internally.

Analog computers are a different class of computing machines and have usefulness mainly in engineering problems. Rather than converting information into discrete numbers (digits) and manipulating them, an analog computer attempts to mimic or physically reproduce by electrical or mechanical devices the way a physical system might respond to stimulii. Analog devices

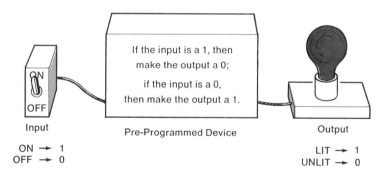

FIGURE 2.19. A simple pre-programmed digital device. If the input digit is 0 (or OFF) the output is 1 (or ON) and vice versa.

generally have no discrete states, but rather vary smoothly and continuously.†
A speedometer, for example, is an analog device that expresses the speed of a
car in terms of the angle the speedometer needle makes with its zero speed
position. A thermometer (See Figure 2.20) relates the temperature of a
substance to the length of the indicating liquid. The most common analog
device used for arithmetic is the slide rule. Here physical lengths are marked
with logarithmic scales so that addition or subtraction of lengths is equivalent
to multiplication or division of the numbers marked on those scales. Regular
addition or subtraction could be included by linearly marked lengths scales,
but the resulting accuracy is not great enough to justify the extra effort.

The idea behind analog computers is that when a physical system is described by a mathematical model it is frequently found that electrical or
mechanical devices can be connected together so that they have the same or
similar mathematical description. Addition, subtraction, multiplication, division, and more advanced, but extremely useful, operations such as differentia-
tion and integration can be simulated by analog devices. Since results from
this type of machine are not discrete quantities, but can vary in a continuous
fashion, the precision of the results will depend on the electrical or mechanical elements used.

†Actually, discontinuous mathematical functions can be represented through special devices.

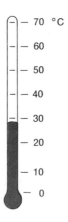

FIGURE 2.20. The thermometer as a simple analog device. Temperature is
proportional to the length of the liquid column. Changes in the temperature
cause the liquid to expand or contract, thereby altering the length of the
column. The temperature scale is calibrated by two measurements of defined
temperature, such as 0° C for such as water freezing and 100° C for boiling
water. After marking the length of the column for these two temperatures,
the intermediate temperature scale is found by dividing the distance between
the two known points into 100 parts, each of which corresponds to 1° C.

There are at least two important distinctions between digital and analog computers. First, as mentioned, digital machines use discrete, coded information whereas analog computers use continuous data. This means that analog devices cannot work with alphabetic type data. Secondly, analog computers lack the internal program control unit which is a vital part of digital computers. In more abstract terms, we find that there is a fundamental difference between the manipulation of information as done by digital computers and the mimicking of physical behavior accomplished in analog computers.

Problems that are easily handled by an analog computer can also be solved by digital machines, but usually with the penality of lengthy and sophisticated programs. In some instances both types of machines can be combined into a *hybrid* computer to exploit the advantages of each. Such combinations are frequently found in machinery control applications that require rapid control of complex processes.

Further information about analog and hybrid computers can be found in the referenced material at the end of this chapter. Only digital computers will be discussed in the remainder of this text.

REFERENCES TO FURTHER READINGS

FORSYTHE, A. I., KEENAN, T. A., ORGANICK, E. I., STENBERG, W.
Computer Science: A First Course. New York: John Wiley & Sons, 1969.
An introductory text devoted to algorithms and data structures.

KORN, G. A., and KORN, T. M.
Electronic Analog Computers. 2nd Edition, New York: McGraw Hill, 1956.

LIGOMENIDES, P.
Information Processing Machines. New York: Holt, Rinehart & Winston, 1969.

RALSTON, A.
Introduction to Programming and Computer Science. New York: McGraw Hill, 1971.

RICE, J. K., and RICE, J. R.
Introduction to Computer Science. New York: Holt, Rinehart & Winston, 1969.
Provides a large number of problems in different disciplines with introductions to FORTRAN AND ALGOL.

WALKER, T. M., and COTTERMAN, W. W.
An Introduction to Computer Science and Algorithmic Processes. Boston: Allyn and Bacon, 1970.
An introductory text which emphasizes the use of algorithms and flowcharts through use of FORTRAN IV.

KEY WORDS AND PHRASES TO KNOW

ADDRESS	HOLLERITH CODE
ANALOG COMPUTER	HYBRID COMPUTERS
ALGORITHM	INFORMATION SYMBOLS
CENTRAL CONTROL UNIT	INPUT/OUTPUT UNITS
CENTRAL PROCESSING UNIT	INSTRUCTION
CHARACTER CODE	MACHINE LANGUAGE
COMPILER	MEMORY UNIT
DATA	OPERATING SYSTEM
DIGIT	PROGRAM
DIGITAL COMPUTER	STORAGE LOCATION
DIGITAL DEVICE	TIME SHARING

EXERCISES

1. Using the Yellow Pages of a telephone directory make a list of the different computing and programming services available in your vicinity.

2. What are the important differences between a digital computer and a digital device?

3. Explain the principle functions of a digital computer's four main organizational units.

4. Why is it useful for the instruction set to be stored within the memory unit of a digital computer?

5. Explain why addresses are needed to identify the individual storage locations of the prototype computer described in the first section of this chapter.

6. How many different patterns can be created using a block of eight switches (each switch has two positions, ON and OFF)?

7. Suppose that you are given a block of switches. Using the switches to generate coded patterns, what is the minimum number of switches in the block that can represent a character set composed of the upper case alphabetic characters (A to Z), the numerals 0 to 9, the four arithmetic operations, the left and right parentheses, a special replacement symbol, $\leftarrow$, and the following punctuation (;,:,=)?

8. A digital computer works through counting while an analog computer operates

through measuring. Can you think of situations in which analog computers might be more useful than digital computers?

9. Several analog devices were mentioned in the text. What others can you name? List both the quantity measured and its analog.

10. Is it possible for an analog computer to work with alphabetic data? Why?

11. Considering relative speeds of operation, what difficulties might arise in a hybrid computer?

12. What are the differences between standard computing languages and machine languages?

13. What is an algorithm? Can you think of any problems involving algorithms for which solutions do not exist?

14. Describe several common algorithms.

15. Make a list of the standard computing languages available in your computer center. Explain their particular areas of usefulness.

16. List specific jobs in hospitals for which computers are well suited. For each job give the reason why a computer is useful.

17. Relying upon your present understanding of digital computers, explain the types of task best suited for computers.

18. Thinking ahead, what types of occupations will computers and associated mechanization eventually replace? What economic factors could prevent such replacements?

19. What are the three steps needed to solve a problem using a computer?

20. Why is a compiler needed?

21. Using the Standard Binary Coded Decimal (SBCD) character code given in the Appendix II, translate the following message:

    110011 011000 010101 110000 010011 100110 100100 100111
    110100 110011 010101 101001 110000 101001 010101 110101
    100110 100011 110100 110011 011001 100110 100101 110000
    011001 110010 110000 011000 010101 101001 010101

22. Translate the following numbers, stored with the Extended Binary Coded Decimal Interchange Code (EBCDIC):

    11111001 11110001 11110100
    11110110 11110111 11110000 11110010
    11110101 11110100 11110111 11110001

23. Translate the following external data into the card punch code listed in Appendix I:

        PENCIL:=B**2 − 4*A*C;
        ITEM[J, K]:=1.2@ + .03*P/Q;

PROBLEMS

1.   Assume that you are the designer of a money changing machine which dispenses coins upon demand. In the machine the coins are arranged in columns and during any single dispensing operation only one coin can be taken from each column. What is the minimum number of columns required to give any amount up to one dollar? Note that several columns may dispense the same coins.

2.   Following the example shown in Figure 2.2, write a similarly detailed program to compute the product $(X + Y) * (X - Y)$ where X and Y are numbers given to the program. What is the minimun number of addresses needed for this program, assuming each cell has its own address?

3.   Write out the steps needed to search a list of ten names to find one particular name. Use the same technique as in Figure 2.1. Indicate which instructions are needed to modify the internal order in which instructions are chosen.

three

Computers, Algorithms, and Flowcharts

THE ROLE OF COMPUTERS

What is a digital computer? The complete answer to this question is complex for, like a tree with its roots, branches, and leaves, many different levels of structure and perception are involved. To a digital engineer the computer may appear as a large collection of individual devices whose behavior depends upon the structure of certain esoteric materials. To a systems designer, this microscopic detail is blurred into the functions of the internal organizational units. To the computer linguist, the computer is a machine that can be used to create new formal languages advancing the ideas of machine communication and information processing.

To most people, however, the digital computer is an electronic machine that can be used to solve certain types of problems. For their uses, the details of the internal mechanisms seem unimportant in comparison to the idea of a computer as a tool for processing information. Yet, because computers are machines, intelligent use of their attributes cannot be made without some feeling for the computer as it appears in different levels of complexity.

Advances in computer technology and applications during the past 20 years emphasize the usefulness of computers as tools to aid humans in the solution of complex problems. In fact, through a slight exaggeration it might also appear reasonable to identify computers themselves as problem solvers. It is just at this point, however, that it is necessary to establish a fundamental distinction between the problem solving roles of humans and the computational skills of computers. Since computers lack the elusive, creative aspect of the human mind, they can solve problems only in the sense that they can apply certain procedures (or algorithms) that outline specific actions. These actions, when taken in a certain order, will lead to definite results. Whether or not these results solve the original problems cannot be determined by the computer: the computer has done its job by following the specified steps and the algorithms. From this viewpoint, it is humans who must be regarded as the problem solvers and algorithm writers. Computers remain in a subsidiary role as algorithm followers capable of aiding in specific tasks.

PROBLEM SOLVING AND COMPUTER APPLICATIONS

Today there are at least five major areas where computers have had significant impact upon society as algorithm followers. These areas include:

Scientific Applications—The solution of equations describing mathematical models of various processes. Simulation of behavior. Analysis of data. Direct analysis and control experiments.

Business Applications—The solution of business overhead mathematical models. Inventory control. Analysis of data. Planning and estimation. Financial accounting. Maintenance of personnel files.

Control Applications—The use of computers to control tools and factory processes according to pre-established programs.

Communication—Control of communication networks. Telephone dialing and billing. Maintenance of systems. Optimization of routing. Encoding and decoding of transmissions.

File Control—The storage and retrieval of data including updating, cross-referencing and linkage of associated data lists. Inventories, data banks, airline, hotel and car reservation systems, and accounting systems are included.

The problems associated with these computer applications are not trivial, and enormous efforts have been required to create operable systems. To solve the problems associated with each of the tasks listed above, lengthy algorithms have been developed which consider in excruciating detail all possible alternatives.

At this point the meticulous steps involved in creating large algorithms may appear overwhelming. But it is important to realize that while the internal structure of some algorithms may be complicated, the four basic steps needed to use the computer to aid in problem solving are relatively direct. Taken in order, these steps are:

1. Define the problem in terms of specific, calculable objectives
2. Develop the algorithm needed to reach the objectives
3. Verify that the algorithm works
4. Convert the algorithm into a computer program

In this chapter and the next, our principle attention will be directed towards Steps 1 through 3 with emphasis upon the development of algorithms having an internal logical structure compatible with computer operations. The actual translation process needed in Step 4 is not discussed in this text since it involves the specific structure of a particular computing language. Such details, although important to the actual use of the computer, are less demanding than the need to learn the general framework of computer algorithms.

PROBLEMS AND ALGORITHMS

Problems frequently begin as questions which reflect a need for new information. Often problems can be expressed in mathematical form in which the values of certain quantities must be found. Other problems concern the storage and retrieval of data, the comparison of data, the processing of data according to certain steps, and so forth. Typical problems solved using computers range from direct calculation to the management of large data files. Some recent computer tasks include:

The operation of a Federal Data Bank where biographical, economic or other data for any citizen can be rapidly stored and retrieved by authorized users (whether or not to establish the data bank is not a legitimate problem for the computer)

Design and testing of a system to analyze cardiovascular motions

Aid in scouting and game preparation for professional football

Establishing a medical illness data bank that would assist physicians in clinical diagnosis

Calculating the height of a flooding river

The use of a computer-aided teaching system for elementary school pupils

Guidance and control for a spacecraft mission to Jupiter and the outer planets.

To solve a problem it is necessary to define a set of specific goals. These goals answer the question "What needs to be done?" Next, a set of sequential steps must be formulated giving detailed instructions for the way the goals can be reached. These instructions correspond to the question "How do we do it?" By its own nature a computer is not capable of selecting the goals. The computer's job as an algorithm follower is to carry out the sequence of instructions given by the computer programmer.

As discussed in the preceding chapter, we frequently refer to the list of steps needed to solve a problem as an *algorithm*. An algorithm can be more formally defined as

a finite set of unambiguous instructions which provides solutions to a particular class of problems.

One common example of an algorithm is the Federal Income Tax return. These forms give general rules enabling people to compute their income tax. The rules specify particular operations and calculations without prior knowledge of the various numbers or results.

Other examples of algorithms are found in cookbooks, model kit instructions, formulas for making chemicals, and even the steps needed to make a telephone call. The five steps below illustrate an algorithm for using a telephone correctly:

Here's how you may be sure of getting your party more often when you dial:

1. Look up the number in the latest directory,
2. Write down the number,
3. Remove the receiver from its cradle and listen for a dial tone,
4. Dial the number correctly,
5. Wait a minute before you decide your party isn't home.

Because Steps 3 and 4 of this algorithm are ambiguous, another algorithm is also provided to telephone subscribers giving more detail about the mechanics of telephone use:

You'll get quicker service when you dial if you follow these simple steps:

1. Listen for the dial tone. This tone is your signal that the equipment is ready to take your call.
2. Dial each digit of the number in its right order, drawing the dial all the way to the finger stop, removing your finger and letting the dial return naturally, without forcing or hurrying.

As another illustration, an algorithm can be written to describe *the way to find words in a dictionary*. (The *italicized* words describe the *objective* of the algorithm.) Following almost intuitive steps, we obtain:

1. Determine the first letter of the word
2. Find the page of the dictionary where this letter first appears
3. Determine the next letter of the word
4. Find the page where these letters first occur in sequence
5. Continue Steps 3 and 4 for succeeding letters of the word until correspondence is obtained between the desired word and the word listed in the dictionary.

This algorithm, written as a series of steps, illustrates several important points. First, although there are just five commands, the actual number of operations needed to find a word is much greater since Step 5 introduces a continual repetition or *looping* until the word is found. Secondly, the algorithm is partially defective since it is possible that the word we are seeking may not be included in the dictionary. In this case Step 5 will be inadequate when no correspondence can be found. Additional steps describing what to do with cases of verbs, plurals, and so forth must also be provided if the algorithm is to be adequately precise.

Finally, note that the word-finding algorithm involves *labeled* steps, (i.e. it is a *labeled algorithm*). In our previous algorithms such labels were unnecessary and action passed from one step to the next without difficulty. When a repetitive looping is needed, however, labels become important and the sequencing of steps cannot be done without them.

While algorithms are designed to yield results in a step-by-step fashion, many problems are too complex to be analyzed in such a way. Chess, for example, cannot be played according to an algorithm, since the vast number of alternatives and their consequences rule out any algorithmic analysis. Intuition, experience, guess, opinion and other similar terms arise from attempts to base future actions upon experiences of the past. These methods are *heuristic* in nature, meaning that the correct solutions are sought through reference to best guesses which have been successful in the past.

Heuristics provides rules that often lead to a reduced search in problem solving. Thus, an algorithmically programmed computer solves problems by following carefully outlined steps. A heuristically programmed computer, in contrast, would seek solutions through reference to past experience in attempts to obtain optimal results. Consequently, there can be no guarantee whether or not a heuristically programmed computer will be able to solve a particular problem.

The ideas of adaptive learning and behavior implicit in heuristically programmed computers go far beyond the ordinary theories describing the use of algorithmically programmed computers. Although many of the newer research areas of computer science are related to heuristically programmed computers, their level of discussion lies beyond an introductory text. Several references to current work in this area are given at the end of this chapter.

Returning to the topic of computer applications, we see that there are many problems which, because of their complexity, can not be solved through algorithms. If we can find one algorithm for solving a particular class of problems, however, it is often the case that several alternate algorithms will yield the same result. Algorithms are seldom unique. However, when we consider the economy of steps and the degree of complication it is usual to find one "best" algorithm.

ALGORITHM DESIGN AND FLOWCHARTS

To illustrate the methods of algorithm design, consider the organization of clinical medical services as they could be applied on a hypothetical basis. Doctors are faced with the task of attempting to return ill patients to good health. A rough guide to the steps that most doctors use to heal their patients is listed here. Algorithm Objective: To provide medical treatment which optimizes healing. Steps:

1. Learn about the patient's problem
2. Examine and test the patient

3. Consider the symptoms

4. Hypothesize the nature of the illness or malady

5. Consider further medical laboratory tests

6. Initiate a treatment

7. Following progress of patient and repeat Steps 3 through 6 until good health is achieved

We note that many additional details could be included in this algorithm specifying more exactly the types of treatment, the ways in which a patient's progress is monitored, how a particular treatment is decided upon, and so forth. However, as it stands above the medical care algorithm provides us with at least the basic steps involved in clinical diagnosis and treatment.

Several points about this algorithm can be emphasized. First, the algorithm can not guarantee success in all applications since with our present state of knowledge, all persons must eventually die. Therefore, the goal of the medical care algorithm must be to provide optimal diagnosis and treatment within the constraints of current knowledge and technology. Secondly, this algorithm, like all algorithms, presents a set of steps which, if followed in the stated order, can cure patients whose ailments are not too disastrous. The importance of this ordering can be seen since it would be clearly unwise to consider Step 6 before Step 2, while Step 1 is of great importance even if the patient is not sufficiently rational to describe his problem.

For convenience algorithms are often expressed as *flowcharts* so that the sequential instructions can be seen in graphical form. Figure 3.1 shows such a flowchart for the medical care algorithm, ignoring the looping implicit in Step 7.

The symbols START and END in this flowchart show us where the algorithm begins and stops. Each instruction in the flowchart is enclosed in a box and the shape of the box is related to the type of instruction enclosed. The square boxes of this figure, for example, indicate commands for action. The *flowline* connecting the boxes serves as the guide ordering the successive steps of the algorithm.

Once an algorithm has been expressed in flowchart form, a careful examination can be made to detect any logical inconsistencies or possible improvements. For example, in the medical care algorithm the doctor may decide, after listening to a patient's description of his difficulty or after making an initial examination, that no further action is needed or that a specialist should be consulted. Alternate courses of action such as these present *branches* in the flowchart of the algorithm and introduce the need for a new type of flowchart box: The *decision box*.

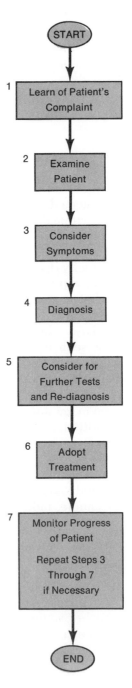

FIGURE 3.1. A first flowchart for the algorithmic approach to medical care.

A decision box is represented as

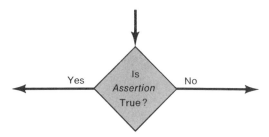

If the contained assertion is true, the flowline follows the "Yes" direction. If it is false, the flowchart leads to a branch in the other direction.

As an indication of the usefulness of the decision box, consider in more detail Step 1 of the medical algorithm. Suppose that a patient appears in the doctor's office, states that his condition is serious and stands awaiting action. Clearly, the flowchart of Figure 3.1 must be altered to include the need for immediate medical treatment. One possible alternative course of action is shown in Figure 3.2 in which there is a decision box containing the question "Is emergency treatment needed?"

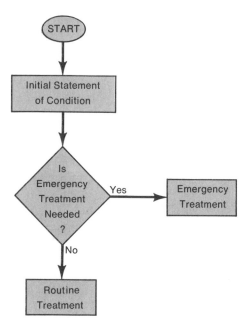

FIGURE 3.2. The decision box which determines when emergency treatment is needed by the patient.

The branch corresponding to "No" leads into the previous sequence of instructions. The branch following the "Yes" exit of the decision box leads to a new series of actions on the part of the doctor. As might be expected, these emergency actions are substantially different from those corresponding to the "No" exit.

Action in a flowchart proceeds from one process box to the next along a single flowline path until a decision box is reached. In the decision box the conditions specified by the assertion are tested, giving a subsequent branching of the flowline. Branches in the algorithm flowline which develop from a decision box are called *conditional branches* because they direct the original single flowline into two separate paths according to the *conditions* expressed by the assertion. The question inside the decision box must always be such that either a "Yes" or "No" answer is adequate. If a decision involves more complicated questions, these must be decomposed into simple units until all possibilities can be answered by a series of "Yes" or "No" responses. The reduction of complex problems to a sequence of what appear to be simple questions admitting only a yes or no answer can be a difficult process, because not only are all intermediate shades of opinion suppressed, but also a bias could easily exist in the question itself.

Another feature of Figure 3.2 is the use of a process box to indicate the *entry of data* into the medical care algorithm. As shown, the doctor can receive information about the patient's condition directly, by medical records, or through statements from other people. The details of the transmission of data need not be elaborated upon, however, since the actual means by which the data are obtained are unimportant to the rest of the algorithm.

We have seen how the use of a *decision box* creates a branch in the flowline of a flowchart. Decision boxes can also lead to another important type of flowchart connection: The *loop*. A *loop* is a type of branch which permits the flowline to return to a previously executed portion of the algorithm. One example of a loop was included in the word-finding algorithm on page 67. Another example of a loop is shown in Figure 3.3 as part of a simple algorithm to help students complete homework problem assignments. In this case the student completes one assigned problem, then asks if another problem should be done. If "Yes", he returns to a new problem; if "No", he has completed his problem assignment and can proceed with his next task.

Loops are important because they permit us to perform many successive, nearly identical operations. Loops can be dangerous, however, if the assertion needed to escape from the loop is incorrectly phrased. In this case the sequence of steps becomes trapped in the loop and a continual repetition occurs.

Using the idea of branching to alternative flowlines, let us continue that portion of the medical care algorithm associated with the decision "Yes,

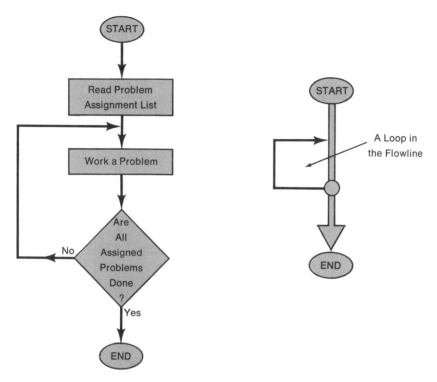

FIGURE 3.3. The homework assignment flowchart with a flowline loop.

emergency treatment is needed." For such a situation, rapid steps must be taken to help the patient. Figure 3.4 indicates a program branch that will provide the patient with this emergency medical care. In addition to the immediate response, we see that the emergency treatment is further strengthened through the addition of a loop which ensures further care if the initial treatment has not succeeded in returning the patient to a reasonable state of health. Note again that the repetitive action provided by loops gives algorithms great power to accomplish a large succession of simple tasks over and over again.

The first decision box in the algorithm shown by Figure 3.4 is interesting in this regard because it divides the algorithm into two separate parts. This branching is absolute in the sense that each branch flowline remains independent with separate terminations.

Returning to the main body of the medical care algorithm, Steps 3 through 6 are of particular importance since they describe the way in which a new condition (the patient's symptoms) is checked against a large body of data (the accumulated medical knowledge of illnesses and bodily malfunctions) to de-

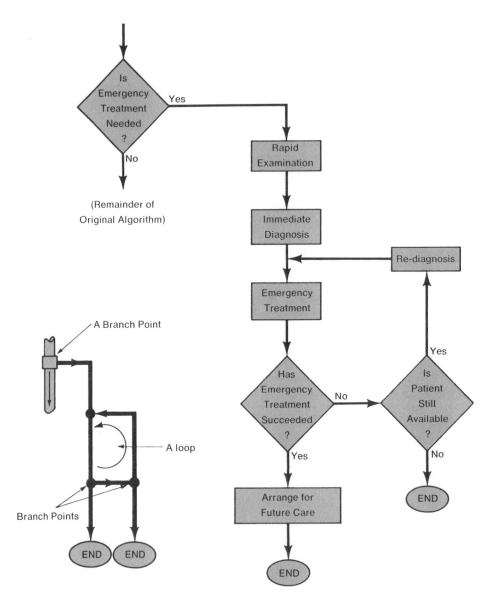

FIGURE 3.4. The emergency treatment part of the medical care algorithm.

termine both the nature of the problem and the treatment needed to return the patient to good health. The flowchart of Figure 3.5 illustrates one approach that can be used to implement Steps 3 through 6. First, the abnormal conditions of the patient are recorded. Next, these symptoms are compared with a

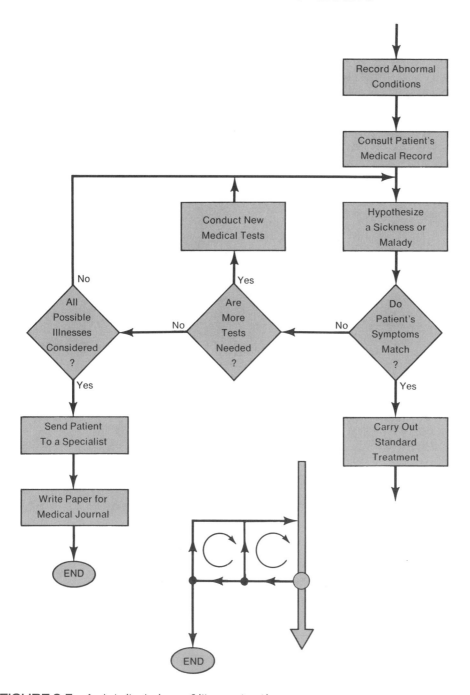

FIGURE 3.5. A detailed view of illness testing.

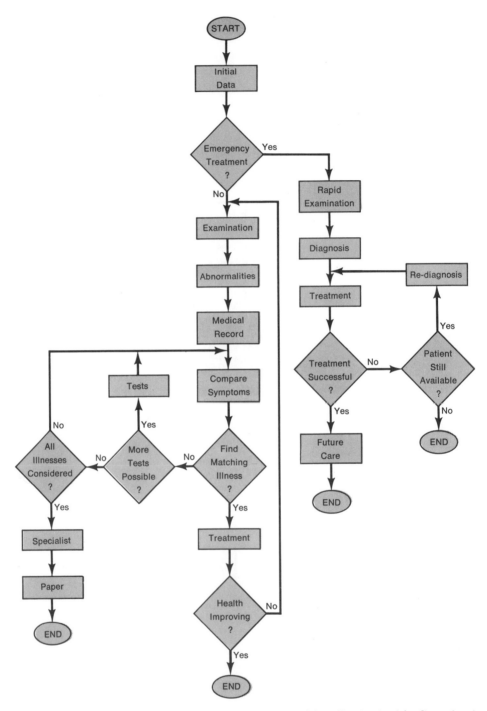

FIGURE 3.6. The complete medical care algorithm illustrated in flowchart form.

list of known illnesses and malfunctions until a correspondence can be found. If a correspondence is found, treatment is prescribed. If no correspondence occurs, the patient must continue to undergo tests performed by another doctor having a more specialized knowledge of the particular symptoms and related illnesses.

The final arrangement of our medical care algorithm can now be presented using the details of the preceding paragraphs. The result, shown in Figure 3.6, presents a reasonably realistic flowchart followed by doctors in the care of patients. At several points in the flowchart decison boxes select possible courses of action and lead to either alternative branches of the program or repetitive loops. We see how consideration of particular aspects of the original flowchart (See Figure 3.1) has led to a substantial increase in detail.

The essential structural paths of the medical care algorithm tend to be obscured by the process and decision boxes. A clearer view of the flowlines can be obtained from Figure 3.7, where the flowlines of alternative branches and loops are made evident. Branch points are indicated by large black dots, while loops are shown by solid arrows. The action flows through different parts of the algorithm in response to the conditional branches. It ends either with a cure or the loss of the patient.

While the practical importance of the medical care algorithm cannot be taken too seriously, it provides an interesting illustration of algorithmic analysis. The medical care algorithm emphasizes the need to design al-

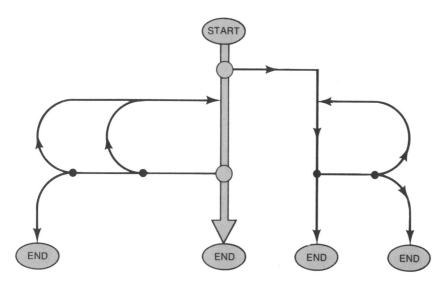

FIGURE 3.7. Flowlines of the medical care algorithm with branches and loops.

gorithms to meet a broad variety of conditions through decision-making networks which channel the action into the responses appropriate to the particular case being considered.

ALGORITHMS, FLOWCHARTS, AND COMPUTERS

An algorithm must provide an unambiguous, ordered set of instructions which lead to a solution for a certain class of problems. For simple tasks, algorithms can frequently be written in an abbreviated form of a *natural language* such as English. This was done, for example, with our first expression of the medical care algorithm on page 68. More complex algorithms with branches and loops soon show us, however, that natural language is not an adequately precise means of algorithmic expression. To overcome this difficulty, flowcharts provide us with an algorithm language through which we can express various operations in terms of geometric shapes and introduce logical ordering through spatial location and flowlines.

The elements of the flowchart language presented in the last section are:

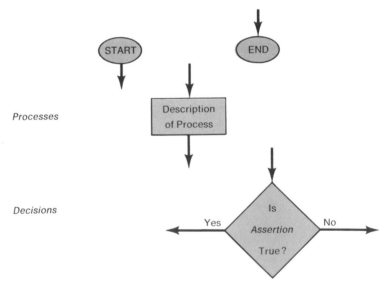

While these diagrams are adequate as a basic flowchart language, some improvements can be made to permit a better expression of algorithms. Before introducing these new elements, however, more needs to be said about the practical uses of flowcharts.

Most flowcharts are developed as an intermediate step in preparing problems for computer solution. It is probable that some day algorithms written in a simplified form of natural language will be acceptable instruction sets for computers. Until then, however, the conversion of algorithms to the formal statements of computer languages must be made by programmers and the best language for the expression of algorithms will remain the flowchart.

The value of flowcharts in preparing computer programs can be considerably increased by designing the flowchart language to treat information flow and flowchart actions (in the process and decision boxes) in a way similar to the actual operations that occur in a computer. This fundamental similarity of operation does not limit the flowchart to a particular computer language, but ensures a minimal amount of difficulty in the final conversion of the algorithm to an operating computer program.

In the following paragraphs the introductory discussion of computer structure given in the last chapter will be used to show basic ways various types of data can be handled inside computers. This involves both the ideas of *variables* and the formation of different types of arithmetic and alphanumeric *expressions*.

VARIABLES

When we use a computer we are interested in obtaining values for different quantities. These quantities are not always mathematical in nature and may involve such varied tasks as comparison of data, finding the best routing for a cross-country telephone call, or choosing the electrical voltages needed for the operation of equipment in an automated factory.

Quantities which can take different values in the course of computations are called *variables*. In a computer, values of variables are contained in separate memory storage locations in the computer memory. To identify these storage locations so that the data stored in them can be used in computations and other operations, we normally lean on mathematical tradition and invent variable names such as X, Y, HEIGHT, NUMBER, and so forth. By doing this we are able to specify operations on and between the different variables irrespective of the values actually stored in the memory storage locations. Operations like "Is X the same as Y?" or "Divide HEIGHT by WIDTH" express general relationships independent of the value of the quantities themselves.

When a variable is named, a link is established between the variable name and one particular storage location in the computer memory. (See Figure 3.8.) Thus, the use of a variable's name in a computer program is actually a reference to the contents of the associated storage location where the value of the variable is stored. A question such as "Is X greater than zero?" is equivalent to asking "Is the content of the storage location we call X greater than the value zero?"

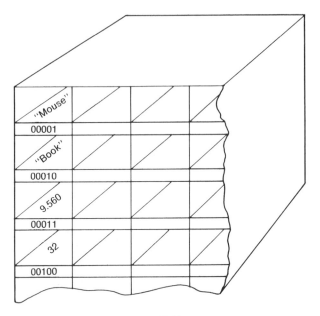

Linkage Table

Variable Name	Memory Address
X	00001
Y	00010
House	00100
Number	00011

FIGURE 3.8. Storage of data in the computer memory.

The content of a storage location may be interpreted as a number, as alphabetic characters, or simply as a string of digits (0s or 1s), depending upon the use for which the variable is intended. Remember, the variable name is only an identifier for a particular memory storage location and that we may repeatedly *change the value of variables by changing the contents of their storage locations*.

There are three main classes of variables used in computers:

1. numerical variables
2. alphanumeric variables
3. logical variables

As might be expected, *numerical variables* have their value represented by numbers. *Alphanumeric variables*, in contrast, have values composed of strings of alphabetic characters, numerals, or other symbols. *Logical variables* are restricted to just two values TRUE or FALSE or sometimes as YES or NO.

Each of these classes of variables has a certain area of usefulness. Numerical variables, for example, are the common quantities of mathematical calculations. With alphanumeric variables it is possible to store and manipulate ordinary written information such as text material, biographical and inventory data, personnel files, and so forth. Finally, certain operations of mathematical logic require the use of logical variables. As discussed in the following sections, each class of variables has its own set of fundamental operations by which variables can be combined, compared, or otherwise manipulated.

REPLACEMENT OF VALUES

The most basic operation in a computer involves *changing the value of a variable*. This is accomplished through *replacement* of the existing value stored in the computer memory by another value. When the existing value is replaced by a new value, the old value is lost forever. Replacement, which is the same as the substitution of a new value, is a destructive operation.

A convenient operation symbol for replacement is ←. If we use this symbol between two variables

$$A \leftarrow B$$

we interpret this as meaning *"Replace the current contents of the storage location corresponding to A by the current contents of B."* The previous value of A is lost, while the value stored under the label of B remains unchanged. Following the replacement operation, the value of A will be the same as the value of B.

A more general form for the replacement operation can be written as:

$$\boxed{\text{variable} \leftarrow expression}$$

The *expression* on the right hand side of the arrow may be a constant or a single variable such as:

$$\boxed{A \leftarrow 3.14} \qquad \boxed{\text{HEIGHT} \leftarrow 10.}$$

or
$$\boxed{C \leftarrow B} \qquad \boxed{D \leftarrow \text{FISH}}$$

These replacements result in the variables on the left hand side of the arrow being given the values associated with the quantities on the right hand side. Replacement with explicit numbers, or constants, permits us to know immediately the current value of A and HEIGHT. The values stored in C and D, however, are not known to us directly since they depend upon the values stored in B and FISH before the operation was carried out. During the process of replacement the values of B and FISH remain unchanged (i.e. the values assigned to C and D are *copies* of the values stored under the names B and FISH).

Numerical Replacements

$$A \leftarrow B * C - 3$$

Before			After	
A	1		A	3
B	2		B	2
C	3		C	3

Alphanumeric Replacements

$$X \leftarrow Y$$

Before			After	
X	"cat"		X	"mouse"
Y	"mouse"		Y	"mouse"

FIGURE 3.9. Examples of numerical and alphabetical replacements.

The term *expression* is actually more general than simple constants or single variables. The term *expression* means any series of data operations among constants and variables that leads to a single value which can be stored in the location identified in the replacement statement. The replacement

$$\boxed{\text{VOLUME} \leftarrow \text{LENGTH} * \text{WIDTH} * \text{HEIGHT}}$$

means that the current values of LENGTH, WIDTH, and HEIGHT are to be multiplied together with the resulting number placed in the storage location assigned to the variable VOLUME. Although expressions based on arithmetical operations between variables ($*$, $/$, $+$, $-$) are easiest to visualize, other data operations such as comparison of alphabetic data or the operations on logical variables are frequently useful.†

When a replacement operation is executed by a computer, the following steps are involved:

a. Copies of the current values of variables used in *expression* must be fetched from their locations in the computer memory

b. *Expression* must be evaluated, using the rules associated with the operation symbols appearing in *expression*, and reduced to a single value

c. The value which results from the evaluation of *expression* must be transferred to the storage location assigned to variable.

Some examples of replacement statements are shown in Figure 3.9.

We note that the value corresponding to *expression* is computed by taking current values of the variables involved from their respective storage locations and performing the requested operations. As a result, it is frequently found that the new variable value is determined by an *expression* which involves the use of the current variable value. For example, the replacement statement:

$$\boxed{A \leftarrow A + 1}$$

means: Take the current value of A, add one to it, and store the result back in the location corresponding to A. If the current value of A is 100, following execution of the above replacement instruction the storage location corresponding to A will hold the value 101.

There are several things one can not do with replacements. The operations

$$\boxed{expression \leftarrow another\ expression}$$

---

†A discussion of logical variables is given in Chapter Ten.

are impossible to carry out because there is no unique way to determine the value for each of the elements of *expression*. The replacement of the existing value of variable with the value of the expression is a one-way operation in which many separate values are combined into one. The reverse decomposition of a single value into many separate values cannot be done.

EXPRESSIONS

The rules for forming expressions are different with numerical, alphanumeric or logical quantities. Years of experience give us some confidence with numerical variables and constants. The ideas behind alphanumeric and logical expressions, in contrast, may be somewhat new.

In the following paragraphs the basic ideas of arithmetic and alphanumeric expressions are discussed. The presentation of logical variables, constants, and expressions is slightly premature at this point and will be deferred until Chapter Ten.

Arithmetic Expressions

Consider first the class of numerical quantities. Since the values associated with these quantities are numbers, the basic operations include addition (+), subtraction (−), multiplication (*), division (/), and exponentiation (↑). Arithmetic expressions are built of numerical variables or constants separated by the arithmetic operation symbols. Examples of valid arithmetic expressions are:

$$A * B$$
$$X/Y$$
$$\text{HEIGHT} + \text{WIDTH}$$
$$\text{MEN} - \text{BOYS}$$
$$S \uparrow T \quad (\text{means } S^T)$$

The forms of several of the arithmetic symbols used here differ from those normally encountered in mathematics. The new symbols have evolved with computer usage and are frequently used in flowcharts and computer programs. As such they are artificial and serve only to indicate to us the nature of the operations. Thus, while the symbols used here are convenient, the symbols used in a particular computer language to carry out the same operation may be very different from those used in the flowchart language.

To prevent misunderstanding it is necessary for all operation symbols in computer-oriented algorithms to be explicitly placed between variables and constants. The expression

$$B^2 - 4AC,$$

taken from the quadratic formula of algebra, is a good example of implied products. Before this expression can be used in a flowchart or computer program it must be rewritten as

$$B \uparrow 2 - 4 * A * C$$

to distinguish the implied multiplications from a possible variable named 4AC.

When an expression such as the above is actually evaluated (i.e. when numerical values are substituted for the variable names) it is necessary to ask, "Which operations are done first?" For instance, we could write the last expression in at least four different ways using parentheses to indicate possible groupings:

$$B \uparrow (2 - 4) * A * C$$
$$B \uparrow (2 - 4 * A) * C$$
$$B \uparrow (2 - 4 * A * C)$$
$$(B \uparrow 2) - (4 * A * C)$$

From experience we know that only the last form is correct. The formal basis for such evaluations follows from certain mathematical conventions establishing a *precedence* among operators in any arithmetic expression. Referring to Figure 3.10, we see that exponentiation is always to be performed first, acting upon the next leftward constant or variable. Next come multiplication and division, followed by addition and subtraction.

As an example, suppose we wish to evaluate the expression

$$A * B + C - DOG \uparrow CAT - FOX$$

where A, B, C, DOG, FOX, and CAT are names for numerical variables. The order of evaluation using replacements would be

$$T1 \leftarrow DOG \uparrow CAT$$
$$T2 \leftarrow A * B$$
$$T3 \leftarrow T2 + C$$
$$T4 \leftarrow T1 + FOX$$
$$RESULT \leftarrow T3 - T4$$

Level	Operation Name	Symbol
First	Exponentiation	↑
Second	Multiplication Division	* /
Third	Addition Subtraction	+ −

FIGURE 3.10. Precedence order for arithmetic binary operands.

where T1, T2, T3, and T4 are temporary variables used to store intermediate values. The result of the evaluation is stored under the name RESULT.

The rules of the precedence table can be altered to some extent through the use of parentheses: Quantities enclosed in parentheses are treated as subunits of the expression which give one value following the indicated internal operations.

When we evaluate the expression

$$A+B*C+D$$

using the values A = 10, B = 3, C = 5, D = 10, we compute

$$10 + 3 * 5 + 10 = 35.$$

With parentheses, however, we can alter this equation to

$$(A + B) * C + D$$
$$(10 + 3) * 5 + 10 = 75$$

or

$$A + B * (C + D)$$
$$10 + 3 * (5 + 10) = 55$$

or

$$(A + B) * (C + D)$$
$$(10 + 3) * (5 + 10) = 195$$

Clearly, parentheses, when used as "separators" to mark the boundaries of groups of items, are a powerful tool that reduce confusion when algebraic expressions are reduced to the arithmetic expressions of flowchart and computer programs.

The evaluation of expressions can also be done pictorially. Using our previous example, we can decompose the operations to the form

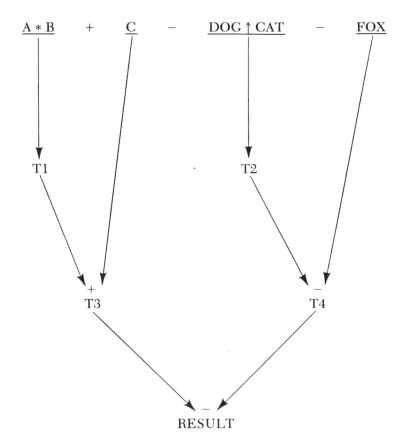

where again T1, T2, T3, and T4 are used to store intermediate values. The value of such a representation is twofold. First, it emphasizes the sequential nature of the evaluation process with the formation of intermediate quantities. Secondly, it prepares the way for discussions of compilers and translators in which standard language expressions are converted into explicit machine language computer commands.

A more complex decomposition procedure must be made for cases where parentheses are present. For example,

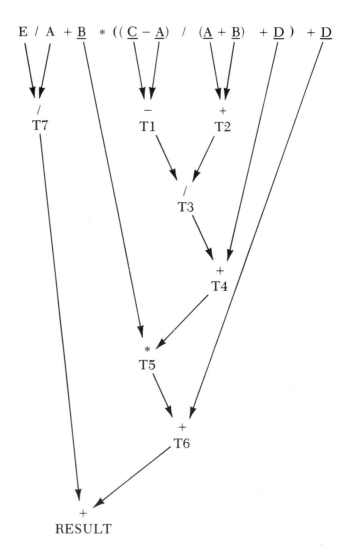

The ordinary arithmetic operators $+$, $-$, $/$, $*$ and $\uparrow$ are always used with two *operands* which provide the data values for the actual operation. Examples might be $3 * A$, $A + B$, $4 /$, $(A + 3) / (B + C)$, and so forth. Operators which require two operands are called *binary operators* (i.e. $+$, $-$, $*$, $/$ and $\uparrow$ belong to this class). A second class of operators is possible for addition and subtraction when expressions such as $\underline{-A}$ + B, C + $\underline{(-D)}$, $\underline{+}$ FOX + DOG are used. In these cases, the underlined symbols for addition and subtraction are used as *unary operators* and special steps must be taken in their evaluation when they occur in conjunction with binary operators. Usually, parentheses can be placed to clarify the intended operations.

$$- A + C \text{ becomes } (- A) + C$$
$$X \uparrow - Y \text{ becomes } X \uparrow (-Y)$$
$$B / + A \text{ becomes } B / (+A)$$
$$\text{but } -A \uparrow X \text{ is usually } - (A \uparrow X) \text{ and not } (- A) \uparrow X$$

More About Arithmetic Variables

Up to this point we have tacitly assumed that the arithmetic operations leading to the evaluation of an arithmetic expression are relatively self-evident. Thus, it might seem that an evaluation of an expression such as A / B with A = 4, B = 8 should give the value 0.5. While such a result is certainly correct in a mathematical sense, computers are slightly eccentric in their treatment of numbers as a consequence of the different ways integer and decimal point numbers are stored in the computer memory. A complete discussion of the relevant number storage ideas is given in Chapter Six. Here, it is sufficient to note that because a computer distinguishes between integer and decimal point numbers, it is necessary to introduce two classes of arithmetic variables: *integer variables* and *real variables*. Integer variables have integer values: real variables have numbers with decimal values (including scientific notation where powers of 10 are present).

Arithmetic Variables

Integer Variables	Decimal-Point Variables
1, -15, 2342, 0	16., -7.3, 1.3×10^4

The existence of two types of arithmetic variables directly affects the fundamental replacement operation

$$variable \leftarrow expression$$

since *expression* can have either an integer or real (decimal point) value which must be converted, if necessary, into a number that is consistent with the class of variable on the left side of the replacement operator. To make these conversions several conventions have been widely but not necessarily universally adopted. The first is:

Convention 1. If the variable is a real variable, the value of expression is converted to a decimal value before replacement.

Example: VR is a real variable. The replacement

$$VR \leftarrow \quad 1 \quad \text{gives a value of} \quad 1. \text{ to VR,}$$
$$VR \leftarrow \quad 2.3 \text{ gives a value of} \quad 2.3 \text{ to VR,}$$
$$VR \leftarrow -5 \quad \text{gives a value of} -5. \text{ to VR,}$$
$$VR \leftarrow \quad 0 \quad \text{gives a value of} \quad 0. \text{ to VR.}$$

Convention 2. If the variable is an integer variable, the value of expression is truncated to an integer value before replacement (all digits to the right of the decimal point are omitted entirely).

Example: VI is an integer variable.

$$VI \leftarrow \quad 2.3 \text{ gives a value of} \quad 2 \text{ to VI,}$$
$$VI \leftarrow \quad 9.0 \text{ gives a value of} \quad 9 \text{ to VI,}$$
$$VI \leftarrow \quad 0.6 \text{ gives a value of} \quad 0 \text{ to VI,}$$
$$VI \leftarrow -1.9 \text{ gives a value of} -1 \text{ to VI.\dagger}$$

The identification of variable types in computer language is done in several ways. In ALGOL, for example, declarations are made at the beginning of all programs, listing the type REAL and the type INTEGER variables. In FOR-TRAN, all variable names must begin with an alphabetic character. Those starting with letters "I" through "N" are automatically typed as integer variables, while all others are assumed to be real variables. Exceptions to the rule are possible too.

Expressions with Integer and Real Numbers

The distinction between real and integer variables and constants affects the evaluation of arithmetic expressions. To see this, consider the replacement

$$A \leftarrow B + C / A + 1$$

where A and C are integer variable, 1 is an integer constant, and B is a real variable. To evaluate the expression on the right side we must mix integer and

†In some computer systems, truncation of a negative number gives the next most negative whole number. In this case such a computer gives the value − 2 to VI.

real values, for example, B + 1. Likewise, the division operator, although it acts on integer variables, would appear to give a real (decimal) value. To guide the evaluation of such mixed-mode expressions, new conventions are needed. Again, however, these conventions are arbitrarily defined and may differ from language to language or even between computers.

Convention 3. If the operands for the binary operators +, −, ∗ and ↑ are both real, the result is a real number. If the operands are both integer, the result is an integer.

Convention 4. If the operands of +, −, ∗ and ← are mixed, one being real and one being integer, the result is real.

Convention 5. The division operator / gives a real result. The division operator ÷ results in a truncated integer.

Examples:

A = 1.5 (real)
B = 4. (real)
I = 2 (integer)
J = −1 (integer)
K = 4 (integer)

A / B	assumes the value	0.375	(real)
A + B	assumes the value	5.5	(real)
A ∗ B	assumes the value	6.	(real)
B ÷ A	assumes the value	2	(integer)
I ÷ J	assumes the value	−2	(integer)
I ÷ K	assumes the value	0	(integer)
K ÷ I	assumes the value	2	(integer)
I / J	assumes the value	−2.	(real)
I / K	assumes the value	.5	(real)
K / I	assumes the value	2.	(real)
A + I	assumes the value	3.5	(real)
A / I	assumes the value	.75	(real)
A ÷ I	assumes the value	0	(integer)

Using the variable names and types listed in the above example, a pictorial decomposition can be made of the replacement

$$\text{IRESULT} \leftarrow K \div A + B * ((I - A) \div (A + B) + J) + J,$$

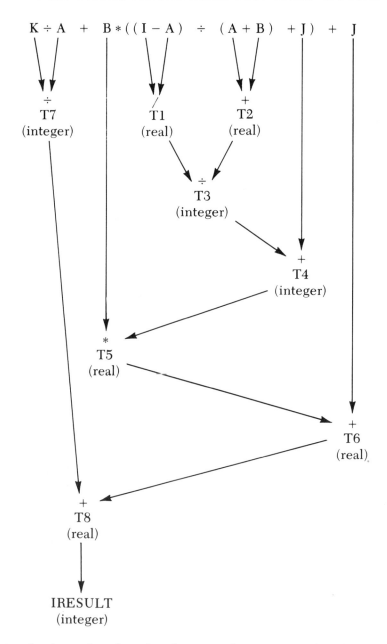

Using the data values listed in the example, IRESULT has the value − 3. If the ordinary division operator / had been used in place of ÷ , what value would have been obtained?

The values contained in storage locations assigned to numerical variables are numbers. As we have seen in the last chapter, other forms of data can be placed in computer storage locations and among these are alphanumeric quantities. Alphanumerics consist of letters, numbers, or special characters. Alphanumeric variables can be represented by ordinary names such as X, Y, HOUSE, and so forth, with their value determined by the symbols contained in the associated memory storage location.

The values corresponding to alphanumeric variables are called *character strings*. Strings consist of sequences of alphanumeric symbols such as those found in text material, inventory descriptors, or other similar quantities. Specific examples of character strings might be:

"H.G.__WELLS;__WAR__OF__THE__WORLDS"
"G1361__MIRO__COMPOSITION__1969"
"YES"
"1253.58"

There are several important points to note about character strings. First, for purposes of notation, a string is contained between quotation marks "———" which indicate the start and end of the material stored within the computer memory. Secondly, blanks are symbols within the string, even though they represent an absence of printing. To avoid confusion, we will indicate blanks in this text with the symbol __ .

A more subtle question involves the string "1253.58" which, except for the quotation marks, would seem to be a value we would normally associate with numerical variables. The distinction lies in the different ways true numbers and character strings are stored within the computer. The quantity "1253.58" would be stored in a memory storage location using the digital code for the symbol 1, followed by the code for the symbol 2, followed by the code for the symbol 5, and so forth. The number 1253.58, if kept in a computer, would normally not be represented in such a symbolic way but would use the much more efficient number storage techniques discussed in Chapter Six.

Since character strings are values, they can be associated with alphanumeric variable names through replacement:

JET ← "123jump"

in which the string on the right side is now the value associated with JET and consists of the ordered codes for the symbols 1, 2, 3, j, u, m, p, and not just the name of some other variable. The indicated replacement causes the old value

FIGURE 3.11. Concatenation is the joining of separate character strings.

of JET to be discarded and the new value "123jump" to be stored in the memory location assigned to JET.

It is also possible to have an alphanumeric replacement made between two alphanumeric variables:

$$JET \leftarrow PASSENGERS$$

This replacement takes the current nonnumerical value of PASSENGERS and stores it under JET. Operations such as this permit internal transfer of symbolic data.

The next step, internal operations leading to string manipulation of alphanumerical expressions, is somewhat more complicated than the ordinary arithmetical operations between numbers. As indicated below, there are four basic string operations. The first operation, *concatenation*, involves the formation of a single string by linking together in chain-like fashion two other strings. (See Figure 3.11.) Introducing the symbolic concatenation operator $\oplus$, concatenation between strings can be accomplished as

Page 95   "abcd" $\oplus$ "efgh" gives "abcdefgh"

"john_" $\oplus$ "von_neumann" gives "john_von_neumann"

The same operator can be used between alphanumeric variables:

$$ALPHA \oplus OMEGA$$

$$BOOK \oplus PENCIL$$

Of course, the current character strings associated with these alphanumerical variables are not known. The resulting alphanumerical expression gives, however, a single string which could be used in a replacement statement

$$RESULT \leftarrow ALPHA \oplus OMEGA$$

Owing to its nature, multiple concatenations can be done

$$LIST \leftarrow A1 \oplus A2 \oplus A3 \oplus A4 \oplus \text{"end\_of\_string"}$$

with LIST representing the value of one long string.

Concatenation builds sequential strings from smaller strings. The next two string operations act upon a single string: the first, by obtaining a substring of sequential characters from the original setting: the second, through insertion of a new character string within the original string.

To indicate the formation of a substring (See Figure 3.12), the operator *sub* [*string, k, l*] is used. Here *string* indicates either an alphanumerical variable name or an actual string and the integer *l* indicates the number of consecutive characters to be removed from *string*, starting leftmost with the *k*−th symbol of *string*. For example,

$$sub \ [\text{``the\_\_injury\_\_of\_\_time''}, \ 15, \ 4]$$

would give the substring "time". A more indirect way of obtaining the same result would be

$$\text{LIST} \leftarrow \text{``the\_\_injury\_\_of\_\_time''}$$
$$\text{RESULT} \leftarrow sub \ [\text{LIST}, \ 15, \ 4]$$

with RESULT now containing the string "time".

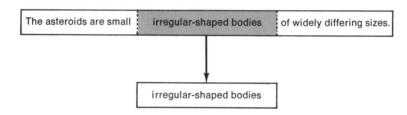

FIGURE 3.12. Formation of a substring from another string.

The insertion of a substring (See Figure 3.13) into another string can be done with the operator

$$insrt \ [string1, \ string2, \ k]$$

which means, insert *string2* into *string1* at the point following the *k*−th character of *string1*. Thus, the operation . . .

$$\text{LIST1} \leftarrow \text{``in\_\_the\_\_month\_\_of\_\_may''}$$
$$\text{LIST2} \leftarrow \text{``merry''}$$
$$\text{RESULT} \leftarrow insrt \ [\text{LIST1}, \ \text{LIST2}, \ 7]$$

gives the variable RESULT the value "in__the__merry__month__of__may".

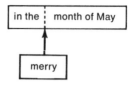

FIGURE 3.13 Insertion of a string to form a larger string.

The same operator can be used to operate on strings alone:

$$NOW \leftarrow insrt \; [\text{“1256”}, \text{“34”}, 2]$$

assigns the string "123456" to NOW.

The final string operation to be introduced, *loc*, is much more subtle than *insrt*, *sub*, or concatenation. The purpose of

$$loc \; [string1, string2]$$

is to search *string1* to see if it contains *string2*. (See Figure 3.14.) If it does, *loc [string1, string2]* is given a numerical value corresponding to the position of the left–most character of *string1* where *string2* begins. If there is no correspondence between the two strings, this value is set to zero.

The observable aspect of a comet is the extensive tail which is developed and irretrievably lost during passage through the inner solar system.

FIGURE 3.14. Search of a character string to find whether or not a specified substring is present.

To illustrate the use of this operation, let

TEXT ← "Farewell!_Thou_art_too_dear_for_my_possessing,
_and_like_enough_thou_knowest_thy_estimate."
HUNTED ← "possessing"

so that the numerical variable POINTER given by

$$POINTER \leftarrow loc \text{ [TEXT, HUNTED]}$$

would have a value of 36. Thus, the *loc* operation organizes a search through TEXT in an effort to find the string represented by HUNTED. If HUNTED were different, say

$$HUNTED \leftarrow \text{``sonnets''},$$

then $$POINTER \leftarrow loc \text{ [TEXT, HUNTED]}$$

would result in POINTER being given the value zero (i.e. the string "sonnets" was not contained in TEXT).

Alphanumerical expressions are formed through the use of the basic string operations. In some computer languages (FORTRAN for example), the manipulation of strings and other text material is difficult and the operations discussed here are not available. A further difficulty arises from the limited storage space actually available in a memory storage location. Here we have tacitly assumed that alphanumeric values can be strings of any length. Actually, there is a limit to the number of character symbols which can be stored in one location and new methods must be used to store large amounts of sequential alphanumeric data. Unfortunately, the precise methods of storing and processing such data vary between languages and computers so that it is not yet possible to describe a general approach.

COMPUTER ORIENTED FLOWCHARTS: THE FIRST STEPS

The ideas of variables and expressions can be illustrated through two algorithms: the first involving numerical quantities and expressions and the second derived from the need for nonnumerical data processing.

Temperature Conversion

The object of this algorithm is to convert temperatures measured in degrees Fahrenheit to corresponding Celsius measure. (See Figure 3.15.) The formula expressing the Celsius temperature, T, in degrees Celsius, is
$$T = 5/9 \, (T_F - 32)$$
where T_F is the temperature, measured in degrees Fahrenheit.

To begin, let us define TEMP to be a real variable giving the desired Celsius temperature, while TF is a real variable giving the Fahrenheit temperature. If the value of TF is given to the algorithm through the statement

READ
TF

the algorithm can be expressed in flowchart form as shown below.

Note that the desired result, TEMP, is obtained from the algorithm through

WRITE TEMP. Clearly, both the READ and WRITE statements are simple

forms of the actual commands needed to enter and remove data from a computer system.

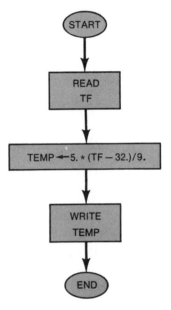

FIGURE 3.15. Flowchart for converting Fahrenheit temperatures to Celsius.

Correcting a String

Let us consider a somewhat more complex problem. Suppose we are given a string of 100 characters that has one incorrect symbol contained within it at the m−th symbol position (we always count from left to right in this string). To correct this error we can take the following steps:

1. Form a substring composed of the first m − 1 symbols (i.e. all characters up to, but not including, the mistake).

  2. Form a substring composed of the last characters extending from m + 1 up through 100

  3. Concatenate the string of Step 1, the correct symbol, and the string of Step 2

These steps are shown in flowchart form in Figure 3.16. We see that the value of m and the correct character are given by the statements READ DATA and READ M, CORRECTION . Here, DATA is an alphanumerical variable

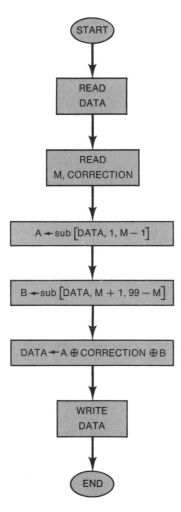

FIGURE 3.16. Flowchart for the correction of a string.

which represents the original error-containing string. M is the numerical variable representing the symbol number for the error. The variables A and B are used to collect the substrings according to Steps 1 and 2, and CORRECT is an alphanumerical variable representing the correct symbol to be placed in DATA. The final action, $\boxed{\text{WRITE DATA}}$, is necessary to obtain the correct form of the character string.

THE USES OF COMPUTERS

The increasing availability of computers during the past 20 years is a tribute to their effectiveness in a broad range of applications. Concurrent with this growth of the computer population there has arisen a modern philosophy which encourages the idea that computers are indispensable partners to the future of mankind. The enthusiasm of this philosophy is enormous and countless success stories can be found in the legends of computer usage. In addition, prognostications based on the growth of technology in the advanced nations of the world indicate that, without computers, the current pace of development cannot be maintained. To provide even the present population of the world with adequate food, fuels, manufactured goods, and information processing, computer-guided data systems are already indispensable.

Many suggestive pressures are inherent in the pervasive computer-partner philosophy. As a consequence, it is easy to overlook the basic limitations of computers and overestimate their capabilities and usefulness. Although not widely publicized, histories of computer-system failures can be found which demonstrate that the computer, like other tools, can be misused.

The decisions leading to grand-scale computer applications are beyond our discussions in this text. Even for more modest tasks, however, one must be continually aware of the possibility that the use of a computer for a particular application may not be cost-effective, when a balance is taken between the value of human labor and machine results.

To evaluate whether a particular problem justifies the use of a computer, there are five basic questions which should be asked:

1. Is problem useful? Is there a measurable benefit?
2. Can problem be defined to permit computational results?
3. Can steps needed to solve problem be expressed in algorithmic form?
4. Is there a need for repeated use of the resulting computer code?

5. Is the cost of labor involved in creating the computer codes needed to solve the problem less than the eventual benefits? That is, will the application of a computer to this problem be cost-effective?

Only after a careful evaluation of these questions should the decision be made to use a computer.

REFERENCES TO FURTHER READINGS

BOHL, M.,
Computer Concepts. Chicago: Science Research Associates, 1970.

DAVIS, E.E. and TRUXAL, J.G.
The Man-Made World. New York: McGraw Hill, 1970.
An interesting exposition of science, mathematics and technology in the modern world. Well worth reading.

DAVIS, G.B.
Computer Data Processing. New York: McGraw Hill, 1969.
Discusses elementary programming techniques with emphasis on data processing.

FORSYTHE, A.L., KEENAN, T.A., ORGANICK, E.L., STENBERG, W.
Computer Science: A First Course. 2d ed. New York: J. Wiley & Sons, 1975.
The chapters dealing with program organization are particularly worthwhile.

GEAR, C.W.
Introduction to Computer Science. Chicago: Science Research Associates, 1973.
An advanced introduction to many of the details of computers and computer programming.

HILL, H.C.
Information Processing and Computer Programming, An Introduction. Los Angeles: Melville Publishing Company, 1973.

ROTHMAN, S. and MOSMANN, G.
Computers and Society. Chicago: Science Research Associates 1972.

WALKER, T.M.
Introduction to Computer Science. Boston: Allyn and Bacon, 1972.

KEY WORDS AND PHRASES TO KNOW

ALGORITHM
ALPHANUMERIC EXPRESSIONS
ALPHANUMERICAL VARIABLE
ARITHMETIC EXPRESSIONS
ASSERTION
BINARY OPERATIONS
CODES
CONCATENATION
CONDITIONAL BRANCH
CONSTANTS
DATA FILES
DECISION BOX
EXPONENTIATION
EXPRESSION
FLOWLINE
HEURISTICALLY PROGRAMMED COMPUTERS
INTEGER NUMBERS
LOOPS
NATURAL LANGUAGE
NUMERICAL VARIABLE
PARENTHESES
PROCESS BOX
REAL NUMBERS
REPLACEMENT
RULES OF PRECEDENCE
STANDARD COMPUTING LANGUAGE
STRING
STRING OPERATIONS
UNARY OPERATIONS
VARIABLE
VARIABLE NAME

EXERCISES

1. Write down the algorithm for finding pleasant music on the radio.
2. Write the algorithm for preparing pancakes.

3. Explain why it might be difficult to write an algorithm designed to bring about the election of a person to public office.

4. Write an algorithm for changing a car's flat tire.

5. Write an algorithm describing the balancing of a check book at the end of the month. Include as many unpleasant details and alternatives as possible.

6. Explain in more detail why clinical medicine is heuristic in character.

7. Write the algorithm for dividing an n-digit number by an m-digit number (assume n > m).

8. Write the algorithm for multiplying an n-digit number by an m-digit number (assume n > m).

9. Write an algorithm for finding a particular book in a large library.

10. Write an algorithm that examines a given word to find any shorter words which may be contained as units within it. Note that the dictionary algorithm will be useful here.

11. Express the following algebraic expressions as replacement statements. Draw the resulting pictorial representations similar to that in the text.

   a. $y = a + b/c$

   b. $x = \dfrac{2a}{1 + a}$

   c. $z = (x + 2)^2$

   d. $y = \dfrac{\dfrac{a}{a + b}}{\dfrac{b}{a + 1}}$

   e. $x = \dfrac{y}{(2 + 3y^2)}$

   f. $S = \frac{1}{2}g\, t^2 + vt + d$

   g. $d = \left(\dfrac{a + b}{a - b}\right)^2$

12. Express the following replacement statements as algebraic expressions.
   a. $X \leftarrow A / B / C$
   b. $HOUSE \leftarrow (ROOF - TOP) / (ROOF + TOP) \uparrow 2$
   c. $Y \leftarrow A / B + A * (1 + B \uparrow 2) \uparrow 2$
   d. $Z \leftarrow A / (A + 1) / (A + 2) / (A + 3)$
   e. $WILL \leftarrow (IDEAS + LAWYER) / TESTINESS / PROVOCATION$
   f. $M \leftarrow (M + A) / (M - A)$
   g. $U \leftarrow X * V / W - Z$

13. Determine the value of the variable A at the points indicated by the arrows adjacent to the following consecutive set of replacement statements.

   $STRING \leftarrow$ "William—desired—to—reign—not—as—a—conquerer—
   but—as—a—lawful—king."
   $NAME \leftarrow$ "J.R.—Green"

$$A \leftarrow STRING + NAME$$

a. → $$TEMP \leftarrow sub \; [A, 35, 9]$$
$$A \leftarrow TEMP$$

b. → $$MISSING \leftarrow \text{", author"}$$
$$A \leftarrow insrt \; [NAME, MISSING, 11]$$

c. → $$A \leftarrow STRING + A$$
$$A \leftarrow loc \; [A, \text{"conquerer"}]$$

14. The short error replacement algorithm of the next to the last secion could have been written to correct misspelled words. Write an algorithm which, given a set of text, searches for a particular misspelled word (given as data) and corrects it.

15. Using the string operations defined in this chapter, write an algorithm which can determine whether or not a word or phrase is palindrome (i.e. whether or not it is the same when read backward and forward).

16.   *"Eway anceday innay anay ingray andnay upposesay utbay*
           ethay ecretsay itssay innay ethay iddlemay andnay owsknay."

Obertay Ostfray

This message has been written in Pig Latin, a form of English popular among children. Special rules govern this language by specifying certain changes in the structure of each word in the original text. These rules to convert English words into Pig Latin are:

1. If a word starts with a vowel, add "nay".

2. If a word starts with a consonant, move the first group of letters before a vowel to the end of the word and add "ay".

Write a flowchart algorithm using the string operators of this chapter to translate Pig Latin text into English.

17. Reverse the steps of the last problem by writing a flowchart algorithm which converts English text into Pig Latin. Discuss any ambiguities which may arise.

PROBLEMS

1. In the final stages of a checker game the arrangement of pieces is often that shown below. Using the indicated square numbers for identification, write the algorithms for Red to win when: a) Black is to move first and b) when Red moves first. For this algorithm assume that jumps of opponent pieces must be made when available. Note that the square identification labels are given in terms of row and column locations.

COLUMN

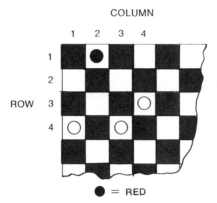

● = RED

2. In the game of NIM a number of sticks, usually 13, are placed on a table. Two players, A and B, take turns removing 1, 2, or 3 of the sticks until one player is forced to take the last stick and lose the game. In actual practice, NIM is not a true game since the player who has the first move can always be defeated through proper moves by the second player. Experience with a few trial games quickly shows that player B will win if he arranges to pick up the sixth remaining stick (i.e. if he can manage to leave five sticks for A).

   After playing a few games, write the algorithm needed for B to win at NIM. Assume that the number of sticks picked up by A is read into the algorithm through repeated READ, A operations.

3. The game of War is played by two children with a deck of 52 cards. To begin the deck is divided evenly. The players then simultaneously show one card. The highest ranking card wins; the cards are given to the winning player and the play repeats until no more cards remain. In the case of ties (when identical cards are shown), the winner of the next play takes the previous cards. The overall winner of the game is determined by counting the number of cards each player has accumulated.

   Write an algorithm to describe the way War is played. Note that this algorithm should not not attempt to describe how to win at War.

4. The card game of Twenty-one, known also as Black Jack, or Pontoon, is played between a dealer and several opponents. In play each person in the game receives two initial cards whose point value (Face cards—10, Aces—11 or 1, all others as indicated value) must be equal to or less than 21. The object of the game is to get more points than the dealer. The point value of any player can be increased by accepting additional cards, one at a time, from the dealer. If more than 21 points are accumulated, however, the dealer automatically wins. If the player receives a jack of spades or clubs and an ace, he or she automatically wins. If the initial two cards formed a pair, the player may split them into two groups and receive extra cards on each group. If a player has five cards and the total is still equal to or less than 21, he or she wins.

Write an algorithm for playing Twenty-one against a dealer. Unlike the previous algorithms, an element of strategy is present since a decision must be made about accepting additional cards. Because we have omitted the betting procedure, this algorithm will not be immediately useful at Las Vegas!

5. The algorithmic steps we use to do multiplication are comfortable and familiar. Nevertheless, they are not at all unique and various other multiplication algorithms can be found. One interesting example of this is the old method of multiplication used by Russian peasants and described below.

To multiply two numbers, two adjacent columns are formed headed by the multiplicand and multiplier. Passing down the left column, numbers are successively divided by two (always ignoring remainders) until the number one is reached. Similarly, the right column is a list of numbers created by successive multiplications by a factor of two. Next, even numbers in the left column and the corresponding right column numbers are cancelled out. The final product is obtained by summing the remaining elements of the right column. An example of the method is shown below.

$$77 \times 11$$

77	11
38	~~22~~
19	44
9	88
~~4~~	~~176~~
~~2~~	~~352~~
1	704
	847 final product

Write a flowchart describing the Russian peasant method of multiplication.

6. Suppose that you are given some large number, N. How can you determine if it is precisely divisible (no remainder) by the integer 12? One rule for such a perfect divisibility is that N be exactly divisible by 3 and the last two digits of N form a number which is exactly divisible by 4. There is little difficulty in determining whether or not the two-digit number formed by the last two digits of N is divisible by 4. The property for divisibility by 3 is slightly more complex, however. The rule is, if the sum of the digits of N is divisible by 3, N itself is divisible by 3.

Using the preceding information, write the algorithm for divisibility by 12 in the form of a flowchart.

More About Flowcharts and Algorithms

MORE ABOUT FLOWCHARTS

The flowcharts of Chapter three were chosen to indicate how problems can be solved using algorithms. These flowcharts were only a first step towards a complete expression of the details of the algorithms, however, since the use of assertions and commands in natural language form often lead to ambiguities. Because we now have some insight into the way variables and expressions are treated in a computer, we can refine our previous definitions for the different operation boxes.

Process Boxes

The symbol

> *process*

is used to summarize the different operations needed to manipulate variables in the algorithm. The most frequent "process" described in a process box is that of replacement, i.e.

> *variable ← expression*

Typical processes might include

> $N \leftarrow N + 1$ $HAT \leftarrow CAT \uparrow 2$ [Numerical variables]

> $NAME \leftarrow$ "123" $ABC \leftarrow XYZ +$ "remainder"   [Alphanumeric variables]

Another use of the process box can be expressed as

> What to do

Here a simple description is given without bothering to present all of the revelant internal operations needed to actually carry out the operation. Examples of this approach might be:

| Compare symptoms with symptoms of other diseases | or | Find the largest number from a set of numbers. |

The previous medical care algorithm and flowchart, Figure 3.6, made exclusive use of such general descriptions. The difficulty with descriptive statements, however, is that they do not represent a sufficiently microscopic view of the actual steps needed to yield the stated result. Descriptions of certain procedures are most useful in the early development of an algorithm when the logical structure of the algorithm must be accurately defined. In the final, computer-oriented algorithm such descriptive procedures must be explained, either through the complete list of steps or through the use of a particular subalgorithm which has separately explained steps and function.

Frequently, the "What to do" boxes define specific tasks such as:

| Find the largest number from a set of numbers | or | Arrange a list of names in alphabetical order |

which are actually subalgorithms or subsidiary sets of actions which are relatively self-contained. Once written, subalgorithms (also called subroutines or procedures) can be used in different algorithms where a particular task must be done. A subalgorithm for computing square roots, for example, would be very valuable for programs of arithmetic computation. If a sufficiently large collection of such subalgorithms were available, creating main algorithms consisting of choices between appropriate subalgorithms would be possible. Further information about subalgorithms is given in the last section of this chapter.

Decision Boxes

Decision boxes are symbolized by

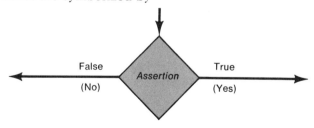

Assertion	Variable Type	Meaning
$A > 0$	numerical	Is the value of A greater than zero?
$B \uparrow 2 \leq 4 * A * C$	numerical	Is the value of $B \uparrow 2$ less than or equal to the value of $4 * A * C$?
$F * A - 3 = BIG$	numerical	Is the value of $F * A - 3$ equal to the value of BIG?
$X = YELLOW$	alphanumeric	Is the value of X the same as the value YELLOW?
$SUN = \text{"hello"}$	alphanumeric	Is the value of SUN the same as "hello"?

FIGURE 4.1.

so that a branch is developed in the flowchart flowline depending upon whether *assertion* is True (Yes) or False (No).

Previously we have used simple verbal assertions such as "Are more tests required?" or "Do more homework problems remain to be done?" For the development of more specific algorithms based on the manipulation of variables, a more precise description of *assertion* is needed.

The simplest form of *assertion* for numerical variables and constants is

$$expression1 \otimes expression2$$

where *expression 1* and *expression 2* are separate arithmetic expressions involving numerical variables, numerical constants, and arithmetic operations. The symbol $\otimes$ represents any one of the arithmetic relational operators shown.

$\otimes$	Meaning
$=$	equal to
$\neq$	not equal to
$\geq$	equal to or greater than
$>$	greater than
$\leq$	equal to or less than
$<$	less than

When a computer evaluates an assertion it executes the following steps:

a.   Values corresponding to variables needed to calculate *expression 1* and *expression 2* are fetched from memory.

b.   The values of the two expressions are computed.

c.   The two values are compared. If the assertion is true [Is *expression 1* $(=, \neq, \geq, >, \leq, <)$ *expression 2* true?] then the algorithm branches to the True (Yes) exit of the decision box. If the assertion is false (No) the False (No) exit is used.

The assertions in Figure 4.1 show the way the relational operators are most frequently used with numerical values.

The relational operators permit us to compare the numerical values of expressions and provide alternative algorithm flowlines which depend upon the result of the comparison. Examples of decision boxes using relational operators to compare two expressions are shown in Figure 4.2.

The decisions relating to alphanumeric quantities are much more restricted than those for numerical quantities. The *assertion* for alphanumeric quantities is usually of the form

$$expression\ 1 = expression\ 2$$

where the alphanumeric expressions can be given by string operations or alphanumeric variables.

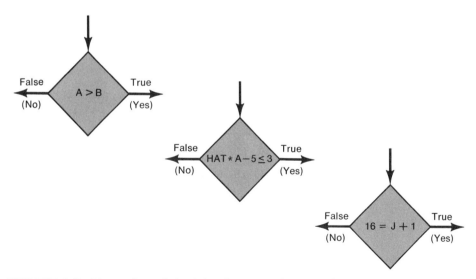

FIGURE 4.2. Examples of decision boxes using relational operators.

Examples such as

assertion	Meaning
J = "ice"	Is the value of J $\left(\begin{array}{c}\text{the same as}\\\text{equal to}\end{array}\right)$ "ice"?
XRAY = GAMMA	Is the value of XRAY equal to the value of GAMMA?
"987" = "how"	Is "987" the same as "how"?

illustrates the use of alphanumeric assertions using both constants and variables. Other relational operators such as $\geq$, $\leq$, etc. have no basic meaning when applied to alphanumeric values without some set of arbitrarily assigned priorities for the groupings of alphanumeric coded characters. For some problems, such as alphabetizing lists of names or arranging alphabetic data, it is possible to construct character codes in such a way that the arithmetic relational operators can be used.

Input and Output Boxes

Up to this point we have not elaborated on the means by which a computer communicates with the external world. It has been sufficient to use the symbols

Read		Write

in our algorithms to show where data values are needed in the course of calculations.

The reason for this reluctance to discuss the way data enters or leaves an algorithm is that the actual mode of communication is relatively unimportant. The data input/output boxes assure that data values are available to the computation or are given as results. It is only in a computer program that a specific form of data communication must be employed.

The most common forms of data input to a computer are punched cards, typewriter keyboards, and magnetic tape. Punched paper tape, magnetic discs, video devices, or direct digital data in the form of electrical pulses can also be used. Data output can be printed pages, punched cards, punched tape, magnetic tape, various visual and audio displays, or direct digital codes to machines. (See Figure 4.3.)

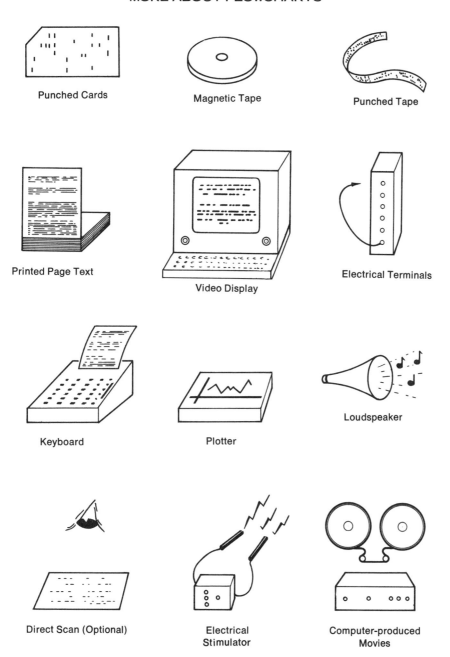

Punched Cards

Magnetic Tape

Punched Tape

Printed Page Text

Video Display

Electrical Terminals

Keyboard

Plotter

Loudspeaker

Direct Scan (Optional)

Electrical
Stimulator

Computer-produced
Movies

FIGURE 4.3. Various computer communication links.

Clearly there exists a vast array of devices which permit a computer to acquire and dispense data. Nevertheless, the goal of such communication is always that of providing information about the values of variables. Data input always results in the assignment of values to variables. Thus, by indicating the name of the variable in a data input box

| READ |
| *variable name* |

we can show which variable should receive a value in the course of an algorithm. This symbol can be interpreted as saying "assign a value to the variable whose name appears within the box." This value is provided later, of course, by the algorithm user. Any previous value the variable may have had before the data input is lost: only the new value will be stored in the memory location corresponding to the variable name.

The use of the symbol

| WRITE |
| *variable name* |

for data output can be interpreted in a similar way: "Make available the value of the variable whose name appears in the box." The value of the variable name which will be given up is the value at that point in the algorithm; it is not destroyed. Thus, if *variable* takes many different values in an algorithm, one must be careful to extract the desired result at the proper point.

Cautionary Comments

The construction of algorithms and flowcharts is a creative process in which the student must apply his intellectual abilities to find a method of solution. Many problems have proved impossible to solve, others have yielded solutions only grudgingly. Unfortunately, there is no general algorithm describing how to develop algorithms. Each problem must be studied objectively to understand: 1.) The nature of the problem; 2.) The tools of analysis needed to solve the problem; 3.) The need for logical ordering of the algorithm steps.

In the following examples we will try to show how these three aspects of problem solving apply to simple problems. You are urged to follow the development closely to see how to arrange the various steps in logical sequence. Creating good algorithms is difficult and you will quickly learn there is an art involved which demands both brevity and style.

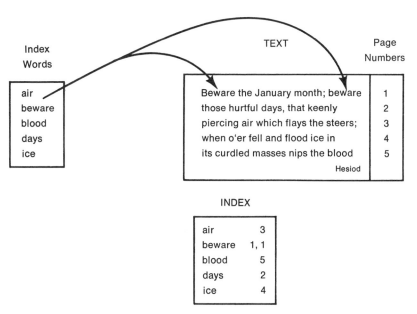

FIGURE 4.4. Illustrating the comparison procedure needed to construct an index.

THE CONCORDANCE PROBLEM

A concordance is a guide to the location of words or short phrases within lengthy texts or reference works. The concordance gives by page numbers all locations of the particular word or phrase. Suppose that we have been given a suitable text and are asked to produce a concordance. In what way should we proceed?

The first step is to create a list of words and phrases which are of particular importance to the book. Next, starting with the first entry of the list, a search is then made through the text keeping track of all places where the entry is mentioned. Once the text has been completely scanned for a given word, the next word is selected from the word list and the process is repeated.

A preliminary algorithm for the construction of an index is shown in Figure 4.4. In the first step we read an entry word. This word is compared with the first text word. If there is no correspondence the next text word is examined. If a correspondence is found, the text word and the page number are printed. The comparison process then continues with the next word until all text words have been compared with the first entry word. We then turn to the second entry word and begin again the search through all text words. This process is repeated until all index words have been compared with the text.

In the course of the algorithm three separate questions are asked:

a.   Is the present entry word the same as the present text word?
b.   Are there any remaining text words to compare with the entry word?
c.   Are there any remaining entry words to be considered?

Figure 4.5 shows an initial flowchart for this algorithm.

We now want to improve upon our algorithm by using variables to represent the different quantities. Let us adopt the following names:

ENTRY is an alphanumeric variable representing the current entry word.

TEXT is an alphanumeric variable representing the current text word.

PAGE is a numerical variable representing the page number for a text word.

MAXENTRY is a numerical variable representing the total number of entry words.

MAXTEXT is a numerical variable representing the total number of text words.

The flowchart of Figure 4.5 can be considerably improved using these variables. First, however, we must ask how we can express the two questions: Are there any more text words? and Are there any more entry words? Through MAXINDEX and MAXTEXT we know the total number of entry and text words to be used. What is needed is some way of *counting* the entry words and text words as they are used by the program. We can then test the two counted numbers of entry words and text words against MAXINDEX and MAXTEXT to find out when the last entry or text words have been used.

To do this let us define a numerical variable N to represent the number of times separate entry words have been read into the program. Then, using the instructions

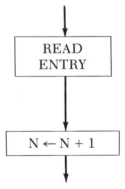

each time a new value is read for ENTRY, the value of N increases by one.

FIGURE 4.5. First flowchart for the concordance algorithm.

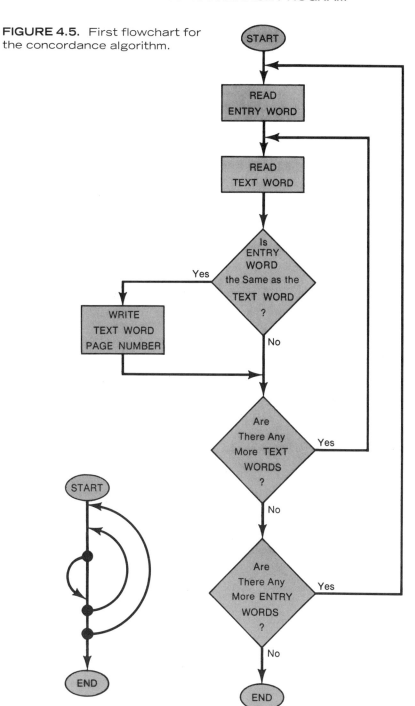

If we then ask

$$\text{"Is } (N < \text{MAXINDEX})\text{?"}$$

and receive a "Yes" answer we will know that there are still some ENTRY words to be read. If the answer is "No" then the last ENTRY value has been used and the program must stop.

When a variable is used to count different processes it is normally referred to as a *counter*. The value of the counter must always be given some *initial value* before it can be used. A replacement statement of the form $\boxed{N \leftarrow N + 1}$ requires that we define at some point an initial value for N. This is best done by the replacement $\boxed{N \leftarrow 0}$ before the first value of INDEX is read into the algorithm.

Summarizing the foregoing ideas, we find that the three basic steps involved in the use of counters to perform repeated operations can be listed as

1. Set an initial value.
2. Arrange for counting.
3. Provide for an exit test.

Using these ideas, the completed flowchart for the indexing problem is shown in Figure 4.6 where two counters, N and M, have been used to keep track of the number of index and text words which have been read. The replacement statements $\boxed{N \leftarrow 0}$ and $\boxed{M \leftarrow 0}$ have been carefully placed to insure that each value of ENTRY is compared with all values of TEXT.

The success of this algorithm depends upon two flowline loops, which are *nested* one inside each other. The inside loop takes one entry word and compares it with the complete text (i.e. every text word). The outside loop ensures that the comparison is made for all entry words.

In general, program loops are valuable because they allow repetitive calculations to be made as long as some *assertion* is maintained. The program loop has a significant danger for the unwary algorithmist, however. If the *assertion* in the decision box is not phrased properly, it may well happen that the program will be trapped in the loop without being able to exit to the remainder of the algorithm. Two examples of simple loops are shown in Figure 4.7 to illustrate trapping and nontrapping. The algorithm segment on the right results in a repeated looping. The lefthand segment completes its looping in a certain number of cycles (How many?) and continues on to the next statement after the decision box.

FIGURE 4.6. Final flowchart for the concordance algorithm.

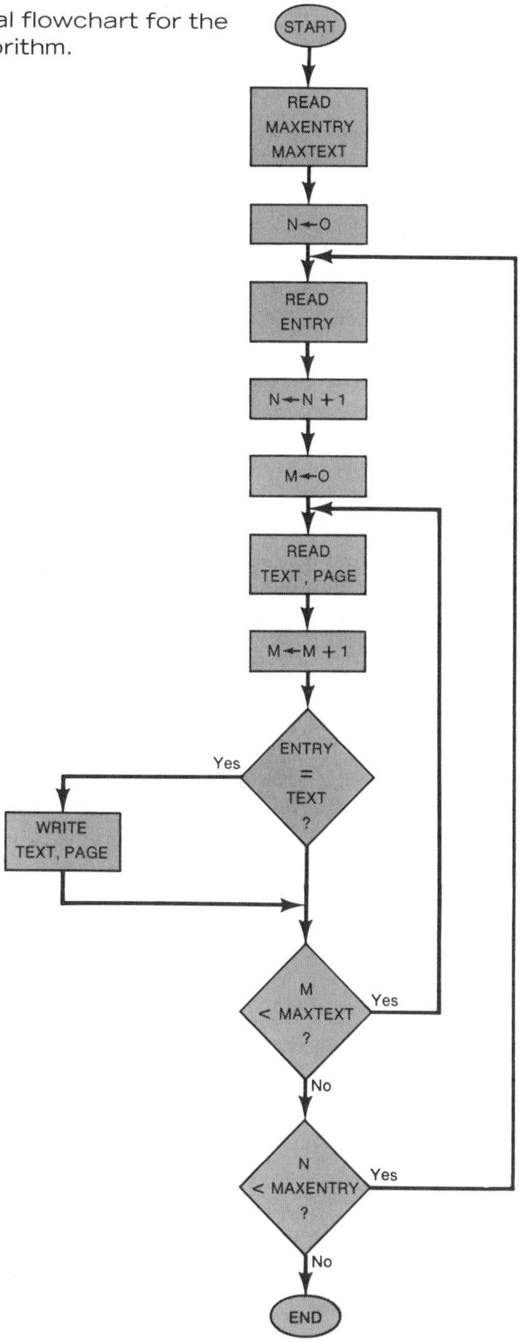

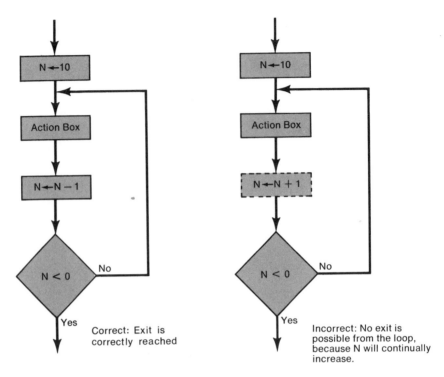

FIGURE 4.7. Two examples of looping with counters.

COUNTERS AND LOOPS

The counters introduced in the concordance algorithm were used to create loops which could be repeated as long as some condition was fulfilled. The three steps involved in setting up the loops (initialization, incrementing, testing) are relatively straightforward and the way they appear in the flowchart of Figure 4.6 is ideal for translation into the various dialects of the FORTRAN language. For ALGOL and PL / 1, however, these three steps do not appear as separate statements or processes, but rather have been cleverly compacted into a single programming statement. Consequently, for these languages it is valuable to define a new flowchart process box which expresses looping in a more realistic way.

As shown in Figure 4.8, the *iteration box* incorporates the initialization, incrementing, and testing of loops into one graphic form. The essential features of our former method of looping are present in the *iteration box*, being expressed in terms of a counting parameter which, for convenience, we will call K.

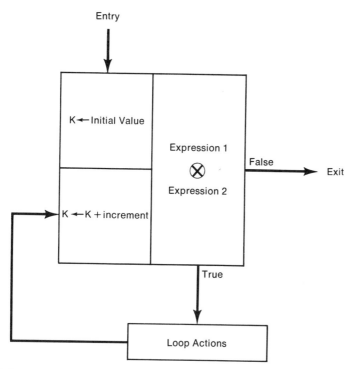

FIGURE 4.8. The iteration box is a process box which incorporates initialization, incrementing, and testing in a way convenient for translation of algorithms into ALGOL and PL/1.

As shown, the compartments of the *iteration box* include:

1. A replacement statement to define the initial value of K;
2. An iteration replacement which specifies the increment by which K is to increase after each execution of the loop;
3. The testing which uses a relational operator ($\otimes$) for arithmetic expressions.

In operation, the value of K is assigned its initial value, the assertion *expression 1 $\otimes$ expression 2* is tested and, if the assertion is true, the flowline leads into the loop computations. Following this, K is incremented and the assertion is reevaluated. The incrementing, testing, and loop computations continue until the assertion is found to be false and the flowline exits from the iteration box.

To show the value of the iteration box, the flowchart for the Concordance Algorithm has been redrawn as shown in Figure 4.9. In this form the translation of the algorithm can be readily made into the advanced control state-

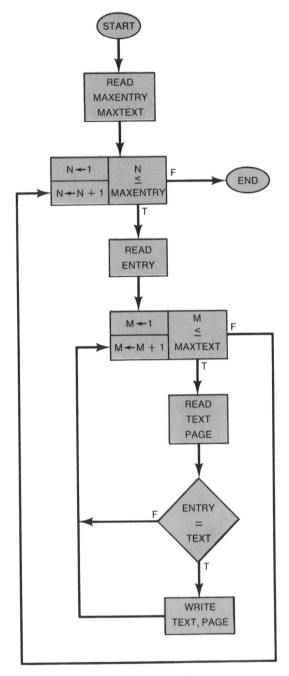

FIGURE 4.9. A revised Book Concordance flowchart which uses two nested iteration boxes.

ments of ALGOL or PL/1. To show the usefulness of the iteration box another flowchart example of a practical problem is introduced in the following section.

Finding the Largest Number in a List

Suppose we are given a list of numbers having both positive and negative values. How can we find the largest number of the set?

To begin we see that "largest" is a relational concept and a comparison of all elements in the list must be made. One way to start a "largest" number algorithm is to compare the first and second numbers. The larger of the two is then compared with the third number in the list and the larger is selected. This process is continued until the last list element has been compared with the "largest" value previously obtained. The number remaining after the final decision is "largest". A preliminary algorithm using this approach is shown in Figure 4.10.

Let us now express this simple algorithm in terms of appropriate variables that can be manipulated by a computer. We can adopt variable names as follows:

LARGEST is numerical variable representing the largest number found at some point in the list.

ELEMENT is a variable representing the value of a number in the list.

TOTAL is a numerical variable representing the total number of elements in the list.

K is a numerical variable to be used within the iteration box.

The complete algorithm, shown below in Figure 4.11, works in the following way. To begin with, it is assumed that the first value of ELEMENT is the largest. Succeeding values of ELEMENT are then compared with LARGEST until a larger ELEMENT value is found. The value of LARGEST is then replaced with the new ELEMENT value and the comparison process continues until the input data list is exhausted (i.e. the iteration process is completed when K is zero).

One disadvantage of the present algorithm is that at no time is the complete list of numbers available to the computer. It is not possible, for example, to compare successive pairs of list elements to determine the largest element. The data values are made available to the algorithm one by one and each new value is assigned to the single variable ELEMENT.

Roots of Numbers

The preceding algorithm was designed to solve nonnumerical problems where the principal emphasis is upon search and exchange. For a numerical

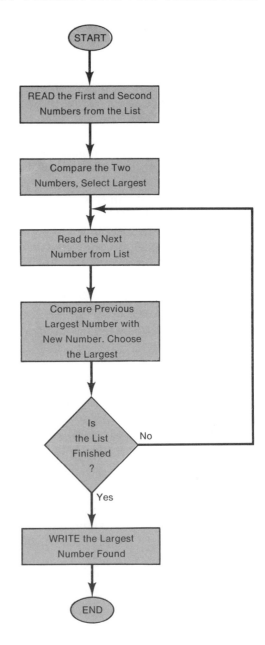

FIGURE 4.10 A first algorithm for finding the largest number in a list of numbers.

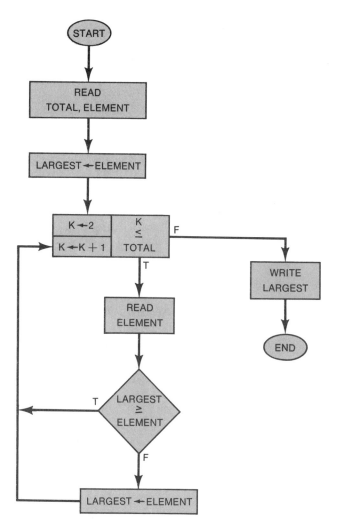

FIGURE 4.11. A flowchart designed to find the largest number in a list of numbers read sequentially into the algorithm.

example, consider the problem of finding the square root of a positive number, N. If we let the variable R represent the square root of N, it follows from algebra that $R = \sqrt{N}$ which, by squaring each side of the equation, leads to the form $R^2 = N$. Our present problem is to find a method for computing the number R which satisfies this last expression.

One convenient algorithm finds the root through repeated approximations which continue until the computed value is very close to the true value. The first written expression of the algorithm can be given as:

1. Make a guess, X, about the value of the square root. (This is a first approximation to R.)
2. Compute the next approximation, Y, to the square root R using the formula

$$Y = .5(X + N^2/X)$$

3. Substitute the new value of Y for the old value of X and recompute a newer value of Y according to Step 2.
4. Continue Steps 2 and 3 until the numerical value of $(Y^2 - N)/N$ is smaller than some small value, E. (This corresponds to the fractional error in finding the square root.) When this relation is satisfied, the value of Y is the computed approximation to the square root, R.

Several comments can be made about the way this algorithm functions. First, although the initial value of X required in Step 1 is almost completely arbitrary, the closer X is chosen to R, the fewer repetitions of Steps 2 and 3 needed to obtain the final answer. An initial guess can be taken as N / 2. Owing to the presence of X in the denominator of the approximation of Step 2, it is not permissible to choose X = 0 as a first or subsequent choice. Secondly, the process of approximation given by the repetition of Steps 2 and 3 is called *iteration*. Examination of Step 4 shows that the iteration will continue until the fractional error in the root is smaller than some predetermined value, E. For example, if an accuracy of 1 per cent is needed, we would continue iterating until†

$$\frac{Y^2 - N}{N} < .01$$

To express the algorithm in flowchart form we can adopt the following variable names:

N—the positive number whose square root is to be found.

R—the approximation to the square root.

E—the maximum permissible fractional error.

The flowchart for the square root algorithm is shown in Figure 4.12. Comparison of this flowchart with the written algorithm reveals an interesting point. While the written form needed the separate variables X and Y, in the flowchart these successive approximations were replaced by the single variable R. This reduced number of variables results from the

†The vertical bars indicate that only the magnitude of the expression is needed; (i.e. if $(Y^2 - N)$ / N is a negative number, it is converted to a positive number before the comparison with .01 is made.

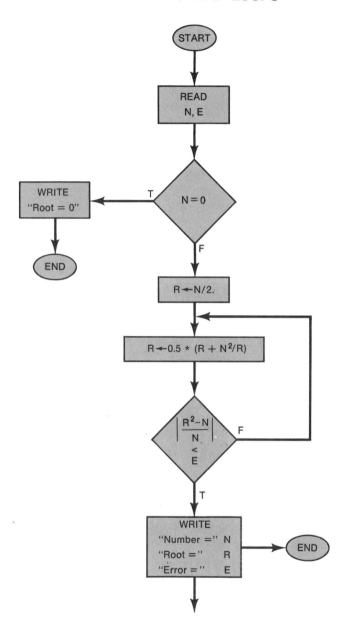

FIGURE 4.12. Flowchart for finding the square root of a number through iteration.

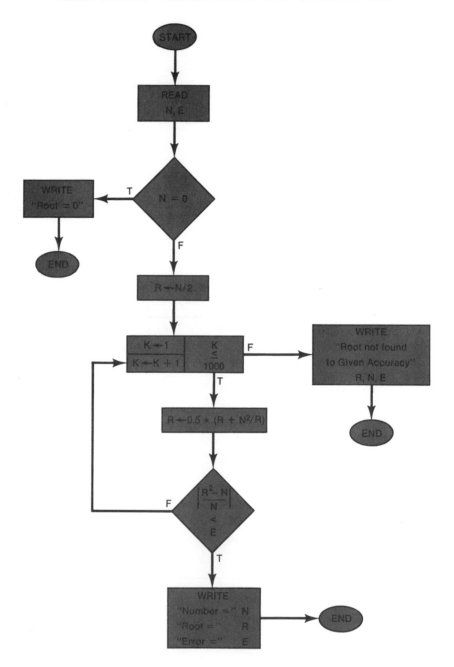

FIGURE 4.13. An improved square root algorithm which uses an iteration box to guard against excessive computation.

fundamental difference between algebraic equality (=) and computer replacement (←). In the flowchart there was no need to define separate values for the old and new approximations since the new value could be directly obtained from the old value.

This algorithm provides an extremely effective means of computing square roots. The convergence towards the true root is very rapid with an improvement of about two decimal places accuracy per iteration after the first few tries. However, if the error, E, is taken too small, the condition given by the final decision box of Figure 4.12 may never be satisfied and continual looping may occur. One way to avoid this is to include an iteration box in the flowchart limiting the number of times that the replacement R ← 0.5 (R + N²/R) can be done. Figure 4.13 shows such a readjustment of the algorithm using an iteration index, K, which is limited to a maximum value of 1000. The root will most likely be found (to an accuracy E) in far less than 1000 iterations. However, it is the decision box within the loop which will normally transfer algorithm control out of the loop into the final WRITE statement. This illustrates a second way to exit from a loop, the first being provided, of course, through the iteration box testing procedure.

Finally, it is possible to rewrite the square root algorithm in a third form that takes maximum advantage of the way an iteration box works. As shown in Figure 4.14, R can be treated as the indexing parameter. As such it can be incremented by a variable T which is just the correction factor needed for each successive iteration. In addition, the test to escape the loop is now phrased in terms of R so that the increments added to R will eventually satisfy the iteration box testing and algorithm control will pass to the WRITE statement. As long as E is sufficiently large so that numerical rounding of numbers within the computer is unimportant, this method will work satisfactorily with a consequent reduction in algorithm length.

COMPOUND RELATIONAL EXPRESSIONS

The functioning of a decision box depends upon the way in which the *assertion* contained within it is expressed. For both numerical and alphanumerical variables the simplest assertion has the form

$$(expression1) \otimes (expression2)$$

in which *expression 1* and *expression 2* are appropriate arithmetical or alphanumeric expressions involving variables, constants and operations. The symbol × represents one of the relational operators defined for the class of variables being operated upon. Simple examples such as:

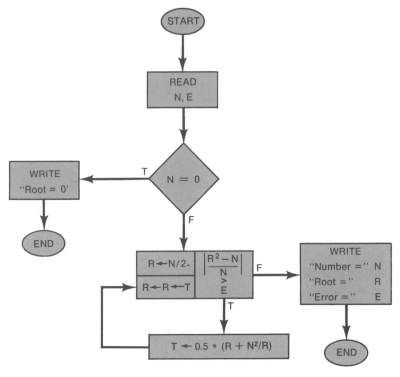

FIGURE 4.14.   The square root algorithm in a more condensed form.

$$\boxed{X > 3} \quad \boxed{Y \le (B\,2 - 4*A*C)} \quad \boxed{FISH = FOOD}$$

$$\boxed{ALPHA * 3 + 2 \ne GAMMA * BETA}$$

illustrate assertions which can be evaluated in a decision box to give a True or False answer.

Frequently we need to impose several simultaneous conditions on different variables in order to introduce a variable testing assertion. For example, the assertions

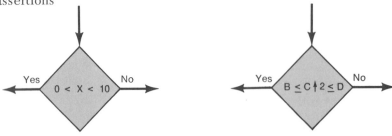

express *compound* conditions which restrict the permissible range of values for X and C↑2. If X or C↑2 have values which lie within the indicated ranges, then the assertion expressed by the compound conditions will be true. Otherwise a "false" decision must be reached.

Compound relational expressions such as $\boxed{0 < X < 10}$ and $\boxed{B \leq C \uparrow 2 \leq D}$ are actually built of two simple assertions:

$$\boxed{\begin{array}{c} 0 < X \\ \\ \text{AND} \\ \\ X \leq 10 \end{array}}$$

$$\boxed{\begin{array}{c} B \leq C \uparrow 2 \\ \\ \text{AND} \\ \\ C \uparrow 2 \leq D \end{array}}$$

where the operation AND means that both statements separated by AND must be true in order for the entire assertion to be true. If, in the first example, the value of X were 12, then 0 < X would be true, but X < 10 would be false so that $\boxed{0 < X \text{ AND } X < 10}$ would be false.

Using AND's, compound conditions can be extended indefinitely with the general form

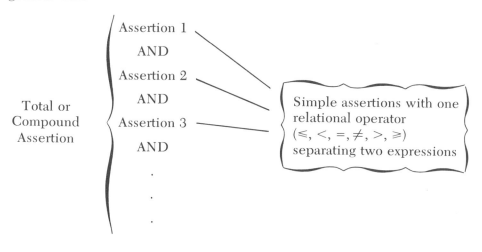

where the assertions involve simple relational operators. In order for the total assertion to be true, all of the simple assertions must be true: compound assertions connected by ANDs tend to be very exclusive so that the failure to meet one assertion results in a total rejection (False) of the proposition made by the assertion. Fortunately, a compound assertion can always be decom-

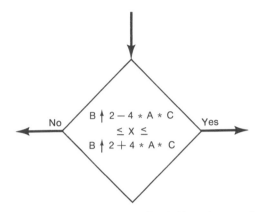

FIGURE 4.15.   An example of compound relational operators.

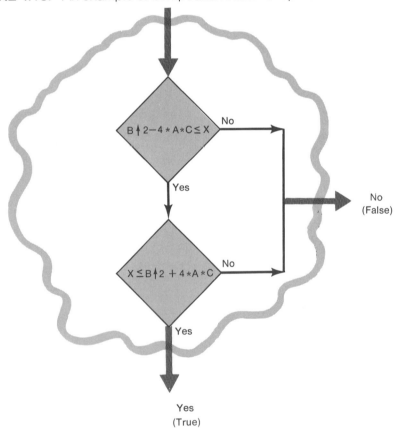

FIGURE 4.16.   A two level compound relational expression decomposed into two simple assertions.

posed into simple separate assertions that can be individually represented by flowchart decision boxes. Thus, the two level compound assertions

$$B \uparrow 2 - 4 * A * C \leq X \leq B \uparrow 2 + 4 * A * C$$

could appear as Figure 4.15 or with decomposition of the original expression into

$$B \uparrow 2 - 4 * A * C \leq X$$

AND

$$X \leq B \uparrow 2 + 4 * A * C$$

as in Figure 4.16.

Multilevel compound assertions can always be constructed out of multiple single level assertions which, through multiple decisions and branching, ultimately evaluate whether the variable value lies within the prescribed ranges. The grouping of such decisions forms a decision "tree" composed of the entire logical network of possible paths.

Simple assertions connected by ANDs tend to reduce the range of variable values which give a "True" decision. Another connector, the OR, can also be used to connect simple relational assertions so that if one or more assertions out of the list of OR-connected assertions is true, then the entire compound assertion is true. OR-connected relational assertions have the form

expression 1 $\otimes$ *expression 2*

OR

expression 3 $\otimes$ *expression 4*

OR

.
.
.

and mean, "If any of the simple assertions separated by OR is true, the entire statement is true. OR compound assertions tend to be very inclusive and nonrestrictive, permitting a wider range of variable values rather than the restricted range associated with AND assertions.

OR statements can frequently be found among eligibility requirements for various organizations. Some automobile insurance companies, for example, often express their criteria for membership in terms of OR assertions. An example might be:

$$\text{XYZ Insurance} \atop \text{Company} \atop \text{Policy} \atop \text{Criteria} \Bigg\{ \begin{array}{l} \text{1. \quad He / She is over 25, OR} \\ \text{2. \quad He / She has had no tickets for 15 years, OR} \\ \text{3. \quad He / She is employed in a regular job, OR} \\ \text{4. \quad He / She is willing to pay high rates.} \end{array}$$

An applicant for a policy with the XYZ Company could obtain a policy if any one of the four criteria were met.

A Grading Algorithm

To show one use of compound conditions, consider the grading policy of Professor I. B. Machine for a basic computer science course. A student can pass the course if he receives a total of 80 points or better when midterm and final examination grades are summed together. If this sum is less than 80, the student can still pass the course provided his homework grade is 90 or better. Otherwise, he will fail and will have to repeat the course.

The flowchart for Professor Machine's computerized grading system is shown in Figure 4.17. The various personal data for each student are read into the algorithm, comparisons are made using preestablished standards, and the results are made available under each student's name along with the three scores upon which the grade is based.

SUBSCRIPTED VARIABLES

Quantities that can change their value in algorithms and computer programs are called variables. In a computer, the value of a variable at a particular time can be found through examination of the contents of the memory storage location assigned to the variable name.

In some ways, the naming of variables with alphanumerical symbols is similar to the old English custom of identifying individual houses by a name rather than the more modern street name/number system. While the house names express much more personal feeling, their use presents substantial difficulty for the British Post Office in its attempt to deliver mail. The problem is that the house names cannot be used to sort the mail, since there is no connection between the house names and geographical location. Street names with addresses help to overcome this difficulty in two ways. First, the number of streets is smaller than the number of houses and second, the numerical order of numbering corresponds to some geographical pattern. (We might also note that Zip Codes are another attempt to designate areas by number rather than by name.)

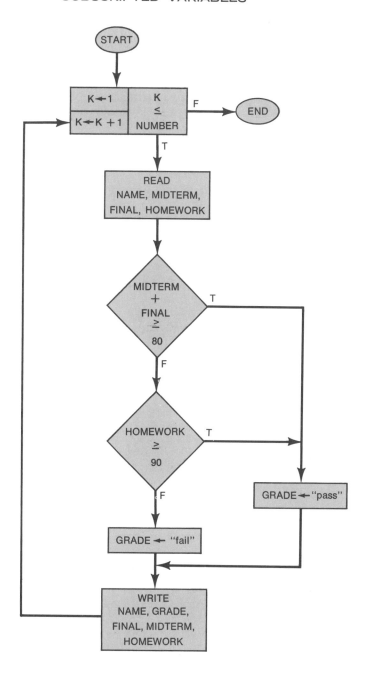

FIGURE 4.17. Professor I.B. Machine's grading scheme.

Similar ideas apply to the naming of variables used in a computer. To apply the name/number concept to variables, suppose that we assign one name (written in terms of alphanumeric symbols) to a set of related variables. Although this group of variables has only one name, we can refer to the individual variables within the group by placing a number after the name. Thus, it seems very natural to say

$$\text{VARIABLE NAME} \begin{bmatrix} \text{First} \\ \text{Second} \\ \text{Third} \\ \text{Fourth} \\ \cdot \\ \cdot \\ \cdot \\ \cdot \end{bmatrix}$$

rather than create an entirely new name for each member of the group.

Variable names composed of alphanumeric characters followed by identifying numbers are called *subscripted variables*. The origin of such labels lies in mathematics where arrangements like:

$$A_1, A_2, A_3, A_4 \ldots$$

are used to specify separate variables usually belonging to some general class.

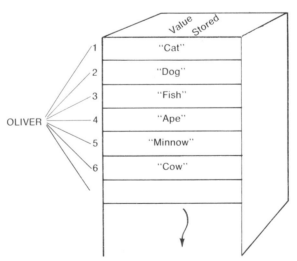

FIGURE 4.18. The subscripted variable OLIVER showing how individual values of the array are sequentially stored in the computer memory.

The lists:

BOX_1 } Post Office Boxes $OLIVER_1$ } Addresses on Oliver Street X_1 } Members of the variable class X.

BOX_2

BOX_3

$OLIVER_2$

$OLIVER_3$

X_2

X_3

illustrate how lists of items can be subscripted to identify individual elements.

One way to write subscripted variable names for use with algorithms and computers would be to simply attach the number at the end so that the number becomes a permanent part of the name:

BOX1	OLIVER1	X1
BOX2	OLIVER2	X2
BOX3	OLIVER3	X3

This would add nothing new to our previous description of variable names, however, since it amounts to nothing more than generating new names with numerals.

The importance of subscripted variables lies in the possibility of designating a particular variable through expressions such as

$$BOX_K, \qquad OLIVER_M, \qquad X_N$$

where K, M, and N are variables whose values the computer must determine in order to find which of the different elements having BOX, OLIVER, or X as a general descriptor are being referenced. In this use K, M, and N point to a particular element of their respective variable names in the same way that an address distinguishes among the many houses along a street. Dipping into mathematical tradition, subscripted variables are often referred as *arrays*.

In the Figure 4.18 the elements of OLIVER are given adjacent storage locations in the computer memory. To refer to one of these locations we must give the variable name (OLIVER) and the subscript value. The subscript is effectively a local address within a variable name similar to a street number.

The value of a subscript may be explicitly given as a number ($OLIVER_9$) or, more importantly, as a variable name whose value must be computed ($OLIVER_M$).

The statement,

$$\text{OLIVER}_5 \leftarrow \text{"elephant"}$$

for example, would place the value "elephant" in position 5 of OLIVER, replacing the previous value "minnow." In a similar manner we could make this same replacement indirectly by

$$K \leftarrow 5$$
$$\text{BOX}_K \leftarrow \text{"elephant"}$$

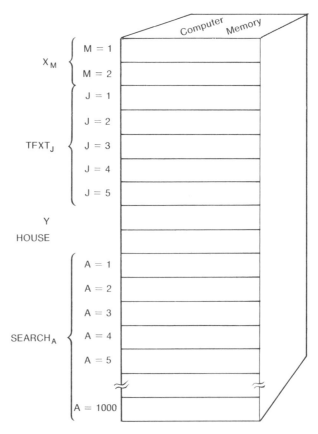

FIGURE 4.19. Storage of subscripted and nonsubscripted variables in the computer memory.

or, even more indirectly, by the steps

$$M \leftarrow \text{``elephant''}$$
$$K \leftarrow 5$$
$$BOX_K \leftarrow M$$

The total number of subscripts allowed for a given variable depends upon the number of elements reserved within the computer memory. (See Figure 4.19.) The subscripts (constants or variables) must have integer values. Both positive and negative integers can be used in computers, but special provisions must normally be taken to define the range of subscript values with a particular computing language. Since we are concerned here with the flow-chart language, we can leave such technical details for the actual flowchart to program translation.

Subscripted variables are of great usefulness in handling groups of related data since we can refer to a single datum by the variable name and the subscript. To illustrate the use of subscripted variables, let us reconsider our previous algorithm designed to find the largest (most positive) number in a list of numbers.

Revised Largest Number Algorithm

One algorithm for finding the largest number in a list of numbers has already been given in Figure 4.11. Because the list of numbers was given to the computer item by item, this method is associated with *external sorting* techniques.

With the introduction of subscripted variables, storing the list of numbers directly within the computer memory is now possible. Using this new approach, the internally stored list can be sorted and otherwise arranged without waiting for the slow process of data reading to be continually repeated. The term *internal sorting* refers to data processing using lists stored directly within the computer memory.

For the present algorithm let us assume that the subscripted variable LIST contains the N individual elements of the data list stored in consecutive locations of the computer memory. To find the largest element of LIST and identify its subscript number, we must compare the values of LIST element by element. Each time that an element is found whose value is greater than the current value of the largest element (called LARGEST), the new value is assigned to LARGEST. At the same time, the subscript value of this new "largest" element is assigned to the variable SUBSCRIPT. The completed flowchart is shown below.

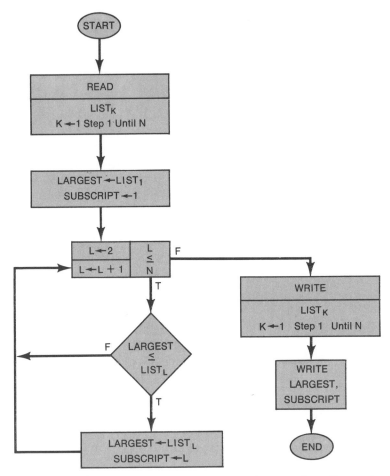

FIGURE 4.20. Revised largest number algorithm using the subscripted variable LIST.

There are several new ideas in this algorithm. (See Figure 4.20.) First, the total number N of data values are read into the computer at the start of the program and stored as elements in the array LIST. The data input order to do this

READ
LIST$_K$
K $\leftarrow$ 1 STEP 1 UNTIL N

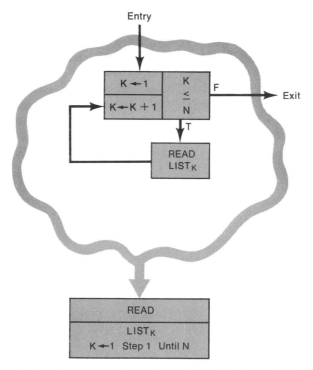

FIGURE 4.21. A simple process box for subscripted variable data input.

is a simplified form of the previous iteration box adapted specifically for the uses of data input. In its more lengthy form, this READ could be represented as shown in Figure 4.21 with the variable K acting as the indexing parameter. The initial and final values of the index as well as the stepping increment must be given to allow the data reading to proceed properly.

In a similar manner, data output for subscripted variables can be completely presented by the process box

WRITE
$LIST_K$
$K \leftarrow 1$ STEP 1 UNTIL N

involving an iteration box looping similar to that shown above.

Returning to Figure 4.20, after all members of the data set LIST have been read into the algorithm, the actual comparison process begins by selecting $LIST_1$ to be LARGEST, and then continuing down the list to $LIST_N$, replacing

LARGEST with new larger values as they are found. Each time a new LARGEST is found, the current subscript value L is assigned to SUBSCRIPT. When the final element of LIST has been tested, the results are then given through the WRITE statement.

An Algorithm for Sorting

As another example of the use of subscripted variables, consider the problem of sorting a list of N numbers into descending numerical order (most positive number first). As an example, if we were given the initial data set $-$ 2, 8, 6, 7, we wish to develop an algorithm which will give the ordered result 8, 7, 6, $-$ 2.

There are many different strategies for solving this problem, each with its own advantages of speed and minimization of memory storage space. The names of a few of these methods, Pigeon Hole, Upward Radix, Natural Merge, Chain Merge, Ancestral, Tournament, Transposition, Bubble, Minima and Quicksort, give a feeling for the wide variety of techniques that have been developed.†

One of the simplest sorting methods uses two arrays, one which contains the initial list of numbers and a second which gives the sorted list. To begin, we can identify each number of the unsorted list as an element of the subscripted array, X. Such an array is shown below for the brief list of numbers given above.

Array X

Element	X_1	X_2	X_3	X_4	X_5
Value	$-$ 2	8	6	7	empty

The algorithm for the Two-Array Sort then proceeds to arrange the N elements of X in the following way:

1. Find the largest element of X, store it as the first element of the array SORT.

2. Find the next largest element of X, store it as the next element of SORT.

3. Repeat step 2 until all elements of X have been transferred to SORT.

---

†Thirty-two methods have been examined by Rich, R. P., *Internal Sorting Methods Illustrated with PL/1 Programs.* Englewood, N.J.: Prentice Hall, 1972.

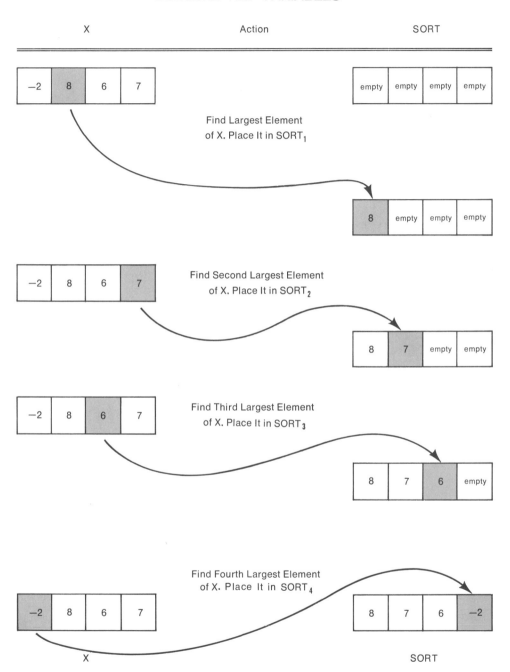

FIGURE 4.22. Operation in the Two-Array Sort.

The sequence of steps needed to sort the data set $(-2, 8, 6, 7)$ via the Two Array Sort is shown in Figure 4.22. The most important problem in writing an algorithm for the Two-Array Sort involves the identification of the progressively smaller elements of X which are to be transferred to SORT. In the first step, the largest element of X can be found through direct comparison of all elements. If we now try to find the second largest element of X through the same type comparison, some care must be taken since the previously found largest element is still present in the array. One way to avoid this difficulty is to change the value of the elements of X as they are identified and transferred to SORT. The new values are arbitrary, of course, but must be chosen so that they will not interfere with the comparison process. For the present example let us choose the value -1000 which is far more negative than any number on the list given previously.

The flowchart shown in Figure 4.23 illustrates the final algorithm in a computer compatible format. The variables X and SORT represent the initial and final arrays, respectively, while N is the total number of elements of X to be sorted into descending numerical order.

In operation, the Two-Array Sort algorithm uses two loops with iteration boxes. Within the inner loop the elements of X are compared to find the largest value using the variable BIG and a subscript indicator, LINDEX. When all passes through the inner loop have been completed, the proper value is assigned to $SORT_K$ and X_{LINDEX} is assigned the value -1000. The outer loop then gives a new value to K and the process is repeated.

There are two immediate disadvantages to the Two-Array Sort. The first is the need to provide an extra data array to store the final sorted number list. This extra array requires computer storage space which, for some programs, may not be readily available or convenient to use. In fact, as shown later, one array is adequate to sort the initial data.

The second disadvantage of the Two-Array Sort lies in its comparison scheme which ignores any partial ordering already existing in the data. If there are N elements in the array, a total of $N(N - 1) / 2$ comparisons must be made to complete the sort, irrespective of the initial order.†

---

†To obtain this result, note that we must compare each element of the array once with every other element. If there are N elements, then $(N - 1) + (N - 2) + (N - 3) + \ldots + 2 + 1$ is the total number of comparisons (but not interchanges) which must be made. By adding the $(N - 1)$ terms of this series twice we get

$$2S = (N - 1) + (N - 2) + (N - 3) + \ldots + 2 + 1$$
$$+ 1 + 2 + 3 + \ldots (N- 2) + (N - 1)$$

which gives

$$2S = N + N + \ldots + N$$

with $(N - 1)$ terms. Thus, $S = (N - 1)N/2$ comparisons must be made.

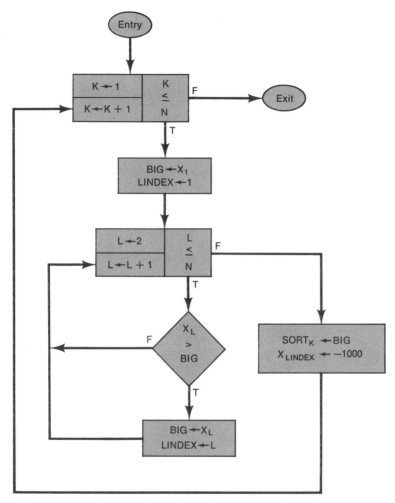

FIGURE 4.23. Flowchart for the Two-Array Sort algorithm.

THE BRUTE FORCE SORT

The Two-Array Sort uses computer storage space at the expense of simplicity. With just slightly more care, the need for the array SORT can be eliminated and the array X can be used to store the final result. One technique, for doing this, which we call the Brute Force Sort, is outlined below.

Brute Force Sort

1.   Find the largest element of $X_1 \ldots X_N$. Store it in X_1. The old value of X_1 is placed in the largest element's former location.

2.   Examine the subarray $X_2 \ldots X_N$, find the largest element, store it in X_2 after transferring the former second element to the location of this new largest element.

3.   Continue the process started in step 2 for successive sub-arrays until the final subarray has only one element.

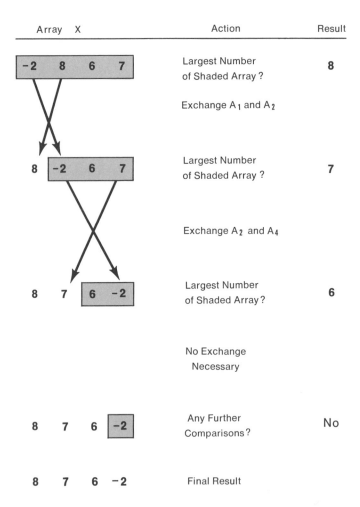

FIGURE 4.24.   Illustrating the Brute Force Sort.

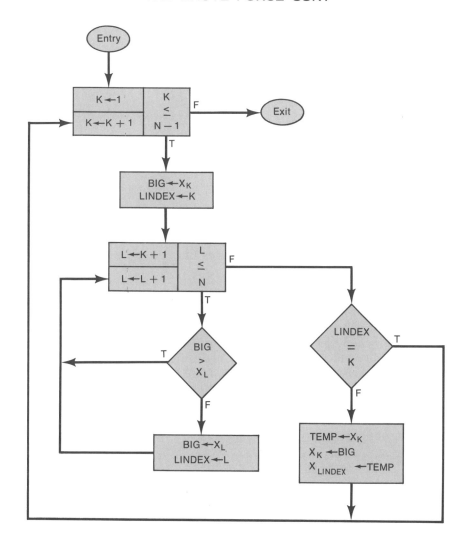

FIGURE 4.25. Flowchart for the Brute Force Sort algorithm.

To illustrate the method, Figure 4.24 has been prepared showing the steps taken to sort the data file (− 2, 8, 6, 7). It is readily apparent that the operation of this method is again laboriously methodical, because it involves repetitious comparison and exchange irrespective of any already existing internal order.

The most difficult step of this algorithm is the special care which must be taken to prevent the destruction of element values during the exchange process of Step 1. For illustration, suppose that it is necessary to exchange the values of X_K and X_J. This can be done through the sequential replacements

$$\text{TEMP} \leftarrow X_K$$
$$X_K \leftarrow X_J$$
$$X_J \leftarrow \text{TEMP}$$

which preserve the intermediate value of X_K and interchange the values of X_K and X_J.

The complete flowchart for this algorithm is shown in Figure 4.25. Note the care that has been taken to compare a given element against all remaining elements of the array before the comparison/interchange is done. The greatest advantage of the Brute Force Sort is the fact that its comparison scheme like that of the Two-Array Sort ignores any ordering which may already be in the data.

The Bubble Sort

The Two-Array Brute Force Sorts are convenient to describe, but mediocre in performance. The Bubble Sort, in contrast, is moderately efficient at sorting, especially when the data set is partially ordered. But the penalty for this efficiency is a somewhat more complex algorithm.

The Bubble Sort for placing the elements of an array X in descending numerical order starts at the first element, X_1. X_1 is compared with X_2. If $X_2 > X_1$, we exchange the values. Next, we compare X_2 with X_3 and, if $X_2 < X_3$ we

X_1	X_2	X_3	X_4	Comparison	Action
−2	8	6	7	Is $X_1 > X_2$?	No, interchange
8	−2	6	7	Is $X_2 > X_3$?	No, start bubble
				Is $X_1 > X_3$?	Yes, stop bubble
8	6	−2	7	Is $X_3 > X_4$?	No, start bubble
				Is $X_2 > X_4$?	No, continue bubble
				Is $X_1 > X_4$?	Yes, stop bubble
8	7	6	−2	Final Result	

FIGURE 4.26.　The basic steps involved in a Bubble Sort illustrated for the data set (−2, 8, 6, 7).

prepare to interchange. Before doing so, however, we want to insure that X_3 will be correctly placed with respect to X_1. To do this we compare X_3 with X_1. If $X_3 > X_1$, we make the replacements $X_1^{NEW} \leftarrow X_3^{OLD}$, $X_2^{NEW} \leftarrow X_1^{OLD}$, $X_3^{NEW} \leftarrow X_2^{OLD}$ so that, in effect, the value of X_3^{OLD} has bubbled up through the array to its correct position. If, on the other hand, $X_3 < X_1$, then we make the replacements $X_2^{NEW} \leftarrow X_3^{OLD}$, $X_3^{NEW} \leftarrow X_2^{OLD}$ which is just a simple exchange.

After the bubbling process has been completed, action resumes at the point X_3 where we left off. Starting downward, X_3 is now compared with X_4 and, if $X_3 < X_4$, the possibility of vertical motion must again be considered. Steps of this nature continue until X_{N-1} has been compared with X_N. A simple example of the Bubble Sort is shown in Figure 4.26 for our earlier data set ($-2, 8, 6, 7$).

The flowchart for the Bubble Sort progresses at two levels. In an outer loop we keep track of progress down the array through an index K which increases in steps of 1 until $K = N - 1$. The details of this outer loop are shown in Figure 4.27.

Within the inner loop two operations are called into action when the bubbling process is needed. First, we must store the value of X_{K+1} in a temporary location while we find the proper level for the value of X_{K+1}. As X_{K+1} is compared upwards (to smaller subscript values) we successively push element values downwards until the comparison $X_{K+1} > X_J$ ($J = K - 1, K - 2,$

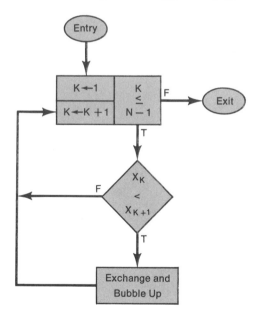

FIGURE 4.27. The outer loop of the Bubble Sort algorithm showing the downward progress through array X.

.., + 2 + 1) yields a negative result. As shown in Figure 4.28 the upwards comparison and downwards push are best accomplished through a negative stepping of an internal looping index.

The complete Bubble Sort Flowchart is shown in Figure 4.29. If the initial data set is initially in the correct order, the outer loop test $X_K < X_{K+1}$ insures that only $(N - 1)$ comparisons will be made. If the initial data set is initially in the correct order, the outer loop test $X_K < X_{K+1}$ insures that only $(N - 1)$ comparisons will be made. If the initial set were in precisely the reverse order, $N(N - 1)/2$ comparisons would be needed to order the set. Since neither case would be regarded as typical, the real number of comparisons for the Bubble Sort must lie between $(N - 1)$ and $N(N - 1)/2$.

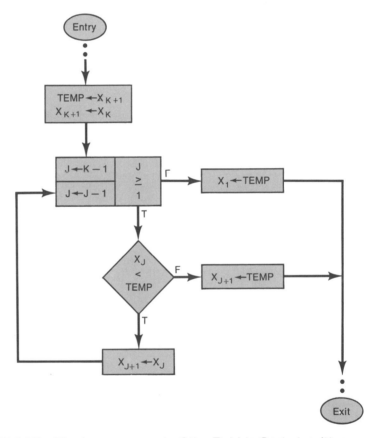

FIGURE 4.28.   The inner segment of the Bubble Sort algorithm.

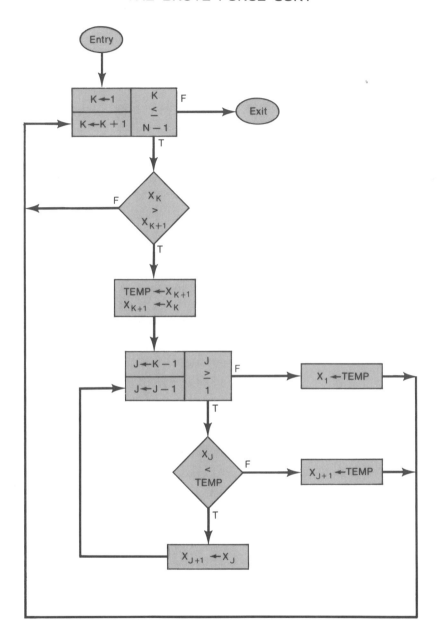

FIGURE 4.29. The final Bubble Sort algorithm.

Multiple Subscripts

To continue the discussion of subscripted variables, there is no particular reason to restrict ourselves to a single subscript. Multiple subscript variables of the form

$$Variable\ Name_{J,K,L,M.\,.\,.}$$

refer to variables whose values can be determined only after the value of all subscripts J, K,. . . have been specified. Each different set of subscripts defines a new quantity which is given a separate storage location in the block of memory reserved for the "variable name". The total number of storage elements associated with "variable name" is simply the product of the total number of values assigned to each subscript.

Large amounts of computer storage can be quickly filled with multidimensional variables. For example, the variable $BOX_{J,K,L}$ where J, K, and L each take values 1 to 10, would require 1000 separate storage locations to take care of the array elements (i.e., $Box_{1,1,1}$, $BOX_{1,1,2}$, up to $BOX_{10,10,10}$).

There are many uses for variables having multiple subscripts since they provide handy keys to different data storage locations. Problems of physics and mathematics use variables with multiple subscripts for vector and matrix operations. In addition, the structure of many data files is closely related with the use of several identifying subscripts.

A simple illustration of two dimensional variables can be found in the game of tic-tac-toe. (See Figure 4.30.) Suppose that we let the variable $T_{J,K}$ represent the state of a tic-tac-toe game with J being the row number, ranging from 1 to 3, and K being the column number, also ranging from 1 to 3. With this notation, each square of the tic-tac-toe board is associated with one of the nine elements of T. Before the first move of the game we set all elements of T to zero (i.e., $T_{1,1} \leftarrow T_{1,2} \leftarrow T_{1,3} \leftarrow \ldots T_{3,3} \leftarrow 0$. The marks needed to identify the spaces taken by each player can be taken as $+1$ and -1, respectively. Thus, the first move of a game might be

$$T_{3,3} = -1$$

$T_{1,1}$	$T_{1,2}$	$T_{1,3}$
$T_{2,1}$	$T_{2,2}$	$T_{2,3}$
$T_{3,1}$	$T_{3,2}$	$T_{3,3}$

FIGURE 4.30. Views of a tic-tac-toe board using subscripts as identifiers for positions.

The second player might counter with

$$T_{1,1} = +1$$

The first player then sees his opportunity and takes

$$T_{1,3} = -1$$

To avoid a loss, the second player must take

$$T_{2,3} = +1$$

but the move

$$T_{3,1} = -1$$

will win the game for the first player.

Using a doubly subscripted variable, an algorithm can be written for attempting to win at tic-tac-toe. While the algorithm cannot guarantee a win, it will always produce at least a tie. In this case, unlike chess, the moves are sufficiently limited to permit a logical analysis to be made based on all possible future positions of the markers.

The winning combinations for tic-tac-toe occur when the sums of the rows, columns, or diagonals are equal to +3 or −3. One can make a flowchart to test a given tic-tac-toe matrix to see whether a win has occured by cycling through the winning combinations of subscripts to search for a win. If a win is found, the winner is identified. If not, a message saying "tie game" is written.

SUBALGORITHMS

In the preceding flowcharts there have been several opportunities to create subalgorithms out of small, repetitive sections of the main algorithm. Although a precise definition of subalgorithm is difficult to phrase, the meaning is straightforward: Subalgorithms are any set of actions which are relatively isolated from the main flow of the algorithm and accomplish some specific task.

In effect, subalgorithms are convenient building blocks for larger algorithms. When organized properly, a group of subalgorithms may allow many different tasks to be done within the body of the main algorithm. Certain subalgorithms are absolutely essential. For instance, mathematical functions like the square root or the trigonometric sine and cosine are in such great demand that the subalgorithms for these quantities are actually provided by programs within computer systems. Thus, the concept of a subalgorithm is also carried over into computer languages where subroutines or procedures can be made available to assist with certain common calculations or data manipulations.

There are two different levels of subalgorithm use. The first is local as in the medical algorithm where subalgorithms may be written by a programmer to assist with logical ordering of a complex main algorithm. The second is that subalgorithms can be written for general use by programmers to accomplish various tasks ranging from data sorting to the solution of simultaneous linear equations. The advantage of these general subalgorithms is that they provide a specific service without the necessity for a programmer to investigate their internal operation in full detail. Data are given to these subalgorithms, manipulation occurs internally, and the results are then returned for whatever use they are intended.

To identify subalgorithms, alphanumeric descriptive names can be chosen. SQRT, for example, might represent a square root subprogram for FORTRAN or ALGOL, while EXCHANGE would be an appropriate name for the Bubble Sort comparison and exchange processes. With the use of such names, however, there comes a subtle change in the meaning of the term subalgorithm. Before, the subalgorithm was simply a collection of operations grouped together for use at different points in the main algorithm. Now, however, subalgorithms assume a more independent existence. Whenever the subalgorithm name is mentioned in an algorithm, the flowline control passes from the main algorithm to a separate set of steps where it remains until control is passed back to the main algorithm. Thus, each time a subalgorithm name is mentioned, the algorithm control moves to the same set of instructions.

This independent existence for the named subalgorithm is convenient in several ways. First, it permits the use of generally available subalgorithms as building blocks. Second, the actual steps need to be written only once instead of each time the task needs to be done.

The function of a subalgorithm is to take information from the main algorithm in the form of the values of particular variables, process these values internally, and return the results to the main algorithm. This implies that there is a need for linkage of data between the main and subalgorithms. Since subalgorithms are separate entities, their internal operations are defined in terms of a specific set of variable names and constants. In general, the variable names of the subalgorithm will not be the same as those of the main algorithm.

If the algorithms are expressed in computer language, how can we transmit data values collected under one set of names into a subalgorithm where, although the desired operations and steps are done, a different set of variable names is used?

The complete answer to this problem must be deferred to Chapter Eight since an understanding of the actual internal operation of computers is involved. For now, it is adequate to say that certain adjustments can be made within the computer memory so that the internal storage addresses of corresponding main algorithm variables and subalgorithm variables become the same. By doing this, two names can temporarily refer to the same memory storage location.

For the purposes of algorithms, a simple symbolic method of data linkage can be adopted. (See Figure 4.31). This is done by providing a list of the variables whose values are to be communicated into and out of the subalgorithm. To be consistent, this list can be placed in brackets after the subalgorithm name. Thus, the name EXCHANGE (A, B) in a main algorithm could indicate a subalgorithm whose task is to exchange the current values of the main algorithm variables A and B.

Suppose, however, that the author of EXCHANGE had written his subalgorithm using the variable names X and Y. Since X and Y represent the values to be linked with any main algorithm he would have written the name of the subalgorithm as EXCHANGE (X, Y) with all internal steps made in terms of the variables of X and Y.

It is at this point that the computer system decides to link the variables A and B with X and Y (assuming that the algorithms are written in a computer language). On the basis of the order of the variables within the brackets, the computer recognizes that A corresponds to X and B corresponds to Y. Thus, the value of A in the main algorithm becomes the value of X in the subalgorithm and likewise for B and Y. This linkage means that when the value of X or Y is changed in the subalgorithm, the values of A or B are also changed.

This linkage between the main algorithm and the subalgorithm is completely general. Thus, the successive use of EXCHANGE (A, B) followed by

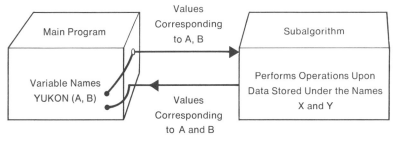

FIGURE 4.31. Linkage of variable names between the main algorithm and a subalgorithm.

EXCHANGE (TEST, NOW) in a main algorithm presents no difficulty since the first call for EXCHANGE (A, B) links A to X and B to Y while the second call EXCHANGE (TEST, NOW) links TEST to X and NOW to Y. (See Figure 4.32.)

Up to this point the name of a subalgorithm has had no intrinsic value. It has been only a convenient identifier. This is not always true, however, and to see why, consider our previous square root algorithm. Since there is a widespread need for finding square roots, we could define a subalgorithm according to the adopted method of linking variables as SQRT (N, R) where N is the number whose root R is to be found.

Although correct, such a method is inconvenient since the call to SQRT(N, R) would have to be made before the value of R could be used. To overcome this inconvenience, *function subalgorithms* are used when the result of the subalgorithm operations is a single value. This value is available whenever the function subalgorithm name is mentioned and is given directly to the name itself. SQRT (A), for example, is a function subroutine in FORTRAN which has a value corresponding to the square root of a number A. In a similar manner, the functions SIN(X), COS(TEST), LOG(XRAY) give single values computed for the current value of the variable listed in parentheses. Several examples are shown:

$$Y \leftarrow A * B * SQRT\ (C)$$
$$PEN \leftarrow SQRT\ (B \uparrow 2 - 4 * A * C)$$
$$RATIO \leftarrow SIN\ (X)\ /\ COS\ (Y)$$

A large number of arithmetic function subalgorithms are provided in the standard computer languages and can be used directly within replacement expressions.

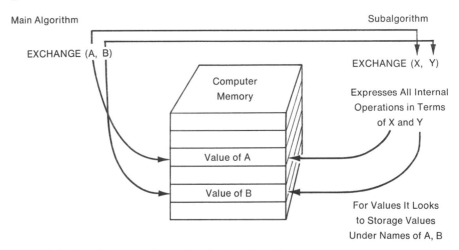

FIGURE 4.32. A basic view of subalgorithm linkage.

References to Further Readings

Many of the texts listed at the end of Chapter two and three provide excellent material for further reading. Additional, more specialized references which may be of use are given below.

JACQUEZ, J. A.

A First Course in Computing and Numerical Methods. Reading, Mass: Wesley Publishing Company, 1970.

KNUTH, D. E.

The Art of Computer Programming, Vol. 1, Fundamental Algorithms. Reading, Mass.: Addison-Wesley Publishing Company, 1969.

MURACH, M.

Principles of Business Data Processing. Chicago: Science Research Associates, 1970.

STARK, P. A.

Introduction to Numerical Analysis. London: The Macmillan Company, 1970.

KEY WORDS AND PHRASES TO KNOW

ALPHANUMERIC EXPRESSION
AND
ARRAY
ASSERTION
BRANCH
BUBBLE SORT ALGORITHM
COMPOUND RELATIONAL EX-
   PRESSION
COMPARISON / INTERCHANGE
CONDITIONAL BRANCH
COUNTER
DECISION BOX
EXPRESSION
FUNCTION SUBALGORITHMS
INITIALIZATION OF COUNTER
INTEGERS

ITERATION BOX
LINKAGE
LOOP
LOOPING
MULTIPLE SUBSCRIPTS
NESTED LOOPS
OR
POINTER
PROCESS BOX
RELATIONAL OPERATORS
SUBALGORITHM
SUBSCRIPT
SUBSCRIPTED VARIABLE
TEMPORARY VARIABLE
TRAPPING IN A LOOP
UNCONDITIONAL BRANCH

EXERCISES

1. Evaluate the truth or falseness of the following assertions using the listed values.

   a. A * B/C > D?

   b. (A +B)/(C +D) ≤ −1?

   c. A/C/D ≠ 1?

   d. −A ↑ 3 + D > 3?

   e. B/A/C/D = D − 2 * A?

Variable	Value
A	−1
B	0
C	1
D	2

2. A *counter* is a simple way of keeping track of the number of times a loop is used. In the partial algorithms shown below the variable K is given the initial value of 0. How many times will the loop be used in each example before the assertion is satisfied and the algorithm proceeds to the alternate branch? What is the value of K?

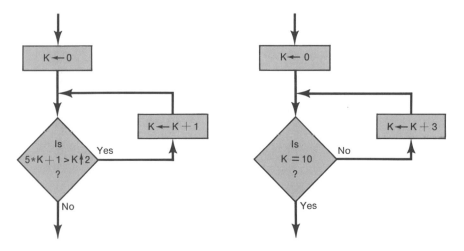

3. Explain why there are only two forms of the relational operator for alphanumeric variables. Can you think of a set of relational operators which would work in ordering text data alphabetically?

4. The algorithm shown in Figure 4.6 loops to a new index word when the number of text words, as counted by the variable M, is equal to or less than MAXTEXT. This is an awkward method, however, since it requires that we count the actual number of text words in advance. A simpler way to end the loop would be to have a codeword such as ENDOFTEXT placed after the last (textword, page) data card. The next to the last decision box could then test to see when this card was reached. In a similar way, an ENDOFINDEXWORDS card could be used in place of MAXINDEX to terminate the algorithm. Rewrite the flowchart for this algorithm with these changes.

5. Make a list of the data input devices available at your computer center. Do the same for the data output devices.

6. In the following portion of an algorithm there are several WRITE boxes. Acting as computer, find the values given by each WRITE statement.

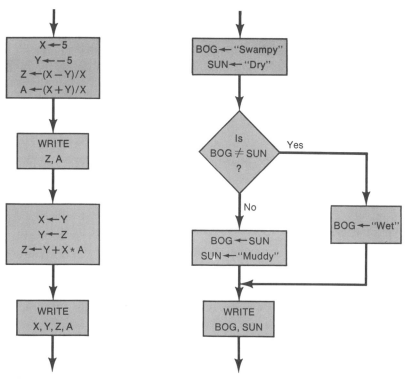

7. Explain why the indexing algorithm of Figure 4.6, if converted directly to a computer program, would present an undesirable method of data card reading.

8. The flowchart for the largest number algorithm of Figure 4.11 reads the first value of ELEMENT outside the comparison loop. Revise the algorithm so that all values of ELEMENT are obtained inside the loop.

9. Find a way to eliminate the variable TOTAL from the algorithm of Figure 4.9 so that we can find the largest number from a number list of arbitrary, unknown length.

10. Decompose the following compound relational expressions into simple assertions illustrated in flowchart language.

   a. $X * Y > Z$ AND $Z \neq Z + X/Y$
   b. $(A + B) \neq C$ AND $A/B + C > D$ AND $X < C$
   c. $A > B$ OR $B \geq D$ AND $A < C$
   d. $X \neq Y$ OR $X \uparrow 2 < Y \uparrow 2$ OR $X > 10$

11. Write an algorithm in flowchart language which will determine if a person is eligible for the insurance policy issued by the XYZ Insurance Company. Data input should include values for the variables AGE, TICKETS, EMPLOYED, and PAYRATES.

12. In most classes "incomplete" grades are possible when illness or other problems interrupt a student's studies. No provision for such a grade was included in Professor Machine's grading algorithm. Change the algorithm to include "incomplete" grades and also to eliminate the necessity for the variable NUMBER.

13. The subscripted variable BOAT comprises five elements. Using the information given below, compute the values of the five elements

Variable	Value
A	0
C	1
D	2
X	3
J	4

$BOAT_X \leftarrow X * A$

$BOAT_{(J-D)} \leftarrow BOAT_X$

$BOAT_C \leftarrow C \uparrow - X$

$BOAT_J \leftarrow BOAT_2$

$BOAT_{(X*D-1)} \leftarrow X * D - 1$

14. Suppose the doubly subscripted variable $X_{J,K}$ has subscript values in the ranges $-1 \leqslant J \leqslant 25$ and $1 \leqslant K \leqslant 10$. How many computer storage locations are required for X?

PROBLEMS

1. Write an algorithm for the conversion of numbers written with Roman numerals into the decimal system.

2. Write an algorithm for the conversion of decimal numbers into numbers written with Roman numerals.

3. From algebra the values of x which satisfy the quadratic equation

$$ax^2 + bx + c = 0$$

are given by

$$x_1 = \frac{-b + \sqrt{b^2 - 4ac}}{2a}$$

$$x_2 = \frac{-b - \sqrt{b^2 - 4ac}}{2a}$$

Write a computer algorithm to compute x_1 and x_2 when the values of a, b and c are given. Note that you will need to test the value of a to make sure it is nonzero. If a is zero, then there is only one root given by $x = -c/b$. In a similar manner, if $b^2 - 4ac$ is negative a special message will be needed to indicate that the square root of a negative number was encountered: Terminate the problem in such a case. Test your algorithm with the following data

a	b	c
0	1	1
1	−1	−2
1	2	2

4. The value of π (Pi) is a fundamental geometrical constant which relates the area of a circle, A, to the radius: $A = \pi r^2$. Since antiquity various methods have been used to compute approximate values of π. These methods almost always involve the summation of a series of numbers derivable from trigonometry. For example, the series derived in 1674 by Leibnitz is

$$\pi = 4 \left(1 - 1/3 + 1/5 - 1/7 + 1/9 - 1/11 + \ldots\right)$$

which if summed over a sufficiently large number of terms, gives the value

$$\pi = 3.1415926536\ldots$$

The major difficulty with Leibnitz's method is that it involves differences between progressively smaller numbers so that the convergence to an accurate result is very slow (several thousand terms are needed to give six decimal place accuracy). However, if we group the pairs of positive and negative numbers given in Leibnitz's formula and carry out the subtractions directly, a more rapid convergence is reached. With this method the basic formula becomes

$$\pi = 8\left(\frac{1}{1 \cdot 3} + \frac{1}{5 \cdot 7} + \frac{1}{9 \cdot 11} + \frac{1}{13 \cdot 15} + \frac{1}{17 \cdot 19} + \ldots\right)$$

Write an algorithm which computes the value of π for N terms using both series. Compare the results by computing the fractional differences obtained by subtracting the two values and dividing the result by the second, more precise value.

5. Suppose an irritated sportsperson drops a golf ball on a concrete floor from a height of 10 meters. If each bounce returns the ball to 90 per cent of the height of the previous bounce, write an algorithm which counts the number of bounces the golf ball makes before the bounce height is less than 1 meter.

6. The greatest common divisor of two positive integers, M and N, is the largest integer which divides evenly (no remainder) into M and N. The algorithm for finding the greatest common divisor was first found by the Greek geometer Euclid (~300 B.C.) and expressed in the following way:

    Divide the smaller integer into the larger integer. If the remainder is zero, the smaller integer is the greatest common divisor. If the remainder is not zero, we repeat the division process by identifying the remainder as a new smaller integer and dividing it into the previous smaller integer. The process is continued until a zero remainder is obtained. The divisor of this final division can then be identified as the greatest common divisor of the original two integers.

    Write this algorithm in complete flowchart form using appropriate variable names and the computer oriented operations described in this chapter.

7. A modern gravel factory uses a computer system with automated sensing devices to package its products. Rocks of random sizes and weights are dumped in a large bin. One by one the individual rocks are placed in an electrical measuring device which determines the weight in grams and the maximum diameter in centimeters. The rocks are then sorted in appropriate bins according to the following rules:

    If the maximum diameter is 2 cm or less and the weight is: less than 50 gm → bin A; from 50 to 100 gm → bin B; greater than 100 gm → bin C.

    If the diameter is greater than 2 cm and less than 4 cm and the weight is greater than 100 gm → bin D. Otherwise the gravel is placed in bin E.

    Write an algorithm in flowchart form which accomplishes the separation process.

8. The difficulty in sorting alphabetic information lies in making a correspondence between the symbols and alphabetical order (which is in arbitrary ordering!) Suppose that we wish to develop a scheme to alphabetize words. To do this we convert each letter of a word into an integer number in the range 1 to 26 with A given the value 1, B the value 2, and so forth. In this notation the word CLASS would appear as

3	12	19	19

Let us now define a doubly subscripted variable $TEXT_{L,M}$ with the first subscript, L, referring to different words and the second subscript, M, referring to the individual letters within the L-th word. For example if the first two words are

CLASS	3	12	1	19	19
NOTES	14	15	20	5	19

the values of TEXT are:

TEXT$_{L,M}$	Value	TEXT$_{L,M}$	Value
1,1	3	2,1	14
1,2	12	2,2	15
1,3	1	2,3	20
1,4	19	2,4	5
1,5	19	2,5	19
1,6	0	2,6	0
1,7	0	2,7	0

where the maximum value of M is 7.

It is now possible to alphabetize a list of words by numerically comparing the different elements of TEXT. We first examine TEXT$_{L,1}$ for all values of L (i.e. we are looking for all words in the list which begin with A). Those words which have the value 1 for M = 1 must then be examined for M = 2,3,4, etc. in order to arrive at the alphabetical ordering.

Rather than writing a complete algorithm for alphabetic ordering of a long list of words, write a subalgorithm which carries out the comparison process for two words (TEXT$_{1,M}$ and TEXT$_{2,M}$) to determine their alphabetic order. Assume that the words have no more than 7 characters each and that zeros indicate the absence of a letter.

9. Write an algorithm with a flowchart which will permit a computerized money changing machine to return the proper number of pennies, nickels, dimes, quarters, and dollars for any given amount of money. The algorithm should choose the coins such that as few coins as possible are needed.

10. The number sequence

$$0, 1, 1, 2, 3, 5, 8, 13, 21, 34, 55 \ldots$$

is known as the Fibonacci sequence in honor of Leonardo of Pisa (Filius Bonaccii, son of Bonaccio), one of the most famous mathematicians of the European early middle ages.† The rules governing this sequence are rather simple. If we identify each term of the series as a subscripted variable so that $S_0 = 0$, $S_1 = 1$, $S_2 = 2$, $S_3 = 3$ and so forth, the entire sequence can be derived from the relations

$$S_0 = 0 \quad S_1 = 1$$
$$S_{N+2} = S_{N+1} + S_N$$

where N is equal to or greater than zero. Thus, after the first two terms, new terms are found by summing together the preceding two terms.

---

†Further information about Fibonacci sequences can be found in the Fibonacci Quarterly Journal available in most University or College libraries.

Write an algorithm to create the Fibonacci sequence up to N terms. Verify the relation

$$S_N{}^2 - S_{N+1} \times S_{N-1} = (-1)^N$$

for each value of n greater than one.

11. The Thirteenth Century manuscript *Liber Abbaci* by Leonardo of Pisa poses the following question, "How many pairs of rabbits can be produced from a single initial pair in the period of one year?" To solve this problem, certain rather abstract assumptions were made:

   a.   Each pair of rabbits reproduces at a constant rate of one new pair (a male and a female) each month.

   b.   Each new pair of rabbits becomes fertile one month after birth.

   c.   No deaths occur

   Write a flowchart to find the number of rabbit pairs present after a period of X months has elapsed following the birth of an original pair of rabbits. If the month by month pair population is listed in sequence, the result should be identical with the Fibonacci sequence discussed earlier.

12. The rabbit population of Problem 11 grows rapidly as time passes owing to the fact that no deaths occur. In a natural environment, predators and sickness will eventually act to keep the rabbit population in equilibrium. To see the effect of these factors, suppose that the probability of a rabbit pair dying in any given month is 10 per cent. If we let N represent the number of rabbit pairs at the end of any month (just before the new rabbits are born), then $0.0001 N^2$ rabbit pairs can be assumed to die without progeny. Since rabbit pairs cannot be divided into fractions, the actual number of death in any month must be $0.0001 N^2$ rounded to the nearest integer.

   Write an algorithm to compute the monthly population of rabbit pairs. How many months elapse following the first few generations before the long term rabbit population is stable to within 5 per cent?

13. A prime number is an integer that cannot be factored into the product of two smaller integers. Examples include 1, 2, 3, 5, 7, and so forth. Suppose we wish to write an algorithm to compute a list of all prime numbers equal to or less than some maximum positive integer N. We can procede in the following way:

   A.   Fill an array $PRIME_J$ with values given by

$$PRIME_J \leftarrow J$$

for all integer values of J from 1 to N.

   B.   The elements of PRIME represent all integers lying between 1 and N. We now want to eliminate, or set to zero, each of the elements of PRIME whose value, or subscript, is a multiple of two smaller integers.

C. To accomplish B. we first set to zero all elements of PRIME whose subscripts are multiples of 2 (i.e. $PRIME_2$, $PRIME_4$, $PRIME_6$ and so forth). This process is then repeated for the multiples of the integers 3, 4, 5 up to and including $\sqrt{N}$.

D. After setting to zero all elements of PRIME having subscripts which are multiples of smaller integers, the remaining non-zero, elements of PRIME are just the prime numbers in the range 1 to N. The list of prime numbers can then be written by ignoring the zero value elements of PRIME.

Using the flowchart methods of this chapter, write an algorithm to compute prime numbers using the technique described above.

14. Suppose you are given an array, BOX_J, having elements with J ranging from 1 to 100. It is desired to invert the original list of values of the elements so that Box_1 is given the value of BOX_{100}, BOX_2 will have the value of BOX_{99} and so on until BOX_{100} is given the value of the original (not the new) BOX_1.

Write an algorithm with a flowchart to carry out this interchange of values. (Hint: Be sure to avoid losing half the array. Use a temporary storage location.)

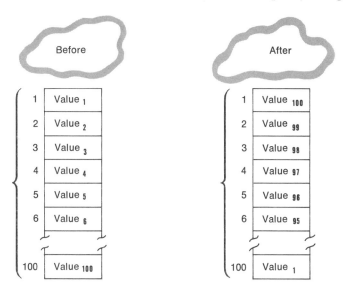

15. The use of computerized grades and class lists have been applied to Madame Badin's computer science class. Each student is identified by a six-digit number and at the end of every quarter grade lists are published giving the student numbers in numerical order and the corresponding grades (also digitized so

$A \to 4$, $B \to 3$, $C \to 2$, $D \to 1$, $F \to 0$). A portion of a typical grade list is shown below.

Original Grade List

Student	Grade
1 0 5 0 6 0	2
1 0 5 0 7 5	4
1 0 6 1 1 3	3
1 0 7 0 0 1	2
2 1 9 1 3 4	1
2 2 6 3 4 1	0
2 2 6 3 4 2	4
6 1 1 4 3 2	3
7 0 0 0 0 0	2
7 0 1 1 2 1	2

Unfortunately, Madame Badin has just been asked to provide a new list of student rankings, identifying first those students who received As, then those with Bs, and so forth. Thus an algorithm must be written to convert the original grade list into a ranking list. Because there are a large number of students, it is necessary to arrange that the student numbers be listed in numerical order within each grade category, as shown

Final Ranking List

Grade	Student
4	1 0 5 0 7 5
4	2 2 6 3 4 2
3	1 0 6 1 1 3
3	6 1 1 4 3 2
2	1 0 5 0 6 0
2	1 0 7 0 0 1
2	7 0 0 0 0 0
2	7 0 1 1 2 1

Write the algorithm needed to carry out this task. *Hint:* the student identifiers are too large to be used as subscripts directly. However, since the number of students in the class is relatively small (compared to the magnitude of the student identification number) we can define the subscripted arrays STUDENT$_J$ and GRADE$_J$. The values of these arrays then contain student identification numbers and the grades, respectively. The sorting operations can then by carried out by searching for the desired values of GRADE$_J$ and locating the student number through the corresponding value of J.

16. Consider a simple polynomial such as $X^3 + X^2 + X + 1$. Suppose that you are given a value of X (say, 5) and asked to evaluate the resulting value of the polynomial. How would you do it? Your first impulse might be to write the value as $5^3 + 5^2 + 5^1 + 1$, do the implied multiplications, then the additions for a total of 9 arithmetic operations to get the answer, 156.

    While such a procedure works, it is not the best method for finding the value of the polynomial. To see this suppose we rewrite the original polynomial as $[(X + 1) X + 1] X + 1$ so that if $X = 5$ we have $[(5 + 1) 5 + 1] 5 + 1$ or a total of 5 operations. If we were dealing with large polynomials it would be progressively more economical to group the values of X rather than attempting to multiply out the individual terms.

    The form of a general polynomial of the n-th order (n is an integer) is

    $$a_n X^n + a_{n-1} X^{n-1} + \ldots a_1 X + a_0$$

    where the coefficients are given numbers and there are $(n + 1)$ terms to the entire polynomial. Such a polynomial can be factored into the form

    $$(\ldots (((a_n X + a_{n-1}) X + a_{n-2}) X + \ldots (a_2 X + a_1) X + a_0$$

    which involves just n multiplications.

    To evaluate the polynomial we find the product $a_n X$, then add a_{n-1}, multiply the result by X, add a_{n-1}, multiply the result by X, add a_{n-3}, and so forth until all terms are exhausted by the final addition of a_0.

    Write a subalgorithm in flowchart language to evaluate a n-th order polynomial. Assume that the coefficients a_n are elements of an array A.

17. Large businesses keep many lists of account numbers. These lists have essential uses, among them being the identification of customers, providing current files of credit card holders, keeping current mailing lists, and so forth. Lists or files such as these are not static, but require continual updating with both additions and deletions of account numbers.

    To practice several of the common types of business data manipulations, suppose we are given a master file having a total capacity of 10,000 five-digit account numbers. Account numbers are maintained in this file in numerical order with the smallest number in position 1, the second account in position 2, and so forth. (Note that some account numbers are missing.)

    To carry out the operations discussed in the following paragraphs, it is convenient to give the file the name FILE so that individual account numbers can be referenced as elements of a one dimensional array $FILE_J$, J ranging from 1 to 10,000.

    One of the most common business operations with a master file is the search to determine if a given account number, represented by the variable TEST, is part of the file. Write an algorithm that makes such a search for TEST and gives an appropriate written output. To minimize the number of operations, be sure to use the fact that the file is maintained in numerical order.

The Master File

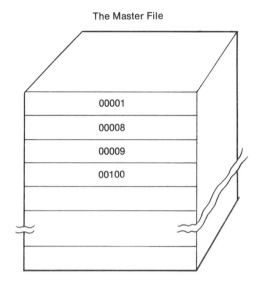

For a second type of data operation, suppose that it is necessary to remove, or purge, various accounts from the master file. If the account numbers to be removed are stored in a second array called $PURGE_K$ (K is in the range 1 to 10,000) in numerical order, write an algorithm which: 1. Removes $PURGE_K$ and 2. Readjusts the master file so that there are no empty elements between filled elements.

Old Master File	Purge List	Intermediate Master File	Final Master File
0 1 0 1	0 2 1 1	0 1 0 1	0 1 0 1
0 1 0 5	0 2 1 6	0 1 0 5	0 1 0 5
0 2 1 1	0	0	0 2 1 3
0 2 1 3	0	0 2 1 3	1 1 2 1
0 2 1 6	0	0	1 1 3 2
1 1 2 1	0	1 1 2 1	0
1 1 3 2	0	1 1 3 2	0
0	0	0	0

18.   The game of Tic-Tac-Toe is a contest between two players (A and B) on a square board divided into nine spaces.

The players put their own marks in vacant squares trying to be the first to arrange three of their own marks in a line along a row, down a column, or across a diagonal. The players alternate turns. Let us assume that A goes first. If neither player gets three marks in a line and no more vacant squares remain, then the game ends in a tie.

The Board

1	2	3
4	5	6
7	8	9

From practical experience we know that a skillful player, when given the first move, can win or force a tie in every game. Clearly, we need a bit more imagination. To add an element of luck, suppose that A and B are not free to choose their moves, but must take squares given to them at random from a shuffled deck of nine cards, each of which has one of the digits 1, 2, 3, ... 9. (If the cards are properly shuffled, the sequence of moves will be random.)

To play this new game of Random Tic-Tac-Toe, the first player draws the first card (value) and makes his mark in the indicated square. The second player takes the second card and enters his mark, and so forth until one of the players wins or the squares have been filled.

Since the moves of Random Tic-Tac-Toe are already determined for A and B, it is not necessary for us to consider the strategy of winning. However, the mechanics of the play are complicated, especially when the various steps are expressed in the algorithmic language of flowcharts. Consider several features of the game:

A. If a card with a particular number on it is drawn from the stack, how do we go about putting our mark in the proper square? Since this is like putting mail in a postbox, let the name of each square, $S_1, S_2, \ldots S_9$, refer to a memory storage location. Initially all squares are vacant. We set their values to zero. Using the correspondence $A \rightarrow +1$, $B \rightarrow -1$, the values of the selected array elements can be changed from an initial empty value of 0 to indicate the proper ownership.

B. How to test for a winner? The easiest way to do this is to note that after five draws we can test the sums $(S_1 + S_2 + S_3)$, $(S_2 + S_5 + S_6)$, $(S_7 + S_8 + S_9)$, and so forth to see if they equal $+3$ (A wins) or -3 (B wins). If there are no sums equal to $+3$ or -3 after nine draws, then the game is a tie.

Using the approach described above, write an algorithm in flowchart language to play the game of Random Tic-Tac-Toe.

19. An interesting extension of the game of NIM presented in the Problems of the last chapter can be made to illustrate a method of learning by a machine. In the algorithm given by Professor H. D. Block of Cornell University, a human player is pitted against an initially naive machine.† In the beginning the machine loses almost all games but, owing to the learning process described below, it gradually improves until after 20 to 25 games it wins every game.

The algorithm needed by the machine can be described as follows: In each of

†See H. D. Block, "Learning in some simple non-biological systems," *American Scientist*, 53, 1965, 59.

four bowls (identified by the integers 0, 1, 2, 3) place three cards numbered 1, 2 and 3. When it is the machine's turn to play (the human plays first) a card is selected at random from the bowl with an identification number equal to the remainder of the number of sticks on the table divided by four. (Suppose 11 sticks remained with the machine to move. The division 11/4 gives a remainder of 3. Therefore bowl number 3 would be used to select the machine's next move.) Further, when the machine loses a game, the last card used by the machine is permanently removed from its bowl. If a bowl which is completely empty of cards is called upon to provide a move, the human player automatically wins.

It is necessary to write an algorithm for the machine's operation. Clearly the bowls can be represented by four doubly subscripted variables with the first subscript identifying the bowl number and the second subscript identifying the three elements which initially contained the values 1, 2, and 3. As the machine learns, certain of these elements of the array will be discarded (i.e., set to zero).

For your algorithm, assume that a subalgorithm RANDOM(K) is available which randomly selects one digit from the list 1, 2, or 3. By using this random number as a subscript number, the requirements of the algorithm described above can be met so that the machine will learn to become proficient at NIM.

20. Modern postal systems are handicapped by the use of handwritten addresses which require visual dispatching. Many efforts have been made to automate the sorting of mail through mechanization of character recognition. There are many difficulties in such a process, yet considerable progress has been made and recognition systems based on computer algorithms are available to work with certain formally shaped letters and digits.

To introduce one method of character recognition, suppose we attempt to detect the letter X when it is written in a special grid. The grid shown below contains both the letter X (composed of five shaded squares) and a pattern which, while similar to X, must be discarded. In general, the pattern for X could appear anywhere within the grid.

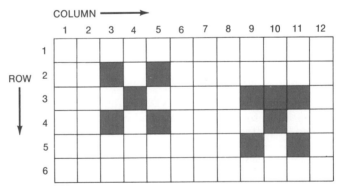

Using a real optical detection system it would be possible to determine the shaded/unshaded state of each box within the grid. For this problem let us suppose that the grid space can be represented by a two dimensional array, $GRID_{I,J}$

for which the subscripts I and J refer to row and column coordinates. To represent shaded boxes we let the corresponding elements of GRID have the value 1 while unshaded squares are assigned the value 0.

For practical application consider a grid which has been divided into N rows and M columns and the pattern of 0's and 1 is given, for example, as shown:

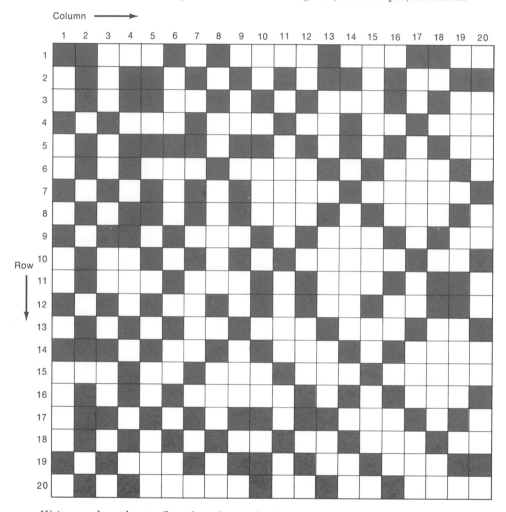

Write an algorithm in flowchart form which:

    a.   counts the number of Xs present in the grid,

    b.   prints the row/column coordinates of the center of each X

    c.   stores the coordinates of the central square of each X in a new array for later reference

21. The game of Monopoly has provided years of entertainment for armchair real estate speculators. A simpler form of Monopoly, called Binopoly (Binary Monopoly), can be used as an object study in computer simulation. In general, simulation provides a powerful technique for studying the behavior of complex, interactive systems such as traffic patterns, population growth, industrial process controls, etc. Through simulations a large number of trials can be made, thereby providing us with the opportunity to examine changes which result from variations in the constraints of the problem. In the present case, for example, changes in the rules of Monopoly like "Go to Jail, do not pass GO, do not collect $200" could be changed to "Go to Jail, pay a $1000 fine" and the subsequent alteration in the length of the game, the rate of accumulation of wealth, and so forth could be studied.

While a simulation algorithm could be developed for the complete game of Monopoly, the resulting flowchart would be complex and include an element of strategy (e.g., a decision procedure to evaluate possible purchases of property). To avoid these difficulties, a simplified game, called Binopoly, is introduced with the following rules:

Rules for Basic Binopoly

1. There are four players, numbered 1 through 4.

2. There are 20 positions on the Binopoly board, numbered 0 through 19. A player moves clockwise around the board from one position to the next. Since the board is circular, moves beyond 19 are recycled through 0, 1, etc.

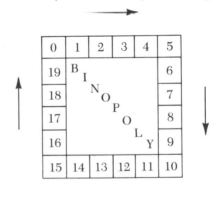

3. All players start at position 0 and have $10 each of Binopoly money.

4. Player 1 goes first by simulating the roll of a die which gives him a random digit, d, in the range 1 to 6. Player 1 then moves forward d places.

5. If the new position of Player 1 is unowned, he must buy it for $1. The BANK receives the $1 and Player 1 owns the position. Play then passes to the next player.

6.   If the new position of Player 1 already belongs to him, he pays nothing. Play then passes to the next player.

7.   If the new position of Player 1 is already owned, a payment of $1 is made by Player 1 to the owner. Play then passes to the next player.

8.   The game continues until one player cannot pay his debts.

Write an algorithm in flowchart form for playing Basic Binopoly. The printout should give a reasonable account of the Players' positions and their wealth at each move as well as identifying the final winner of the game.

22.   The game of Binopoly described in the last problem can be extended with more realistic rules to simulate actual Monopoly. Write an Advanced Binopoly algorithm which incorporates the following rules:

1.   Identify position 5 on the board as JAIL. If a Player lands on JAIL he must pay the BANK a $3 fine and lose his next turn. If the fine reduces his account to less than $0, the game is finished.

2.   Identify position 0 on the board as GO. If a player lands on GO or passes GO during his turn, he collects $1 from the BANK. This payment is added to the Player's wealth before any other transactions are completed.

Note that while Basic Binopoly will normally take about 80 moves to complete, Advanced Binopoly may continue forever (i.e., the equivalent of a time limit should be imposed, which is best done through inclusion of a move counter that limits the total number of plays).

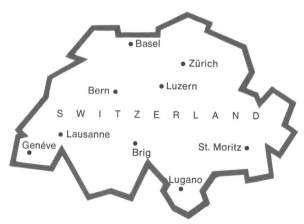

23.   A summer visitor to Switzerland plans to travel to nine towns in the course of her vacation. Since she will use a rental car, she would like to minimize the length of her journey by visiting the towns in an order which will give the least distance travelled. The towns she will visit are Genéve, Lausanne, Brig, Bern, Luzern, Zürich, Basel, Lugano, and St. Moritz. If the visitor is to begin and end her trip at

Distances (Kilometers)

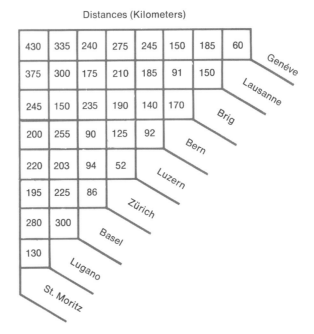

Genéve, write an algorithm in flowchart form which determines the correct order of the itinerary and the total distance travelled.

24. A maze is a confusing, intricate network of passages. Frequently, psychologists probe the learning capacity of rats by requiring them to find their way through a maze in order to receive food or other rewards. When the rat enters the maze for the first time, it searches for the correct path through trial and error, often retracing its steps when a dead end is reached. In subsequent experiments rats are able to find the correct route progressively more rapidly owing to their knowledge derived from previous attempts. Eventually, the rats can move through the maze without error.

   For this problem we want to simulate the behavior of a superbly logical rat (LOGRAT) that must find its way through a maze which is given in terms of a two dimensional grid, as shown below. LOGRAT's initial position is shown and corresponds to the row/column coordinates (1,5). An algorithm is needed to guide LOGRAT through the maze in some logical fashion so that it can traverse any maze successfully to the final coordinates (XFINAL, YFINAL). In the example shown below we have taken the final coordinates as (10, 12).

   Specifically, write an algorithm for LOGRAT which

   a. guides the choice of LOGRAT's next position (LOGRAT cannot move along diagonals, through the walls, or onto a darkened box).

   b. enables him to follow the maze network with the capacity to retrace his steps if he encounters a dead end.

c. enables him to memorize the correct path through the maze so that LOG-RATA, its mate, can pass through the maze without error.

To solve this problem, note that the maze itself can be represented as a two dimensional array, $GRID_{J,K}$, where forbidden squares are represented by some value, say -1. At each move LOGRAT must examine four adjacent boxes or elements of GRID and select its new move from those having a value other than -1. The entire maze can be represented in terms of a tree-like data structure through which LOGRAT must traverse searching for the route to the final position.

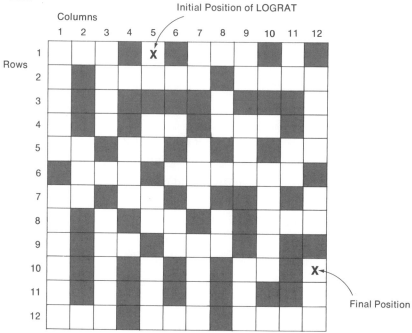

25. In businesses, merchandise is often held in storage to meet sales demands for the periods between merchandise delivery. The control of this stored merchandise is an important factor in the economic success of a business. Various strategies are used to keep the inventory as small as possible while, which at the same time minimizes losses arising from a lack of merchandise. Typically, new stock is delivered to a warehouse following the placing of an order only after some appreciable time lag. Thus, it is clear that if the re-order supply was too small, sales can exhaust the supply of a given item before the next delivery arrives. Hence, some planning based on the rate of sales and the anticipated delivery time is needed to determine the correct inventory level and delivery order size.

For this problem we want to investigate the behavior of a system of manual stock control for tennis racquets. The constraints of this particular inventory control model are as follows:

a. There is an initial stock of 40 racquets.

b. A random integer number of racquets from 0 to 4 are sold each day.

c. The fixed inventory level at which new racquets are ordered is 16 racquets.

d. The fixed order quantity is 40 racquets.

e. At the end of each day an order for new racquets is placed if the stock has dropped to the minimum order level or less.

f. Once the order for new racquets has been placed, it takes 10 days for them to arrive. The units arrive at the end of the day after sales are finished and before the day's inventory has been taken.

g. Once an order for more racquets has been made, a new order cannot be made until the present order arrives.

A simulation should be planned for 50 days. For each day the flowchart should output the following information:

1. The number of racquets sold.
2. The number of racquets ordered.
3. The number of racquets received.
4. The number of racquets in stock at the end of the day.
5. The number of lost sales arising from insufficient stock.

At the end of 50 days the flowchart should compute:

1. The average number of racquets in stock.
2. The average number of sales per day.
3. The average number of lost sales per day.

(This problem was developed by Dr. T. Hankins)

26. In the last problem a simulation algorithm was developed for a manual inventory control model. With the introduction of computers a new ordering strategy is possible:

   a. By computerizing the inventory control process, the delay between realizing that an order must be placed and the arrival of goods is reduced to 5 days.

   b. The minimum order level (MOL) and the order quantity (OQ) are now adjusted from order to order in an effort to meet changing conditions. The formulas adopted to determine the MOL and OQ are based upon corrections to $(MOL)_{OLD}$ and $(OQ)_{OLD}$.

$$(MOL)_{NEW} = (MOL)_{OLD}$$

$$\times \; \frac{\text{(total sales + total lost sales)/(number of days since last order)}}{\text{(average sales per day from the previous order period)}}$$

$$(OO)_{NEW} = (OQ)_{OLD} \times \frac{(MOL)_{NEW}}{(MOL)_{OLD}}$$

To investigate the behavior of this model, a simulation flowchart is needed with the same outputs as were described in Problem 25. Initial values should be MOL = 16, OQ = 40, with average sales per day of 2. Note that MOL, OQ and the average sales per day are not updated until an order is placed.

27. *Baseball by Computer.* Baseball is played using complicated rules enforced by the arbitrary decisions of obdurate umpires. Owing to the highly structured character of the game, it is possible to create a simple simulation model which can be used to compare different teams on the basis of their batting capabilities. While simulated games will never excite the devoted fan, they do provide an interesting exercise in development of algorithms and computer programming.

For the present model we adopt the basic structure of baseball: nine or more innings are played per game, with the visiting team batting first each inning. As in the real game, a team continues at bat as long as the accumulated number of outs is fewer than three. If the visiting team is behind at the end of their turn in the ninth inning, the game is completed at that point; otherwise, the full nine innings are played. If the score is tied at the end of nine complete innings, then one or more additional innings are played as necessary to determine the winner.

The simulation game is played according to average batting statistics of the individual team members. From past performance the probabilities for a given player reaching 1st, 2nd or 3rd base or hitting a home run are known. Examples of these probabilities for the members of two professional teams are given at the end of this problem.

Unfortunately, these probabilities cannot be used directly for the simulation model owing to the discrete character of a batting event (i.e., a batter either reaches a base or is out). One way to decide whether or not a batter reaches base is to convert the separate batting probabilities to ranges of values on an integer batting scale extending from 0 to 999. As an example of this, the batting scale for John Grubb (San Diego Padres) can be cast in the form shown below.

Integer Batting Scale

J. Grubb	Walk	1st Base	2nd Base	3rd Base	Home Run	Out
	0–29	30–253	254–309	310–319	320–340	341–999

With such an integer batting scale, it is now possible to use a random number generator to randomly select an integer in the range 0-999 which, with the batting scale, determine the outcome of the player's turn at bat.

Initially, the order in which players come to bat are given for each team and play begins with the first batter of the visiting team. Specific rules for the subsequent play include the following:

1. A player already on base (1st, 2nd or 3rd) advances two bases when a batter obtains a hit to 1st, 2nd or 3rd base.

2. A player already on base (1st, 2nd or 3rd) automatically scores a run when a subsequent player hits a home run.

3.   When a player advances to 1st base through a walk, players already on base advance one base only if it is necessary to provide space (only one player at a time can occupy a given base).

4.   Stealing, balks, substitutions, multiple-out defensive plays and other fine points of the real game are omitted.

5.   Players remaining on base at the end of three outs are removed from base.

6.   Players bat in the sequence of the original batting list as the innings progress. When all batters have had a turn at bat, the batting list is repeated.

a.   Using the rules described above, create an algorithm in flowchart form for playing baseball according to the simple simulation model.

b.   For computer applications, write a program which plays a complete game using the actual (1973) data for the two professional teams listed below. Arrange the output to give an inning by inning summary of the runs, hits and players left on base for each team. If possible, play ten games to determine the best team.

SAN DIEGO PADRES
(Based on 1973 Data)

Player	Walk†	1st Base	2nd Base	3rd Base	Home run
E. Hernandez	.020	.210	.008	.004	.000
G. Beckert	.025	.220	.034	.000	.000
J. Grubb	.030	.224	.056	.010	.021
W. McCovey	.030	.146	.037	.008	.076
D. Winfield	.025	.220	.028	.007	.021
F. Kendall	.020	.213	.043	.006	.020
D. Roberts	.015	.194	.042	.006	.044
B. Tolan	.010	.150	.030	.004	.020
B. Collins*	.005	.105	.053	.000	.000

OAKLAND A's

Player	Walk†	1st Base	2nd Base	3rd Base	Home run
B. North	.020	.247	.018	.009	.009
B. Campaneris	.025	.200	.030	.010	.007
S. Bando	.030	.179	.054	.005	.049
R. Jackson	.030	.174	.052	.004	.059
J. Rudi	.025	.183	.057	.002	.027
G. Tenace	.020	.172	.035	.004	.047
R. Fosse	.015	.191	.047	.004	.014
D. Green	.010	.202	.051	.000	.009
E. Newson*	.005	.123	.031	.000	.015

*Fictitious pitcher   †Arbitrary probabilities

Numbers for Computers

WHY NUMBERS?

Since digital computers process both numerical and nonnumerical data, it might seem that an entire chapter devoted to numbers and number systems would prove to be very unfair. Yet, appearances are sometimes deceiving and especially so in this case. Owing to their internal structure, computers continually operate in an environment of numbers which are not based upon our ordinary decimal number system. Instead, it is more convenient and economical to use the binary, octal, and hexadecimal systems for different purposes. Any discussion of this diversity of number representation presumes some knowledge of the basic facts about general place value number systems. An introduction to this topic is given in this chapter. The application of these principles to the actual means of computer information storage is made in the next chapter.

NUMBERS FROM PAST TO PRESENT

The most commonly used number system in the modern world is the decimal system. Digits in this system are represented using ten separate characters [0, 1, 2, 3, . . . 9] called the Hindu, Indian, Arabic, European, or Modern numerals. These digits, along with the idea of place value or positional notation, became widely known in Europe only after 1500 A.D. As we have seen in the first chapter, before the year 1500 A.D. written numbers were usually

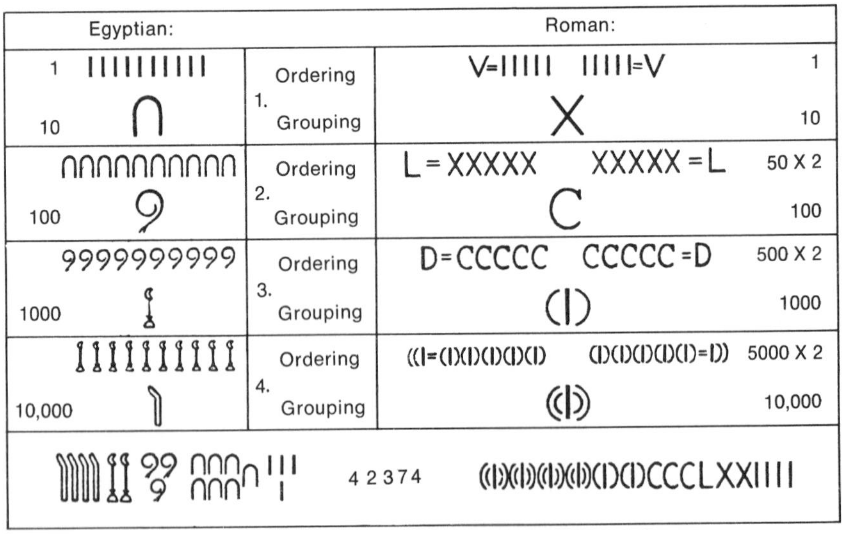

FIGURE 5.1. Comparison of Egyptian and Roman numerals.

expressed with the number value system of Roman numerals or presented in written alphabetic form (one hundred twenty one, for example, as compared with CXXI, and 121).

The path leading to our modern decimal, place-value number system appears to have begun with the primitive idea of *ordering*. With ordering, a one-to-one relationship is created between an object and a symbol. To represent several objects, one uses an equal number of symbols. Thus, for example, a native could count his fish by assigning one stick to each fish. When the native has finished counting, his pile of sticks represents the number of fish caught.

When the pile of sticks (or stones or other objects) becomes too large, one-to-one symbols lead to confusion and the idea of *grouping* is used such that groups of 3, 5, 10, or 20 items are represented by a new symbol. These new groups can themselves be grouped, leading to the transitions

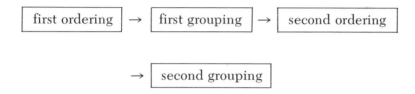

and so forth.

An example of ordering and grouping based on orders of 10 is shown in the Figure 5.1 of early Egyptian pictographic numerals. A similar discontinuous grouping of early Roman numbers is also shown. In contrast to the Egyptian system, the Roman representation is based upon subgroups of 5, 50, 500, etc.

The change from the older order/group ideas to the next level, *gradation by steps*, was first accomplished in most cultures through the verbal expression of numbers. In the order/group method of counting, the individual symbols of the group have no individual names. One accumulates sticks until the group is full, but the individual sticks are not given separate names. In spoken form, languages do give identity to the individual. The counting sequence 1, 2, 3 . . . forms a progression of individual elements which builds upwards to the threshold of 10. Groups of 10 are then built up verbally until a group of 100 is reached. Verbal sequences of this type form step gradations in numbers with the presence of consecutive thresholds.

Studies of language have shown that the verbal expression of numbers in cultures is built long before there is an equivalent written expression. This partially explains why the Roman system of written numerals was based upon ordering and grouping while their verbal system was based upon step gradations:

four thousand	eight hundred	seventy	nine	English written
quattuor mila	octingenti	septuaginta	novem	Latin written
(I) (I) (I) (I)	DCCC	LXX	VIIII	Roman numerals
4879				Place value numbers

The transition from verbal numbers with stepwise gradations to a similar form of written numbers was unique to the early Chinese and Indian cultures. In the Chinese expression, separate characters are used to represent both the nine digits (1, 2, 3, . . . 9) and the ranks of 10 (tens, hundreds, thousands, etc.). (See Figure 5.2.) Thus, the number 1973 was expressed in the form

$$1\,TH\ \ 9\,H\ \ 7\,T\ \ 3$$

with the ranks of ten shown explicitly. Using Chinese characters this number appears as shown in Figure 5.3.

Because the Chinese system represents the ranks of 10 explicitly, there is no need for the symbol 0. The number 1001, for example, is written, and spoken as 1 TH 1.

FIGURE 5.2. Characters used by the ancient Chinese to represent numerals and ranks.

FIGURE 5.3.

Our present number system seems to have originated in India starting with the numerals of Brahmi writings dating to about the second century B.C. As shown in Figure 5.4, the principle of ordering and grouping had been abandoned at that time in favor of encipherment in which each digit had a separate symbol. To some extent, however, the encipherment went too far since not only did the nine digits have symbols, but also each group of 10 and 100. Thus, it was not immediately possible to express numbers in a pure ranking system such as was developed by the Chinese.

The reversion to a pure rank system took place around 600 A.D. in India. Dropping the encipherment of the 10s, the first nine Brahmi digits, modified with time to new forms, appeared for the first time in place-value notation. Unlike the Chinese, the Indians did not keep separate characters to indicate the ranks of 10, but used the relative location of the digits themselves to show the proper rank value. With this method, older numbers which, with excessive encipherment, might have appeared as 500 40 9 could be compressed to the Chinese form of 5H 4T9 or the place-value expression 549.

The transition from explicit ranking to the implicit place-value system was not done without difficulty, since it meant the creation of a new symbol, the zero (the Indians used a dot), having the function of indicating the presence of ranks with no associated digit. In the middle ages this symbol was regarded as an evil, mysterious creation of the Devil which of itself represented nothing but by its presence gave value to other digits.

The westward migration of the Indian numerals was accomplished through the Arabic civilization and its rapid westward expansion. Our present numerals derive from West Arabic numerals which, in their acceptance in Western Europe, underwent further changes in form. Changes in the digit symbols continued through the late fifteenth century until the advent of printing

Units	Digits	1	2	3	4	5	6	7	8	9
Tens	Enciphering	10	20	30	40	50	60	70	80	90
Hundreds and Thousands	Place-value Notation	100	2H	5H	1000	4 Th	70 Th			

FIGURE 5.4. Indian Brahmi numerals.

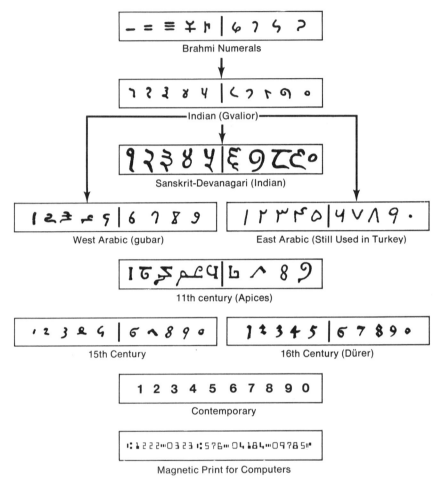

FIGURE 5.5.

stabilized the form of the numerals roughly as the standard set of numerals we know today. (See Figure 5.5.)

NUMBER SYSTEMS FOR COMPUTERS

Our common place-value number system uses 10 separate symbols to represent digits. Other place-value number systems can be easily created by enlarging or restricting the number of allowed digits. As we shall see, the decimal system is not particularly well suited for use by computers. Consequently, other place-value systems have been developed for machine operations.

To distinguish between different place-value number systems, it is often convenient to refer to the *radix*, that is, the number of separate symbols a particular number system uses to represent the basic set of digits. Our decimal system, for example, has a radix of 10, while the binary, octal, duodecimal, and hexadecimal systems have radices of 2, 8, 12, and 16, respectively. With respect to these latter number systems a confusing, but useful, convention has arisen. Each time we create a new number system it is possible to adopt a completely new character set to express the individual digits. With a binary system (radix 2), for example, it would be perfectly acceptable to use character sets composed of (α, β), $(\uparrow, \downarrow)$ or any other two symbols.

The disadvantage of choosing new character sets for each number system lies in the simple difficulty of remembering the new symbols. To overcome this human failing, it has become usual to adopt ordinary Arabic characters for number systems other than decimal. For binary numbers we use the characters 0 and 1, while the octal system uses 0 through 7. To distinguish between digits relating to different number systems, it is often necessary to introduce decimal subscripts giving the radix of the system involved (16_8, 1001_2, etc.).

For number systems having radices greater than 10, the Arabic numerals are insufficient in number to create a complete set of digits. The usual practice for these number systems is to adopt the 10 Arabic numerals and use alphabetic capital letters for the remainder of the character set. Complete character sets for several useful number systems are shown in Figure 5.6.

Place-Value Notation

In the method of *place-value* or *positional notation* the value of a digit in a number is determined by its rank or location relative to the units rank. Thus, each digit in a number has a value determined by an implicit multiplication of the digit by a power of the radix. For the units digit (located immediately to the left of an assumed radix point) the power is zero; the multiplicative factor is 1 in all number systems. For the next leftward digit position the multiplicative factor is $(radix)^1$, followed by $(radix)^2$, $(radix)^3$, and so forth for subsequent digit positions. To the right of the radix point a similar scheme of radix vactor

Radix	Character Set
2	0,1
6	0,1,2,3,4,5
8	0,1,2,3,4,5,6,7
10	0,1,2,3,4,5,6,7,8,9
12	0,1,2,3,4,5,6,7,8,9,A,B
16	0,1,2,3,4,5,6,7,8,9,A,B,C,D,E,F

FIGURE 5.6. Character sets for various number systems.

RADIX OF NUMBER SYSTEM

2	6	8	10	12	16
0	0	0	0	0	0
1	1	1	1	1	1
10	2	2	2	2	2
11	3	3	3	3	3
100	4	4	4	4	4
101	5	5	5	5	5
110	10	6	6	6	6
111	11	7	7	7	7
1000	12	10	8	8	8
1001	13	11	9	9	9
1010	14	12	10	A	A
1011	15	13	11	B	B
1100	20	14	12	10	C
1101	21	15	13	11	D
1110	22	16	14	12	E
1111	23	17	15	13	F
1000	24	20	16	14	10
10001	25	21	17	15	11
10010	30	22	18	16	12
10011	31	23	19	17	13
10100	32	24	20	18	14

FIGURE 5.7. Number equivalents for the binary, senary. octal, decimal, duodecimal, and hexadecimal systems.

multiplication is used with the first place represented by $(radix)^{-1}$, the second by $(radix)^{-2}$, and so on. The total value of a number represented in positional notation can be found by summing together the values (digit × radix factor) of all the individual digit positions.

To illustrate these ideas, consider the number $[638.32]_{10}$, the subscript indicating that this is a decimal number (radix 10). The decimal point is indicated by the symbol (.). The *literal expansion* of this number using the ideas of positional notation is

$$[638.32]_{10} = 600 + 30 + 8 + .3 + .02$$

$$= 6 \times 10^2 + 3 \times 10^1 + 8 \times 10^0 \mid + 3 \times 10^{-1} + 2 \times 10^{-2}$$

$$\left\{ \begin{array}{l} \text{radix point} \\ \text{location} \end{array} \right.$$

Number systems having radices of 2, 8, and 16 are of particular importance to the representation of data in computers and arithmetic operations. Figure 5.7 gives the numerical equivalents of these systems for the decimal numbers 0 through 20. Also included are the equivalents for radix 6 and 12 systems, even though these number systems are not widely used.

From Figure 5.7 we note an interesting fact: The radix of every number system, when expressed using its *own character set*, appears as the characters [10]. If we show the radix by the subscript r, it is clear that the decimal equivalent of $[10]_r$ is not $[10]_{10}$, but some other decimal number which must be calculated through number conversion. To avoid confusion, the number inside the braces [ ] is expressed in the symbols of the chosen system and the radix of that system is written below in our ordinary decimal numbers. For example, $[10]_2 = [2]_{10}$, $[10]_8 = [8]_{10}$, $[10]_{16} = [16]_{10}$.

Despite our unfamiliarity with new number systems, the principles of doing arithmetic calculations in any radix r number system is no more difficult than in the decimal system. The principal differences are found in the results of arithmetic operations, since the changed character set gives answers which are somewhat different than we find in decimal operations (note that $[3 \times 3]_{10} = [9]_{10}$ while $[3 \times 3]_8 = [11]_8$).

As an example of the more important differences, consider the octal (radix eight) number system. The rules of addition and subtraction, which can be deduced from Figure 5.7, show that "10" is reached in the octal system directly after character 7. As in the decimal system, it is possible to count by "10s" and use the combination of characters 10 in the literal expansion of a number. More novel, however, are the rules for multiplication in an octal system, as shown in the octal multiplication table of Figure 5.8. Clearly, to be

0	1	2	3	4	5	6	7
1	1	2	3	4	5	6	7
2	2	3	6	10	12	14	16
3	3	6	11	14	17	22	25
4	4	10	14	20	24	30	34
5	5	12	16	24	31	36	43
6	6	14	22	30	36	44	52
7	7	16	25	34	43	52	61

FIGURE 5.8. Octal multiplication table through $[7 \times 7]_8$.

proficient in octal arithmetic it would be necessary to learn the octal multiplication table at least through $[10 \times 10]_8$ in a manner similar to elementary school children learning their $[10 \times 10]_{10}$ tables in decimal. However, once the rules are memorized, octal arithmetic is neither more nor less difficult than decimal arithmetic.

The general form of a number in the radix system looks like

$$\overset{\lceil \text{sign}}{\pm} \ldots \overset{\lceil \text{digit}}{d_3 d_2 d_1 d_0} \cdot \overset{\lceil \text{radix point}}{d_{-1} d_{-2} d_{-3}} \ldots$$

$$\underset{\substack{\text{digit} \\ \text{identifying} \\ \text{subscript}}}{\big|}$$

so that a literal expansion can be made as

$$\pm[\ldots d_3 \times R^3 + d_2 \times R^2 + d_1 \times R^1 + d_0 \times R^0 + d_{-1} \times R^{-1} + d_{-2} \times R^{-2} + \ldots]_r$$

Here R represents the value of the radix in its own number system (i.e., $[10]_r$). For convenience, the radix powers and the radix r are all given in the decimal system.

Substituting the value of the radix value R = $[10]_r$, expression becomes

$$\pm[\ldots d_3 \times 10^3 + d_2 \times 10^2 + d_1 \times 10^1 + d_0 \times 10^0 + d_{-1} \times 10^{-1} + d_{-2} \times 10^{-2} + \ldots]_r$$

Using the previous expression as a guide, it is possible to perform literal expansions for numbers of arbitrary radix as shown.

Binary $[101.11]_2 = [1 \times 10^2 + 0 \times 10^1 + 1 \times 10^0 + 1 \times 10^{-1} + 1 \times 10^{-2}]_2$
$$= [100 + 1 + .1 + 01]_2$$

Octal $[6741.7]_8 = 6 \times 10^3 + 7 \times 10^2 + 4 \times 10^1 + 1 \times 10^0 + 7 \times 10^{-1}]_8$
$$= [6000 + 700 + 40 + 1 + .7]_8$$

Duodecimal $[B94.A3]_{12} = [B \times 10^2 + 9 \times 10^1 + 4 \times 10^0 + A \times 10^{-1} + 3 \times 10^{-2}]_{12}$
$$= [B00 + 90 + 4 + .A + .03]_{12}$$

Hexadecimal $[FE050.]_{16} = [F \times 10^4 + E \times 10^3 + 0$
$\times 10^2 + 5 \times 10^1 + 0 \times 10^0]_{16}$
$= F0000 + E000 + 50]_{16}$

Conversion of numbers from any number system to the decimal system can be easily accomplished by converting the individual terms of the literal expansion to decimal numbers and carrying out the indicated multiplications and additions.

Examples:

Binary to Decimal

$$[10110.]_2 = [1 \times 10^4 + 1 \times 10^2 + 1 \times 10^1]_2$$
$$\text{But } [10]_2 = [2]_{10} \quad \text{(from Figure 5.7)}$$

Thus,

$$[10110.]_2 = [1 \times 2^4 + 1 \times 2^2 + 1 \times 2^1]_{10}$$
$$= 16 + 4 + 2$$
$$= [22.]_{10}$$

Hexadecimal to Decimal

$$[9E0.]_{16} = [9 \times 10^2 + E \times 10^1]_{16}$$
$$\text{But } [10]_{16} = [16]_{10}$$
$$[E]_{16} = [14]_{10} \quad \text{(from Figure 5.7)}$$
$$[9E0.]_{16} = [9 \times 16^2 + 14 \times 16^1]_{10}$$
$$= 2304 + 224$$
$$= [2528.]_{10}$$

The more general conversion of numbers between two arbitrary radices, r and t, can be carried out using a similar procedure. One difficulty with this method, however, is that all the arithmetic products and summations are carried out with radix arithmetic rules which may not be as familiar as the rules for decimal arithmetic (remember the octal multiplication table of Figure 5.8).

Because our interest in number systems is directed towards computer applications we will concentrate in the remainder of this section upon the techniques needed to conversions between decimal, binary, octal, and hexadecimal numbers. The rules governing number conversion between other number systems are given in the Appendices.

Binary to Decimal Number Conversion

Binary to decimal number conversion can be rapidly done using the literal expansion method. Given a binary number of the form

$$\pm[\ldots d_3 d_2 d_1 d_0 \cdot d_{-1} d_{-2} \ldots]_2$$

where the individual binary digits are represented by the ds, (each d is either 0 or 1) we can make the literal expansion as

$$\pm[\ldots d_3 \times 2^3 + d_2 \times 2^2 + d_1 \times 2^1 + d_0 \times 2^0 + d_{-1} \times 2^{-1} + d_{-2} \times 2^{-2} + \ldots]_{10}$$

or

$$\pm[\ldots d_3 \times 8 + d_2 \times 4 + d_1 \times 2 + d_0 \times 1 + d_{-1} \times 1/2 + d_{-2} \times 1/4 + \ldots]_{10}$$

Substitution of the original binary digits into this expression and subsequent multiplication and addition gives the final decimal equivalent.

Example: Convert $[1011.011]_2$ to decimal

$$\begin{aligned}
[1011.011]_2 &= [1 \times 2^3 + 0 \times 2^2 + 1 \times 2^1 + 1 \times 2^0 + 0 \times 2^{-1} + 1 \times 2^{-2} + 1 \times 2^{-3}]_{10} \\
&= [8 + 2 + 1 + 0.25 + 0.125]_{10} \\
&= [11.375]_{10}
\end{aligned}$$

Example: Convert $-[0.00101]_2$ to decimal

$$\begin{aligned}
-[0.00101]_2 &= -[0 \times 2^0 + 0 \times 2^{-1} + 0 \times 2^{-2} + 1 \times 2^{-3} + 0 \times 2^{-4} + 1 \times 2^{-5}]_{10} \\
&= \quad [0.125 + 0.03125]_{10} \\
&= -[0.15624]_{10} \text{ (Note that the sign makes no difference.)}
\end{aligned}$$

Decimal to Binary Number Conversion

As we have seen, the conversion of a binary number to its decimal equivalent is straightforward. Unfortunately, it is slightly more complicated to convert decimal numbers into binary, because it is necessary to treat the integer (whole) and fractional parts of the decimal number separately.

Suppose we are given the integer (whole) number $[28]_{10}$. The conversion to binary can be made with the following method:

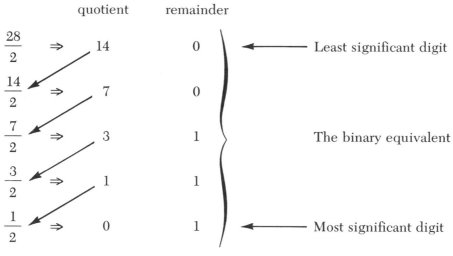

quotient   remainder

$\frac{28}{2}$ ⇒ 14   0   ← —— Least significant digit

$\frac{14}{2}$ ⇒ 7   0

$\frac{7}{2}$ ⇒ 3   1   } The binary equivalent

$\frac{3}{2}$ ⇒ 1   1

$\frac{1}{2}$ ⇒ 0   1   ← —— Most significant digit

Answer: $[28]_{10} = [11100]_2$

This method involves only simple division by 2, keeping track of resulting quotients and a remainder list. This list, when inverted, provides us with the integer binary equivalent.

Example: Convert $[58]_{10}$ to binary

$\frac{58}{2}$ = 19   0

$\frac{19}{2}$ = 9   1

$\frac{9}{2}$ = 4   1

$\frac{4}{2}$ = 2   0   } $= [100110]_2$

$\frac{2}{2}$ = 1   0

$\frac{1}{2}$ = 0   1

For fractional decimal numbers a multiplication method can be used. Suppose we wish to convert $[0.15625]_{10}$ to binary. The multiplication method is:

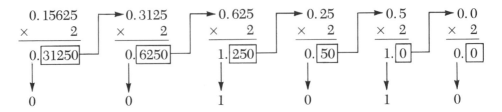

Answer: $[0.00101]_2$

The multiplication method involves continual multiplications by 2 from the fractional part of the preceeding multiplication. The process stops when the fractional part is zero, as shown above. In some cases, there is no exact equivalent between a decimal fraction and its binary version. Only if the decimal number is a fraction such as $1/2$, $1/8$, $1/16$, . . ., or some combination of these can there be a binary fraction of finite length. The implications of this for computer number storage are discussed in the next chapter.

Example: Convert $[0.573]_{10}$ to binary

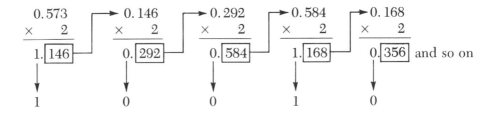

Answer: $[0.573]_{10} = [0.10010 . . .]_2$ to five binary places

Although these last two numbers are not precisely equivalent, we can reach any desired degree of accuracy by carrying out further multiplications.

To convert a decimal number composed of an integer (whole) and fractional part, it is only necessary to convert each part of decimal number separately according to the two methods given above.

Example: Convert $[342.175]_{10}$ to binary

Integer Part:

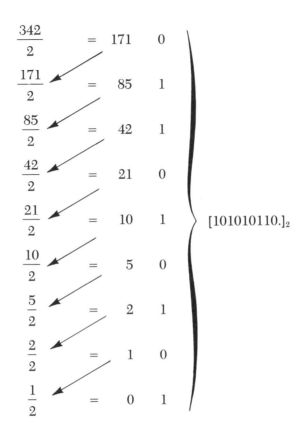

Fractional Part:

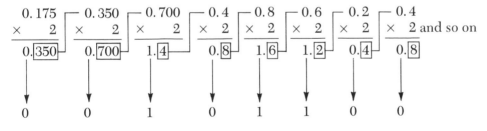

.00101100 . . .

Answer: $[342.175]_{10} = [101010110.00101100 . . .]_2$

The manner in which the multiplication and division methods have been presented may seem somewhat arbitrary. A more detailed discussion and explanation of these methods can be found in the Appendix.

Interconversion of Binary, Octal, and Hexadecimal Numbers

The interconversion of binary, octal, and hexadecimal numbers can be accomplished very readily with the following rules:

A. *Binary to Octal and Hexadecimal.* Starting from the binary point, form groups of three [octal] or four [hexadecimal] binary digits to both the left and the right. Convert each of these groups of binary digits into its octal or hexadecimal equivalent.

Example: Convert $[111110.1011]_2$ to octal

Rewrite the binary number in groups of three digits

$$111 \quad 110.101 \quad 100$$
$$7 \quad\quad 6 \ . \ 5 \quad\quad 4 \quad = [76.54]_8$$

Example: Convert $[111110.1011]_2$ to hexadecimal
Rewrite the binary number in groups of four digits

$$0011 \quad 1110.1011$$
$$3 \quad\quad E \ . \ B \quad = [3E.B]_{16}$$

B. *Octal and Hexadecimal to Binary.* Replace each digit in the octal or hexadecimal number by its binary equivalent.

Example: Convert $[7314.03]_8$ to binary

$$7 \quad 3 \quad 1 \quad 4 \ . \ 0 \quad 3$$
$$111 \quad 011 \quad 001 \quad 100 \ . \ 000 \quad 011 = \quad [111011001100.000011]_2$$

Example: Convert $[FE0.E4]_{16}$ to binary

$$F \quad E \quad 0 \quad . \quad E \quad 4$$
$$1111 \quad 1110 \quad 0000 \quad . \quad 1110 \quad 0100 = [111111100000.111001]_2$$

C. *Octal/Hexadecimal Conversion.* Convert the octal or hexadecimal number to binary using Rule B, then with Rule A re-express the binary number in the desired number system.

Example: Convert $[7740.71]_8$ to hexadecimal

octal	7	7	4	0	.	7	1
binary	111	111	100	000	.	111	001
regrouped binary	1111	1110	0000	.		1110	0100
hexadecimal	F	E	0	.		E	4

Thus, $[7740.71]_8 = [FE0.E4]_{16}$

As discussed later, the interconversion relations provide a rapid means for a space saving presentation of internally stored strings of binary digits as strings of octal or hexadecimal numbers.

Finally, to convert decimal numbers into octal or hexadecimal, it is most rapid to first find the binary equivalent, then regroup to identify individual octal or hexadecimal numbers. The reverse process of octal or hexadecimal to decimal conversion can be most rapidly done through literal expansion.

REFERENCES TO FURTHER READINGS

MENNINGER, K.
Number Words and Number Symbols. MIT Press, 1969.
NASHELSKY, L.
Digital Computer Theory. New York: John Wiley & Sons, 1966. Contains a good description of general number systems and the methods of number conversion.

KEY WORDS AND PHRASES TO KNOW

BINARY   OCTAL
CHARACTER SET   ORDERING
ENCIPHERMENT   PLACE-VALUE SYSTEM
GRADATION BY STEPS   POSITIONAL NOTATION
GROUPING   RADIX
HEXADECIMAL   RANK SYSTEM
LITERAL EXPANSION   ZERO
NONNUMERICAL DATA

EXERCISES

1. Can you explain why $10_2 = 2_{10}$ or $10_{16} = 16_{10}$?
2. Derive the multiplication table for the senary (radix 6) number system.
3. Since we have seen that arithmetic is no more difficult in an arbitrary number system than in decimal, is there any fundamental reason to argue against adopting radix 5 or radix 16 number systems for general use?
4. Perform literal expansions for the following numbers:

   a. 1100.01_2 c. $ABA.A1_{12}$
   b. 707.06_8 d. $F00D.0_{16}$

5. Convert the following numbers to decimals:

   a. 1011011_2 d. $10FEE_{16}$ g. 1435_6 j. 1101_8
   b. 10010_2 e. $A101F_{16}$ h. 1101_2 k. 1101_{16}
   c. 743_8 f. 1001_8 i. 1101_3 l. 1101_{20}

6. Write an algorithm in flowchart form for the conversion of decimal integer numbers to binary.
7. Convert the following decimal integer numbers to binary:

   a. 1000   d. 17
   b. 123   e. 101
   c. 832   f. 192

8. Convert the following decimal fractions to binary keeping eight-place binary accuracy:

   a. 0.123   d. 0.025
   b. 0.001   e. 0.0756
   c. 0.987   f. 0.1251

9. Convert the following decimal numbers to binary keeping eight-place binary accuracy:

    a. 16.43   d. 7.93
    b. 126.125   e. 1.333 . . . (repeating fraction)
    c. 1.001   f. 3.141592

10. Convert the following binary numbers to octal and hexadecimal:

    a. 10110110.10   e. 1101101.
    b. 100001.00101   r. 101101101.001
    c. 11010.0101   g. 101
    d. 11.010101   h. 1111.111 . . . (repeating fraction)

11. Convert the following octal and hexadecimal numbers to binary:

    a. 7407.006_8 e. $FEDC.BA_{16}$
    b. 1430.01_8 f. $F0.110_{16}$
    c. 1672_8 g. 1001.0101_{16}
    d. 1001.0101_8 h. $19.F_{16}$

12. Using the information given in Figure 5.1, express the following decimal numbers in Egyptian and Roman numerals:

    a. 1043   d. 521
    b. 89   e. 66
    c. 10,821   f. 19

PROBLEMS

1. Write an algorithm in flowchart form for the conversion of decimal integer numbers to binary.

2. Write the algorithm describing the conversion of decimal fractions to binary fractions.

3. Write the algorithm describing the conversion of binary numbers to octal and hexadecimal.

4. Write the algorithms describing the conversion of octal and hexadecimal numbers to binary.

six

How a Computer Stores Information

INTERNAL REPRESENTATION OF INFORMATION

Computers process data using instructions stored within the computer memory. Before we can discuss the details of data and instruction operations, however, an explanation is required of the way information of different types is represented within the computer. This subject was briefly mentioned in Chapter two where it was shown that simple codes based upon the two binary characters, 0 and 1, could be used to represent numerals, alphabetic characters, punctuation, arithmetic operators, and other information symbols of the external world. In this section we will probe more deeply into the reasons why such codes are needed and what their relationship is to the basic information storage ability of computers.

The internal functioning of digital computers is closely related to the physical structure of the devices used to store digital information. In operation, the

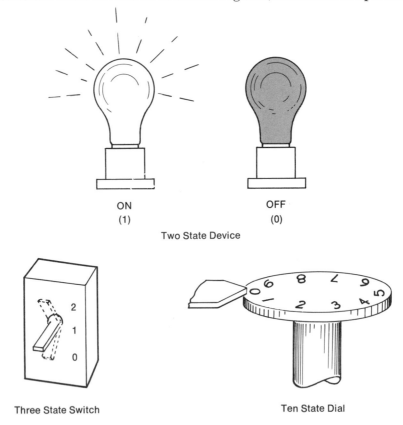

ON   OFF
(1)   (0)

Two State Device

Three State Switch   Ten State Dial

FIGURE 6.1. Digit storage devices.

200

individual cells of the computer memory are designed to accept, store, or return the value of one binary digit upon the command of the computer central control unit. The individual memory cells, like electric light bulbs with their "ON" and "OFF" states, have just two different internal settings, which makes them ideal storage devices for the binary digits, 0 and 1.

At the most fundamental level, the storage of a digit in any type of memory cell can be done only if we establish a one-to-one correspondence between the different states of the cell and the digits of some number system. For example, a light bulb is a two state device which can be used to represent the binary digits 0 ("OFF") and 1 ("ON"). In a similar manner, a switch having

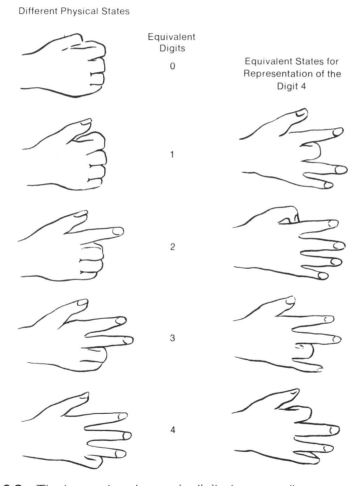

FIGURE 6.2. The human hand as a six-digit storage cell.

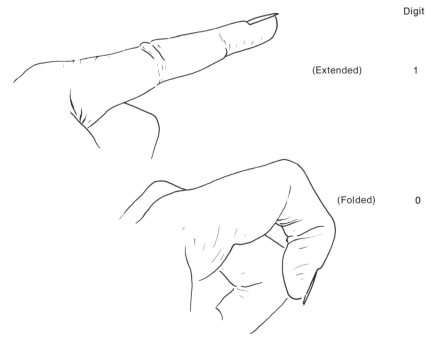

Digit

(Extended)   1

(Folded)   0

FIGURE 6.3. A single finger can be a two-state digit storage device.

three positions could be used for a set of three digits (0, 1, 2) forming the basis of the trinary number system, and a 10 position switch, like the digit wheels of mechanical calculators, can be used for the 10 digits of the decimal system. (See Figure 6.1)

The human hand can also be regarded as a storage device. If we disregard the previous finger positions associated with finger counting, we can look at a hand as a six state device, capable of representing the digits (0, 1, 2, 3, 4, 5) through extension of an appropriate number of fingers. As shown in Figure 6.2, (for the present purpose) the order in which the individual fingers of the hand storage cell are extended is unimportant in determining the state of this storage cell; only the total number of extended fingers matters.

We do not usually think of our hands as six state storage devices. Instead, more attention is given to the individual fingers. In contrast to the method of finger counting, suppose that we consider a single finger as a digit storage cell having two states: finger EXTENDED and finger FOLDED (into the palm of the hand).(See Figure 6.3.) Since there are two states, these two finger positions can be used to represent just two digits, 0 and 1, which form the basis of the binary number system.

At this point it is interesting to compare the separate ideas of the hand viewed as a single six state storage cell and the hand seen as a collection of five independent, two state cells. (See Figure 6.4.) The hand storage cell can be used to represent six digits (0 through 5), while each of the individual fingers, like switches, is restricted to two digits (0 and 1). Previously it was shown that groups of binary digits can be used to represent alphanumeric symbols. In a similar manner, it would be possible to use six state devices (like hands) for the same purpose. The only difference being that, because the digit storage capacity of each six state device is greater than that of a binary switch, fewer six state storage cells would be needed to represent a complete alphanumeric character set.

Although hands (and toes) are sufficient for many simple counting and data storage operations, a more rapid and economical means of digit storage is needed for computers. Modern technology has created several efficient digit storage devices which are widely used as memory cells in computers: Mag-

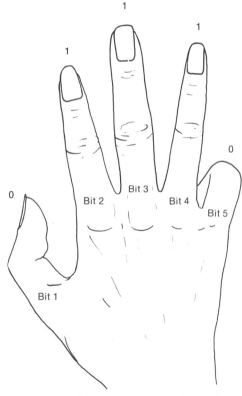

FIGURE 6.4. The human hand seen as a collection of five two-state storage cells.

netic cores and thin magnetic films. These devices depend upon their direction of internal magnetization to represent the value of binary digits. Cores, for example, can be magnetized so that the binary digits 0 (clockwise magnetization) and 1 (counterclockwise magnetization) can be uniquely identified.

In operation, the direction of magnetization of cores or thin films can be found or changed using pulses of electrical current. To illustrate this in a simple way, consider a single magnetic core which is traversed by two wires. (See Figure 6.6.) Suppose that the core is initially magnetized in the clockwise sense and that we send a pulse of current through wire A. This pulse, when it reaches the core, changes the direction of magnetization from clockwise to counterclockwise. This sudden change of direction is sensed by the second wire as an induced voltage pulse which travels along wire B to a detector. In a symbolic sense the core has been asked (by wire A), "Do you contain the digit 0?" and the response, given by wire B, is "Yes".

Suppose now that the core was initially magnetized in the counterclockwise direction. When the current pulse in wire A reaches the core it tries to add to the magnetization of the core. However, because the core is completely saturated in this direction, it cannot change appreciably and no pulse is induced in wire B. Thus, in this case the response to wire A's query is "No, I do not contain the digit 0" so, by inference, it must contain the digit 1.

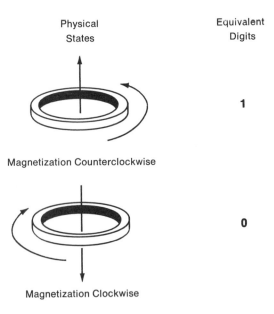

Physical
States

Equivalent
Digits

1

Magnetization Counterclockwise

0

Magnetization Clockwise

FIGURE 6.5. The physical states of a magnetic core.

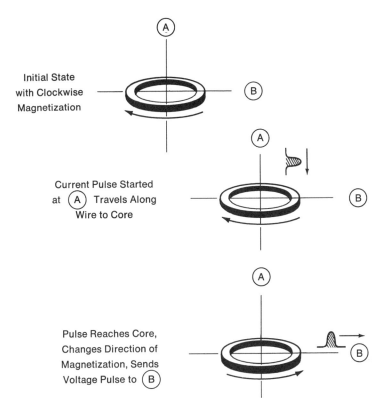

Initial State
with Clockwise
Magnetization

Current Pulse Started
at (A) Travels Along
Wire to Core

Pulse Reaches Core,
Changes Direction of
Magnetization, Sends
Voltage Pulse to (B)

FIGURE 6.6. Interrogation of a magnetic core.

The pulsing method of learning is destructive to the magnetization state of a core, since the previous magnetization state may be changed. Thus, if we wish to retain the stored binary digit following the read cycle, it is necessary to replace the correct digit with a write cycle. This writing involves a logic of the following form: Was the digit read a 0? If YES, then the reading cycle was destructive, the magnetic core now contains a 1 and a 0 must be entered. If NO, then the digit stored was a 0, the reading cycle was nondestructive and nothing needs to be done.

In the past, computer memories have been made of thousands of magnetic cores or thin films, each of which can be found at the junction of three wires, two of which ask questions about the internal magnetization state of a particular core, and a third which gives the answer. Thus, in theory, it is possible to isolate each individual digit storage cell within the computer memory. In modern practice, slightly more complicated groupings of memory elements are used to economize on the number of wires and external electrical devices needed to make computer memory work.

Although the foregoing discussion emphasizes magnetic cores, magnetic thin films, rotating magnetic discs or drums, or even more active electrical circuit elements known as flip-flops are also used within computer circuitry for particular tasks. In each case there are just two identifiable physical states that can be identified with the digits 0 and 1. Consequently, the internal structure of computers must revolve about binary digits and the laws of YES/NO mathematical logic. While such a restricted range of digit values might appear too small to give such devices any practical importance, the digits 0 and 1 form an adequate basis for storing all types of information in a computer. The relative disadvantage of a small range of digits per storage cell is reflected in a larger number of individual cells needed to represent a given code as compared with other devices having more distinguishable internal states. However, the low cost and intrinsic stability of magnetic storage devices provide strong economic advantages and the memory units of all large computers are built using one form or another of magnetic devices.

BITS, BYTES, AND WORDS

The individual storage cell provides the smallest unit of digital information which can be stored within a computer. This basic unit is usually referred to as a *binary digit* or *bit*. Computers are normally built with a large number of bit storage cells to that programs involving extensive instruction sets and data can be stored and processed internally. To be useful, each site of digital information storage must have a unique address so that the contents of the storage location can be transferred or changed upon suitable command by the computer central control unit.

Although it would be possible to construct computer circuits to give individual addresses to each binary digit stored in the computer memory, such an arrangement would be very extravagant. For purposes such as alphanumeric data storage and manipulation, machine instructions, or numerical data, groups of bits are normally stored together under one common address and treated by the computer as a unit of information. In some recent computers the fundamental group of bits is called a *byte*. (See Figure 6.7.) The size of a byte, usually six or eight bits, is chosen so that the byte can store one alphanumeric character using the basic binary character code adopted for the computer. The individual bits of a byte are electrically linked in such a way that a single memory address applies to the entire byte. For such machines the byte is the basic unit of addressable information.

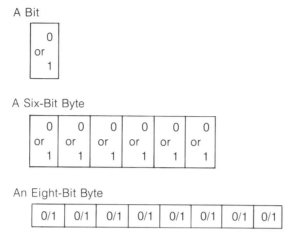

A Bit

A Six-Bit Byte

An Eight-Bit Byte

FIGURE 6.7. A byte is composed of individual bits linked together and treated as a unit.

A good example of the byte can be found in the human hand. As before, instead of viewing a hand as a simple storage cell having six states, suppose we consider each finger of a hand as a separate binary storage cell of two states with an extended finger corresponding to the digit 1 and a folded finger corresponding to 0. Since a hand has five such storage cells (see Figure 6.2), one hand is a byte composed of five bits. If we keep track of which fingers are extended, there are 32 possible finger patterns on a five finger hand. Using the hand byte these 32 different combinations can be used to represent alphanumeric characters and other symbols. The difficulty with a five-bit byte becomes quickly evident, however, since in building a code we find that 26 combinations are immediately taken by alphabetic characters, leaving only six possible combinations for the 10 numerals and any punctuation or special symbols. A six-bit byte, in contrast, provides 64 combinations ($2^6 = 64$), while eight-bit bytes can represent 256 separate characters ($2^8 = 256$).

While bytes are well adapted for character representation and storage, larger organizations of bits must be provided for storage of instructions and numbers. Such a larger unit is formed by linking bytes together to form a *word*. The IBM 360 computer system, for example, uses four eight-bit bytes to form a word. (See Figure 6.8.) The information stored in a word of this type can be directly referenced through the use of one address.

The various addressable groupings of information units are not restricted to bytes and words. It is found, for example, that instructions do not require as

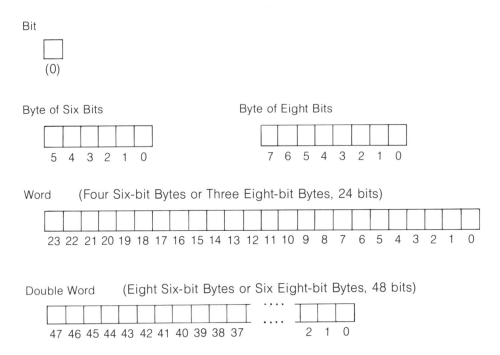

FIGURE 6.8 Typical organization within a computer using six and eight-bit bytes.

many bits as are needed for number representation. Hence, to conserve computer memory space *instruction half words* are often used. Likewise, although numbers are normally represented in words, for more accurate arithmetic it is possible to link two words together to form an addressable *double word*. The ultimate flexibility now available in large computer systems uses *variable length fields* composed of suitably linked bytes referenced by a single address.

From the preceding discussion, clearly the internal grouping of bits, bytes, and words in a computer is not rigid, but can be varied to meet particular data and instruction storage requirements. This flexibility is lacking, however, in many smaller or older computers where the *word* itself is the smallest addressable unit of information storage. In such machines addresses are not provided for the individual character codes corresponding to the bytes, even though the older words normally contain enough bits for six to eight alphanumeric characters. As a result, many tasks involving individual character manipulation become relatively difficult and time consuming using these computers, when compared with similar operations performed with machines having an addressable byte structure.

STORAGE OF ALPHABETIC DATA

Alphabetic symbols and special characters are represented in computers through codes based on sequences of binary digits. Normally at least six bits [$2^6 = 64$ square patterns] are required to establish a unique code set for the 26 upper case letters, the 10 Arabic numerals, various arithmetic operators, and punctuation marks. Most large computers having a byte structure use eight bit character codes [$2^8 = 256$ separate patterns] to take advantage of the larger available character set.

Both the six and eight bit character representations are subdivided into two parts: A *zone* part of two or four bits and a *numeric* part of four bits, as shown in Figure 6.9.

The most frequently used six bit character code is the Standard Binary Coded Decimal Interchange Code (SBCDIC). For eight bits the most widely used code is the Extended Binary Coded Decimal Interchange Code (EBCDIC). A table of both codes is given in Appendix II.

In discussions of binary coded characters it is often inconvenient to write out the six or eight bit sequences. This inconvenience can be substantially

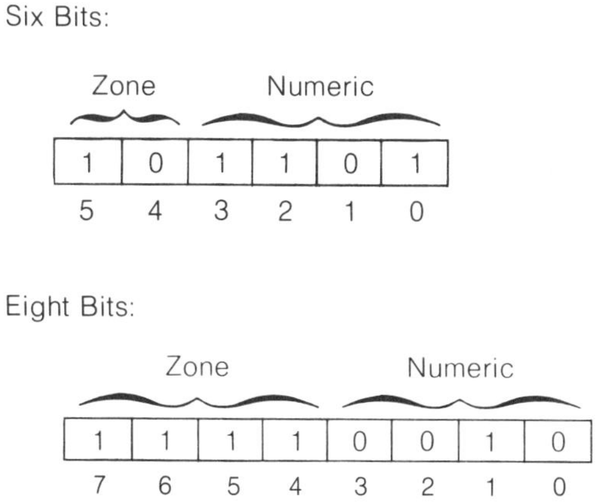

Six Bits:

Eight Bits:

FIGURE 6.9.   Representation of the symbols for numbers using six and eight-bit bytes with zone and numeric fields.

reduced by using the special relationships mentioned in the last chapter existing between the binary, octal, and hexadecimal number systems. If we treat the six and eight bit coded characters as numbers, rather than codes, it is possible to represent six binary digits by two octal digits and eight binary digits by two hexadecimal digits. Examples of this reduced external representation are shown below:

	character	binary code	reduced form
6 bit codes:	B	110 010 6 2	62
	*	101 100 5 4	54
8 bit codes:	B	1100 0010 C 2	C2
	*	0101 1100 5 C	5C

It is important to realize that the reduced form of character codes is never used within computers, but is only a helpful means of abbreviating the internal binary codes for human uses.

The *collating sequence* of a character set is the priority ordering of the individual members of the set. For letters the normally defined collating sequence is the alphabetic order A, B, . . . Z. Although such a priority scheme is completely arbitrary, it is invaluable in text manipulation, searching procedures, and other nonnumerical operations. In the EBCDIC code, alphabetic order is preserved through the magnitude of the binary code for each character interpreted as a binary or hexadecimal number. With the EBCDIC code, alphabetic ordering of ordinary words can be done character by character through comparison of the numerical magnitude associated with each of the alphabetic letters comprising any text material.

Example:

The list of alphabetic characters [A, D, Z, M, G, H] can be alphabetized by arranging the EBCDIC codes in ascending numerical order.

Initial Data

Letter	EBCDIC Code	Hexadecimal Equivalent	Decimal Equivalent
A	1100 0001	C1	193
D	1100 0100	C4	196
Z	1110 1001	E9	233
M	1101 0100	D4	212
G	1100 0111	C7	199
H	1100 1000	C8	200

Final Data

Letter	EBCDIC Code	Hexadecimal Equivalent	Decimal Equivalent
A	1100 0001	C1	193
D	1100 0100	C4	196
G	1100 0111	C7	199
H	1100 1000	C8	200
M	1101 0100	D4	212
Z	1110 1001	E9	233

STORAGE OF NUMERICAL DATA

Digital computers were first developed for assisting in the numerical solution of the mathematical equations of physics and engineering. Today the most exciting areas of computer applications lie in topics related to nonnumerical information processing. Nevertheless, a knowledge of the different ways numbers can be represented in computers gives valuable insight into some particular problems of data storage.

The three most important methods of number representation can be listed as:

1. The fixed point system
2. The binary coded decimal system
3. The floating point system

The Fixed Point System

The simplest and most direct method of number representation in a computer is to regard the n bits of the computer storage location (byte or word) as a binary integer number, keeping the left most bit (bit n − 1) reserved for the sign of the number [0 for +, 1 for −]. Naturally enough, this is called the *sign magnitude* notation. (See Figure 6.10.) The term *fixed point* is also used for this representation, because it is assumed that the binary point exists just to the right of the righthand most, or zero, bit position.

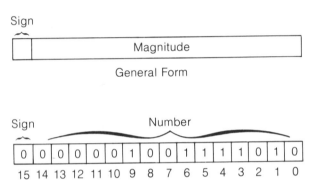

FIGURE 6.10. Representation of a fixed point number in sign-magnitude notation.

Example:

The decimal number $[634]_{10}$ corresponds to the binary number $[1001111010]_2$. and can be represented in a 12 bit word as

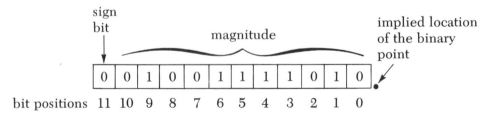

In this 12 bit word, 11 bits are reserved for the binary number, represented using positional notation, and one bit indicates the sign. The implied binary point is located after bit position zero (i.e., it is not given an actual bit position). The numbering scheme reflects the magnitude of each bit position. A 1 in position four corresponds to a numerical magnitude of 2^4.

Decimal Number	Fixed Point Representation	Hexadecimal Number
0000	0000000000000000	0000
120	0000000001111000	0078
−35	1000000000011101	801D
263453	*0011010001100001	*3461
−1050	1000000101100010	8162

sign bit ⟶ magnitude

*Fixed point overflow. $2^{15} - 1 = 32{,}767$ is the maximum permissible decimal number.

FIGURE 6.11. Table of fixed point representations using a 16 bit computer word.

For computers which have n-bit words available for fixed point (integer) number storage, the range in size of decimal numbers which can be stored in the form illustrated above is $-(2^{n-1} - 1)$ to $+(2^{n-1} - 1)$. Sometimes it may happen that an attempt is made to store a number lying outside the possible range of binary representation (i.e., there is an insufficient number of bit storage positions available in the storage location). When this happens a *fixed point overflow* occurs and the leftmost bits of the binary number could be lost. Such a condition is normally detected by the computer system and is brought to the attention of the computer user, often through termination of the program.

Using the sign magnitude method, both positive and negative numbers can be directly represented with fixed point notation. Such an arrangement is somewhat expensive, however, since arithmetic processing units capable of performing both addition and subtraction must be provided. To avoid this difficulty, many computers store negative numbers in the form of *complements* so that subtraction can be done through the simpler process of addition. More details of this method of number representation and its application to computer arithmetic are given in Chapter Nine.

Various fixed point decimal integers are shown in Figure 6.11. Sign magnitude notation is used for negative numbers.

Fixed point integers are frequently used in counting problems in which decimal fractions do not occur. For decimal integers within the allowed range of storage values, there is always an exact binary equivalent. As we may anticipate, such a correspondence is not possible for all decimal numbers involving fractions and a rounding-off of the internally stored binary number is almost always necessary.

Decimal Number	Binary Coded Decimal
0	0000
1	0001
2	0010
3	0011
4	0100
5	0101
6	0110
7	0111
8	1000
9	1001

FIGURE 6.12. Pure Binary Coded Decimal (BCD) conversion table.

The storage of decimal fixed point numbers in a computer using binary numbers requires that special decimal to binary number conversion units be provided. While internal arithmetic operations on fixed point numbers are very rapid, the input/output process of number conversion is relatively slow. One way to overcome this difficulty is to use a scheme of number representation based on binary coded characters. As described below, this approach is used in some computers employed in accounting (business) applications.

The Binary Coded Decimal System

For applications in which the speed of internal calculation is relatively unimportant compared with the input or output of data, storing decimal numbers directly, integer by integer, is possible using the binary character codes discussed previously. Since the speed at which arithmetic operations are performed in this mode of number representation is slow, its principle use lies in nonnumerical applications in which manipulations such as comparison, editing, and ordering are most frequent.

The simplest pure Binary Coded Decimal system, shown in Figure 6.12, is closely related to the six and eight bit codes given in the Appendices. Using four bits, it is possible to represent the symbols 0 through 9. Comparison of

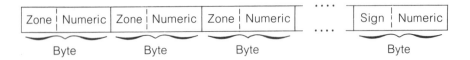

FIGURE 6.13. Binary Coded Decimal storage using a Zoned Mode.

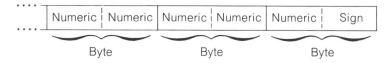

FIGURE 6.14. Binary Coded Decimal storage using a Packed Mode.

the codes of Figure 6.12 with the SBCDIC and EBCDIC codes of the Appendix shows that the pure BCD representation corresponds to the numeric fields of the two codes.

Two forms of BCD number storage are common:

a. The Zoned Mode

b. The Packed Mode

In the Zoned Mode of decimal number storage the entire SBCD or EBCD code is used to fill six or eight bit bytes as shown in Figure 6.13.

The sign of the decimal number is usually placed in the zone field of the rightmost byte using the convention $[+ \rightarrow 1100; - \rightarrow 1101]$ for eight-bit bytes.

In a packed mode, the zone bits are omitted altogether and the sign is kept in the rightmost byte. Such a representation is especially convenient for eight-bit bytes, because two decimal numbers can be placed in one byte, as shown in Figure 6.14.

Examples of decimal number representation using the zoned and packed methods are given in Figure 6.15.

Decimal Number	Zoned Representation	Packed Representation
−064	11110000 11110110 11010100	0000 0110 0100 1101
149	11110001 11110100 11001001	0001 0100 1001 1100
−1280	1111000 11111001 01111000 11010000	0001 0010 1000 0000 1101

FIGURE 6.15. Examples of Zoned and Packed Mode number representation using EBCDIC.

Floating Point Numbers

There are two types of numbers we wish to consider here: a) very large ones which, if written out in full, would require an extraordinary number of binary digits, and b) numbers containing fractional parts which cover the other extreme of very small numbers. In previous sections we saw how fractional parts could be represented in a positional notation with the aid of a radix point. In this section we will discuss how place value notation with a radix point may be exploited to write both fractional and very large numbers that can be readily stored in a computer. The key to this process is knowing where to place the radix point.

The floating point method of storing numbers is derived from scientific notation in which decimal numbers are multiplied by powers of 10. The basis for scientific notation, examples of which are shown below, lies in the literal expansion of a number. Referring to our previous notation of Chapter Five.

Decimal Number	Scientific Notation
438.0	438.0×10^0
	43.80×10^1
	4.380×10^2
	0.4380×10^3
0.00316	0.00316×10^0
	0.0316×10^{-1}
	0.316×10^{-2}

We see that we can shift the decimal point either to the left or right by multiplying the number by positive or negative powers of 10. This is equivalent, of course, to changing each of the exponents in the powers of 10 positional notation. Scientific notation is generally useful for decimal fractions and for very large or very small numbers in cases when writing out the usual decimal number in positional notation would be unwieldy.

The application of scientific notation to computer number storage requires several arbitrary restrictions. First, to keep as many significant digits as possible all numbers must be *normalized* so that the leftmost digit of the number lies immediately to the right of the radix point, as shown below.

Decimal Numbers	Normalized Scientific Notation
4832.1	0.48321×10^4
0.001231	0.1231×10^{-2}
6.88×10^{-4}	0.688×10^{-5}

Next, the internal bits of the floating point data word must be designated so that separate *fields* for the number sign, exponent, and fraction are available.

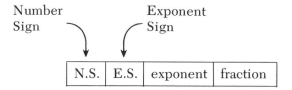

Using the above examples, the symbolic representation of a floating point data word is

| + | + | 4 | .48321 |

| + | − | 2 | .1231 |

| + | − | 5 | .688 |

We have emphasized the use of decimal scientific notation up to this point principally because of its familiarity. In practice, the decimal system is relatively awkward for storing numbers in computers and better use can be made of binary, octal, or hexadecimal scientific notation.

To be specific, let us define the normalized form of a binary number expressed in scientific notation as

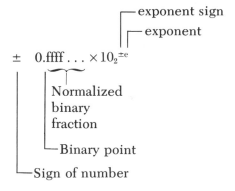

As in decimal normalization, the binary number must be adjusted until the first significant digit lies immediately to the right of the binary point. In this

adjustment process the exponent of $[10]_2$ must also be altered, as shown below:

Decimal Number	Binary Equivalent	Normalized Binary Equivalent
$[11.75]_{10}$	$[1011.11]_2$	$0.101111 \times 10_2{}^{+100}$
$[86.25]_{10}$	$[1010110.01]_2$	$0.101011001 \times 10_2{}^{+111}$
$[0.125]_{10}$	$[0.001]_2$	$0.1 \times 10_2{}^{-10}$

Under the entry for Normalized Binary Equivalent there is a representation using the true binary radix ($[10]_2$) with *binary exponent powers*. This representation is of interest for purposes of computer number storage, since the binary fraction and exponent can be stored as separate binary numbers as in the method shown below:

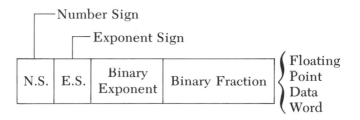

As an example, consider a 48 bit floating point data word. The format of this data word could appear as

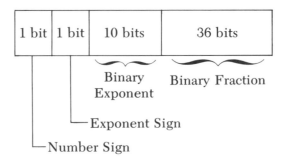

The largest possible positive number which can be stored in the word would look like

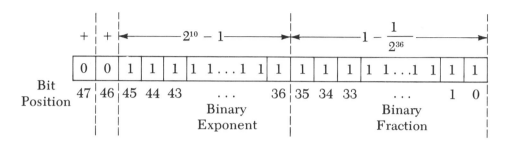

and would have a decimal equivalent of

$$\left(1 - \frac{1}{2^{36}}\right) \times 2^{(2^{10} - 1)} \text{ or about } 10^{+307}$$

The smallest possible positive number which could be represented would appear as (remember that the binary fraction must be normalized)

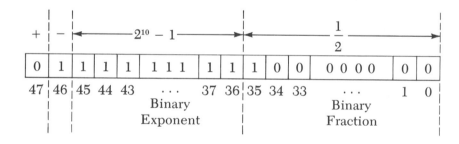

with a decimal equivalent of

$$\frac{1}{2} \times 2^{-(2^{10} - 1)} \text{ or about } 10^{-307}$$

Thus, using this particular 48 bit word structure it is possible to represent decimal numbers ranging from $+10^{+307}$ through 0 to -10^{+307} in steps of 10^{-307}, a finely spaced grid of numbers sufficient for almost all numerical applications. The value zero must be handled as a special case since the fraction is zero; usually the exponent is set to zero as well. If an attempt were made to store a number outside the permitted range, a floating point *overflow* or *underflow* would result, because there would be an insufficient number of bits available in the word to properly represent the number.

The storage of decimal numbers in the form of binary scientific notation is only the first step in the actual methods of floating point representation used in computers. One advanced method, for example, involves the use of hexadecimal arithmetic with binary coded decimal digit representation of the exponent and hexadecimal fraction. The reason for such an arrangement lies both in the attempt to reduce the need for frequent number renormalization following arithmetic operations and the increase in the range of numbers stored.

ROUNDING ERRORS

Owing to their internal structure, digital computers impose certain restrictions on the accuracy with which we can represent numbers. As a consequence, errors are continually introduced in computer arithmetic operations. Normally, these errors are small, amounting at times to a slight change in the least significant digit of an 8 to 12 decimal digit number. But under certain conditions, such as when we need the difference of two approximately equal numbers, these errors can accumulate and the results of the computer arithmetic can quickly become meaningless.

To see how such errors arise, we must remember that numbers are represented in computers using words having a limited number of bits.

For integers and integer arithmetic, when a given number of the result of an arithmetic operation falls out of the range of the computer data word, the computer will attempt to fit as much of the number into the data word as possible. (See Figure 6.16.) Owing to the way integers are stored, the erroneous result may be positive or negative.

With real or floating point numbers, we must consider the way storage is done for simple decimal fractions (such as 1.342, 17.61, 0.0123) and irrational numbers not expressible in any closed form (π, e, μ and other mathematical constants). As shown in the last section, decimal numbers are stored in computers using a binary (or octal or hexadecimal) fractional system. Two immediate problems arise from this transformation. First, there often is no precise equivalence between a binary fraction and a decimal fraction. As a

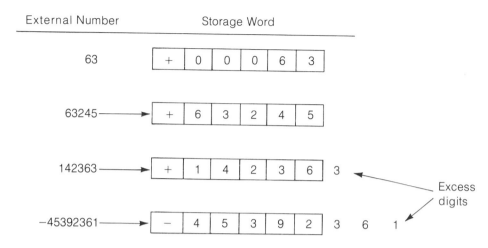

FIGURE 6.16. Storage of integers in a five decimal digit plus sign word. An overflow condition occurs when the external number becomes too large for the available digit spaces.

consequence, errors in numbers can be introduced in the first step of placing external decimal numbers into data storage words.

The second problem relating to the transfer of decimal numbers into the floating point words used in computers revolves around the finite length of the data words. If a given fraction has too many digits, whether binary or decimal, the less significant digits of the fraction are eliminated with a consequent decrease in numerical accuracy.

Taken together, these two problems indicate that it is not always possible to duplicate the precision of real arithmetic using computers even if no additional errors were to be introduced by internal processing. As we shall see, however, not only must we use approximate forms of the true numbers we wish to manipulate, but also the ordinary mathematical operations carried out within the computer lead to even larger errors that can exaggerate further the differences between the results of real and computer arithmetic.

The accumulation of errors in computer arithmetic arises from internal processing when the results of arithmetic operations must be stored in data storage words of finite size. A simple example of this problem can be seen in the floating point multiplication 172. × 833. = 143276. If, for the purposes of illustration, our computer data words were restricted to three digits plus sign, and although both the multiplicand and multiplier fit into the data words, the product is too large and must be shortened through truncation (simply chopping off the least important digits) or rounding. In either case a new approximation has been introduced which will affect the final result.(See Figure 6.17.)

To investigate further the way internal approximations develop, let us make some simple computations using a pseudo-computer word having a length of three decimal digits plus sign. Normally, numbers stored in a computer word would be expressed using binary numbers. The appearance of computational errors, however, appears irrespective of the number system used and for the present purposes it is more convenient to assume that each position of the psuedo-computer storage word contains a decimal digit.

To mimic the behavior of a computer arithmetic unit, we assume that, as illustrated, all operations are truncated (cut off without rounding) to three decimal digits, thereby limiting the accuracy of the results as shown by the last shaded blocks.

$$
\begin{array}{cccc}
3.14 & 4.12 & .123 & 9.43 \\
+\ 7.47 & -\ 1.03 & \times 6.32 & \div\ 1.54 \\
\hline
10.6\boxed{1} & 3.09 & .777\ \boxed{36} & 6.12\ \boxed{33\ ....} \\
\end{array}
$$

To indicate the way errors can accumulate when truncation is present, suppose that we add the truncated version of 2/3 four times:

$$
\begin{array}{rl}
 & .666 \qquad \text{(Note that truncation} \\
+ & .666 \qquad \text{has been applied here)} \\
\hline
1. \quad & 1.33\boxed{2} \\
+ & .66 \\
\hline
2. \quad & 1.99 \\
+ & .66 \\
\hline
3. \quad & 2.65 \\
+ & .66 \\
\hline
4. \quad & 3.31 \\
\end{array}
$$

The result, 3.31, differs from the true answer, 3.33, as a consequence of the truncation procedure. If, however, we carry out the same problem using the techniques of rounding rather than truncation, the computed result is found to be 3.34; too large by .01. From this we must conclude that caution is needed when computer arithmetic involves many repeated operations. Fortunately, internal rounding of results in the central processing unit does help and with

Six Decimal Digits

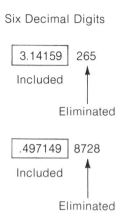

FIGURE 6.17. Two examples of truncation of real constants to six decimal digit plus sign storage words.

computer words of eight to 12 equivalent decimal digits many of the problems apparent in our three decimal place computations are avoided, or at least well hidden.

Finally, computational error voids the basic associative and communicative rules of simple arithmetic. In computer arithmetic the order in which arithmetic expressions are evaluated affects the final result. As an example, the associative rule

$$(A + B) + C = A + (B + C)$$

fails in the truncation mode if sample values are chosen as below:

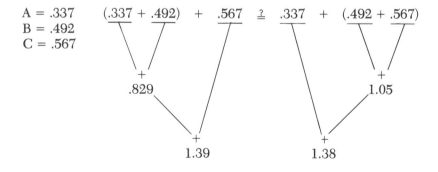

In a similar manner, the distributive law $A * (B + C) = A * B + A * C$ can also fail, as shown below

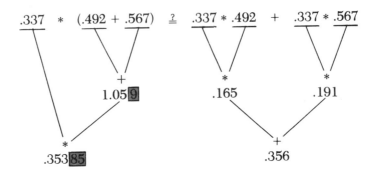

In summary, although the innaccuracies involved in the transition from real arithmetic to computer arithmetic may appear to be small, they are not insignificant. Applications requiring a high degree of accuracy may fail unless special care is taken to avoid unnecessary operations or to enlarge the intrinsic accuracy of the memory data storage words.

THE STORAGE OF LOGICAL DATA

In two prior sections we have discussed ways in which alphabetic and numerical information can be represented and stored in digital computers. We must now introduce a third type of information: *Logical data*. In many ways the processing of logical data is one of the more important functions of a modern digital computer.

A single piece of logical information can have only one of two values, typically represented as YES or NO, TRUE or FALSE, and 1 or 0. A logical, or Boolean, variable is a quantity which can assume only one of two values:

$$X = \begin{pmatrix} YES \\ or \\ NO \end{pmatrix} \text{ or } \begin{pmatrix} TRUE \\ or \\ FALSE \end{pmatrix} \text{ or } \begin{pmatrix} 1 \\ or \\ 0 \end{pmatrix}$$

The answer to the question, "Is Mary here?", could be defined as a logical variable, X, such that X = YES (or TRUE or 1) represents Mary's presence and X = NO (or FALSE or 0) signifies Mary's absence.

Logical data can be represented by several means in a computer. If we use a complete computer word to represent the value of a logical quantity (a wasteful luxury), adopting an arbitrary BCD mnemonic form such as

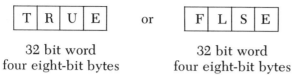

| T | R | U | E | or | F | L | S | E |

32 bit word
four eight-bit bytes

32 bit word
four eight-bit bytes

is possible or a particular binary code such as

TRUE   FALSE

| 000 . . . . .001 | or | 00 . . . . 000 |

32 bit word
four eight-bit bytes

32 bit word
four eight-bit bytes

In both cases there is a large waste of computer storage space, because the basic value of a logical quantity can be expressed with only one bit. Thus, machines which have individual bytes can provide more efficient storage for logical data than with words. The BCD mnemonic form TRUE/FALSE is not implemented in most computers, because the binary strings of a 1 or 0 permits a much more efficient set of operations.

The storage of a single logical quantity can be accomplished in two ways. First a logical variable name, which is associated with a particular memory word can be defined. The value of the logical variable can then be stored as the contents of the storage location and changed through appropriate operations.

Another method of storing logical data in a computer is connected with *logical strings*. In a logical string each bit of a byte (or group of bytes or word) represents a separate logical quantity with the entire string, and the string is identified by one memory address. Such an arrangement provides a very efficient means of storage for large amounts of logical data.

To illustrate the use of logical strings, consider the following situation. Suppose that a school needs to keep an up to date record of the class schedule for each student. To do this the name of each student is associated with the memory address of a sixteen-bit (2 byte) word so that the logical string contained in the data word will apply to one student. Next, a list of classes is made such that each bit of the computer data word corresponds to a particular class. Thus, the logical string for each student will be composed of a sequence of 1's and 0's (1 indicates enrollment; a 0 indicates nonenrollment).

CLASS LIST

LOGICAL DATA WORD

BIT NUMBER	0	1	2	3	4	5	6	7	8	9	10	11	12	13	14	15
	Math 1	Math 2	English 1	English 2	History 1	History 2	Soc Studies	Phys Ed 1	Phys Ed 2	Biology 1	Biology 2	Comp Sci 1	Comp Sci 2			
STUDENT NAME																
Alice A.	0	1	0	0	1	0	0	1	0	1	0	0	1	0	0	0
Ted B.	1	0	0	1	0	0	1	1	0	0	0	0	0	0	0	0
Carol C.	0	0	1	0	1	0	0	1	1	0	1	0	0	0	0	0
Bob D.	0	1	1	0	0	0	0	0	1	1	0	1	0	0	0	0

The contents of the four logical data words would appear as

STUDENT NAME	COMPUTER ADDRESS	BIT NUMBER 0	1	2	3	4	5	6	7	8	9	10	11	12	13	14	15
Alice A.	001	0	1	0	0	1	0	0	1	0	1	0	0	1	0	0	0
Ted B.	002	1	0	0	1	0	0	1	1	0	0	0	0	0	0	0	0
Carol C.	003	0	0	1	0	1	0	0	1	1	0	1	0	0	0	0	0
Bob D.	004	0	1	1	0	0	0	0	0	1	1	0	1	0	0	0	0

We note that bit positions 13 to 15 are vacant and could be used for other purposes.

Although individual class schedules can be provided by this method, more can be done with the strings than just keeping track of the individual students. The total group of student records is a complete tally of the way students are distributed in classes throughout the school. Thus, lists of student names for each class could be compiled by examining particular bits of the data files for the entire student body. Using the above data, for example, we can compile the following class lists in terms of string storage addresses:

Math 1	Math 2	English 1	English 2	History 1
002	001	003	002	001
	004	004		003

Even more detailed analyses of the strings can be made to determine multiple class attendance. For instance, which students attend both Math 2 and Biology 2? From our data list we scan bits number 2 and 10 of each student's data word to obtain the answer: Students 001 and 004.

Manipulation (storage and testing and so on) of data in logical strings will involve examination of individual bits within a word. So far, the smallest unit of information to be manipulated or stored was the character-size byte. The byte is generally the smallest such unit, so in the next chapter we will develop techniques to extract single bits from a byte or a whole word.

More details of logical quantities and their relationship to computer structure will be given in Chapter ten.

REFERENCES TO FURTHER READINGS

MENNINGER, K.

Number Words and Number Symbols. Cambridge, Mass.: MIT Press, 1969. An outstanding reference to the development of numbers and number systems.

NASHELSKY, L.

Digital Computer Theory. New York: John Wiley & Sons, 1966. Explains the operation of various memory devices at an intermediate level. Also presents a more advanced discussion of information storage than given here.

KEY WORDS AND PHRASES TO KNOW

ALPHANUMERIC DATA

BINARY CODED DECIMAL

BINARY DIGITS

BIT

BYTE

CHARACTER CODES

CHARACTER SET

COLLATING SEQUENCE

DOUBLEWORD

EXTENDED BINARY CODED DECIMAL

FIXED POINT REPRESENTATION

FIXED POINT OVERFLOW

FLOATING POINT REPRESENTATION

HALFWORD

LOGICAL DATA

LOGICAL STRINGS

MAGNETIC CORES

MAGNETIC THIN FILMS

MEMORY CELL

NORMALIZATION

NUMERIC FIELD

PHYSICAL STATES OF A STORAGE CELL

SCIENTIFIC NOTATION

TRUNCATION

WORD

ZONE FIELD

EXERCISES

1. How many six state devices (like hands), would be needed to form a byte that could represent the character set listed for the EBCDIC code in the Appendices.

2. Investigate the byte or word structures available in your own computer and explain the use of these structures.

3. Translate the following alphanumeric data from their octal reduced form to binary and alphabetic symbols:

    23 46 44 47 64 63 25 51 62 60 21 43 66 21 70 62 60 64 62 25 22 31 45 21 51
    70 60 24 31 27 31 63 62 12

4. Translate the following alphanumeric data from their hexadecimal reduced form to binary and alphabetic symbols:

    C8 C5 E7 C1 C4 C5 C3 C9 D4 C1 D3 40 C8 C9 E3 E2 40 E3 C8 C5 40 E2 D7
    D6 E3 63 40 F2 F5 F6 40 C3 C8 C1 D9 C1 D3 E3 C5 D9 ES 63 40 E3 C8 C1
    E3 E2 40 Ck 40 D3 D6 E2 12

5. What is the largest integer that could be stored in a 24 bit data word using the fixed point system (leave one bit for the sign of the number).

6. Using a 10 bit word, show the floating point representation for the following decimal numbers:

    a. 45 d. -106
    b. -194 e. 10.3
    c. 949 f. -16

7. Give the zoned and packed mode BCD representations for a 24 bit word (4 bytes) for the following decimal numbers:

    a. $-$ 8032 d.   6432
    b.   10112 e. $-$ 89
    c. 199435.65 f. 90643.1

8. Normalize the following decimal numbers:

    a. -4324.1 d. -1006.12×10^{12}
    b. 0.0123×10^{-3} e.   13
    c.   19.0064   f.   0.01

9. Express the decimal numbers of Problem 8 as normalized binary numbers.

10. Suppose that the fields of a floating point data word are defined as:

bit number	purpose
15	sign
14	exponent sign
10 to 13	exponent
0 to 9	fraction

What are the largest and smallest positive numbers that can be expressed with this floating point data word?

11. Using binary scientific notation, give the octal reduced form for the following decimal numbers expressed in the 16 bit floating point data word described in Problem 10.

a. 1632.41
b. -19.46
c. 1.742×10^{16}
d. -18.3×10^{-10}
e. 100
f. -4321.1×10^2

12. Find the sums $.637 + (.538 + 1.69)$ and $(.637 + .538) + 1.69$ using three significant digits with a) truncation and b) rounding. Is the communicative law valid?

13. The associative law $A(B + C) = AB + AC$ is often violated in computer arithmetic. Using the values $A = 10.6$, $B = 0.053$, $C = 1.01$, determine whether the associative law is valid for a) truncation and b) rounding.

14. Find the sum of 1/3 added 10 times using three significant digits and truncation. Explain why this sum differs from $10 \times (1/3)$.

15. Suppose that you are asked to sum the series $100. + 99. + 98. + 97. + \ldots + 1.$ using a computer which has three decimal digits plus sign storage words. Does the resulting accuracy depend upon whether the series is summed forwards or backwards?

seven

Computer Instructions

MORE ABOUT THE INTERNAL ORGANIZATION OF COMPUTERS

The memory unit of a digital computer is composed of individual binary storage cells organized into addressable groups such as bytes or words. In Chapter Six we discussed the ways in which these groups of bits can be used to store alphanumerical quantities, numbers, and logical data. The storage of such information is a rather passive aspect of the computer system, however, and we now want to describe in more detail the way instructions can be stored in the computer memory to guide the processing of data.

The internal structure of a computer can be separated into four conceptually separate units with individual functions:

1. The central control unit
2. The memory unit
3. The input/output unit
4. The central processing unit

In the sketch shown in Figure 7.1, the connections between these units are shown in terms of data flow (full lines) and command functions (thin lines). As indicated, the principal guidance for the overall computer system is given by

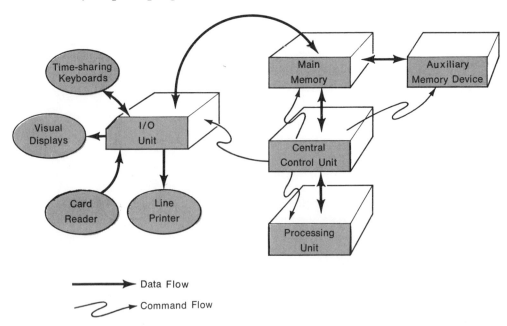

Data Flow

Command Flow

FIGURE 7.1. A schematic representation of the main elements of the digital computer.

232

the central control unit. Using information taken from the internally stored instruction set, the *central control unit* must coordinate the transfer of data throughout the entire computer system, arranging for the use of the central processing unit, guiding the storage and retrieval of data within the memory, and maintaining control of the input and output of data into peripheral computer system devices.

The *memory unit* of a computer provides storage space for both data and instructions. To permit rapid access to this information, each memory storage location has an address, used in the same way that post office box numbers are employed in delivering letters. Addresses are labels which identify the individual storage locations of the memory for data and instruction storage and retrieval.

Actually, most computers have several memories—each having different storage capacities and access times. The main memory, normally built of magnetic cores or thin films, is used mainly for storing program instructions and data files which either are being used or are soon to be used. Since space in the main memory unit is usually limited, auxiliary memories such as magnetic discs, drums, tape or optical storage devices, are also available to provide for the storage of large amounts of data and/or programs that are not currently being executed.

The addresses of most computer memories are usually represented using binary numbers. If we let a represent the binary address of a particular storage location, we can refer to the contents of this location as $C(a)$. From the discussion of Chapters Three and Four, however, we know that names of variables are also associated with storage locations. Thus, there are two pieces of information associated with any variable name: First, the contents of the location or the value of the variable, and second, the actual address of the location. Owing to the one-to-one correspondence between variable names and individual storage locations, variable names such as A, BOX, Z and so forth are actually *symbolic addresses*, because each of these names is associated with a true binary address. (See Figure 7.2.) This correspondence will be used repeatedly in the following sections where it is convenient to use *symbolic addresses* to describe the workings of computer instructions. Since the computer always works with an actual memory address expressed as a binary number, we can assume that all *symbolic addresses* will be converted at some later time to actual memory addresses. This conversion process can be done by the computer and forms an interesting part of the compilation of a computer program into machine language instructions.

There is another important point about the use of names of quantities as symbolic addresses. If the variable name BOX were given as a symbolic address one might ask whether the contents of the memory storage location was being sought (the value of the quantity which we call BOX) or the actual

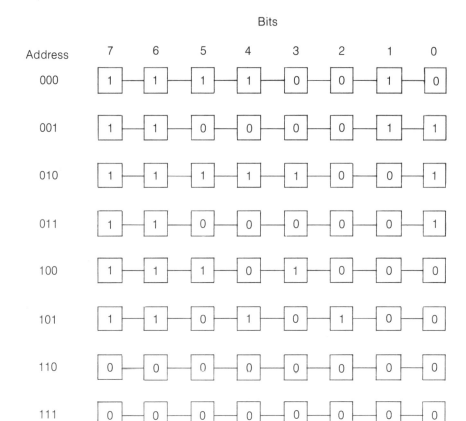

ADDRESS TABLE

Variable Name	True Binary Address	Variable Values [8 bit EBCDIC]
A	000	A ← "2"
BOX	001	BOX ← "D"
CAT	010	CAT ← "9"
X	011	X ← "A"
Y	100	Y ← "Y"
Z	101	Z ← "M"

FIGURE 7.2. Contents of an eight word memory, showing the implied storage addresses and a Table of True Addresses for a list of six variables having different EBCDIC codes.

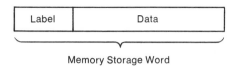

Memory Storage Word

FIGURE 7.3. Illustrating the structure of data which has been content addressed by creating a special field filled with a coded label.

binary address of BOX. Although we will avoid this situation, the basic ambiguity can always be resolved by studying the context in which the variable name is used.

In most digital computers, addresses are associated with definite physical locations of information storage in the computer memory. To extract or store information, reference must be made to the address of the desired location. An alternative way of addressing information is to supply coded descriptions within the contents of the storage location itself. If we then ask for all the data with a particular code, the machine can perform searches throughout the memory to find related data items. This method, called *content addressing*, is found in associative or heuristically programmed computer memories and has many important applications to the manipulation of symbolic information and the development of artificial intelligence. (See Figure 7.3.) Normally, however, such advanced systems rely in some way upon the basic implicit address structure of an addressable memory.

Continuing with our previous discussion of computer structure, the *input/ output unit* of a computer acts as a connection between the external world and the internal storage and computation facilities of the computer system. In most cases the input/output unit is separated from the rapid internal computations of a computer by a buffer storage area. This permits slow electromechanical devices such as card readers, line printers, and magnetic discs to proceed at their own pace without slowing the operation of the main computer.

The *central processing unit* (CPU) provides the calculating power of a computer. The CPU is composed of a number of temporary data storage locations, called *registers*, along with the various devices needed to carry out arithmetic and logical operations. (See Figure 7.4.) The registers, like memory storage locations, are able to store both byte and word information. Since some of these registers provide temporary storage locations for data and other

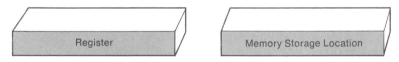

FIGURE 7.4. Registers store bit structures like bytes and words using two—state active devices.

information in various stages of CPU processing, they are frequently called *scratch pad memories*. Unlike simple magnetic cores or thin films, registers are active switching devices which are able to transmit and receive binary coded data from various areas of the computer at higher speeds than is possible with the magnetic cores of the main memory. Data placed in CPU registers, for example, might be subsequently channeled into one of the CPU arithmetic units or sent directly on to the input/output processor. As we shall learn, registers are also useful as *counters* to keep track of instruction addresses, the number of steps taken in repetitive processes, and so forth.

A more detailed diagram of the way information flows between the memory, control and central processing units is shown in Figure 7.5. Here we note three new features:

a.   The Memory Address Register (MAR)
b.   The Memory Data Register (MDR)
c.   The Decoder

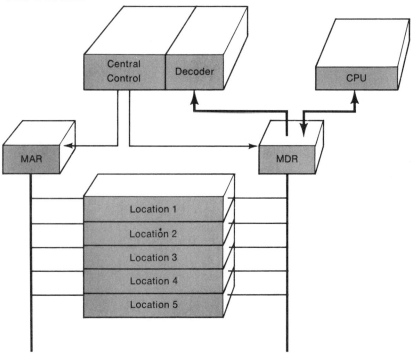

FIGURE 7.5.   A simple view of instruction and data reading and writing. The MAR is the Memory Address Register, while the MDR is the Memory Data Register.

The *Memory Address Register* (MAR) and the *Memory Data Register* (MDR) play important parts in the operation of the computer memory. The memory unit is built in such a way that when a memory storage address is placed in the MAR and a memory "read" operation is requested by the central control unit, a copy of the contents of the storage location corresponding to the address in the MAR is fetched and transcribed into the memory data register. This process can also be reversed so that data placed in the MDR can be placed in any memory storage location by specifying the desired storage address in the MAR and requesting a memory "write" operation. At this level of operation the nature of addresses is most apparent: Addresses describe the location of data and instructions within a computer memory through electrical connections (hardware) alone. When an address is placed in the memory address register, connections are opened to one particular word or byte of the computer memory. Depending upon the command received, information is transferred into or out of the memory.

Although we have repeatedly emphasized that memory storage locations can be used for both data and instructions, no mention has been made of the way instructions are actually used to direct computer operations. Anticipating the more complete discusssion of the next section, instructions are basically coded patterns of binary digits which guide internal processing by the computer system. As indicated in Figure 7.5, the translation of the coded instruction is done by a subunit of the central control unit: The decoder. When the bit pattern of an instruction word is given to the decoder, this device interprets the instruction in terms of the internal actions needed throughout the computer. This, for example, could involve placing a particular address in the memory address register, transfer of data from the memory data register, ordering a multiplication or other arithmetic operation, and so forth.

With this information about the decoder, we can follow the basic cycle of computer operation during the execution of a program. After the completion of an instruction, the central control unit loads the address of the next instruction into the memory address register, then requests a "read" operation which extracts a copy of the desired instruction from memory and places it in the memory data register. In the next step, a path is provided for the transfer of a selected part of the instruction word from the MDR to the decoder. (See Figure 7.6.)

In the decoder one section of the instruction word is examined and recognized as a particular type of instruction; new electrical connections are made throughout the computer to prepare the way for the actual processing of data by executing the instruction. When the actions called for by this instruction have been completed, the central control unit determines the memory address of the next instruction and the cycle of instruction-fetch and operation is repeated.

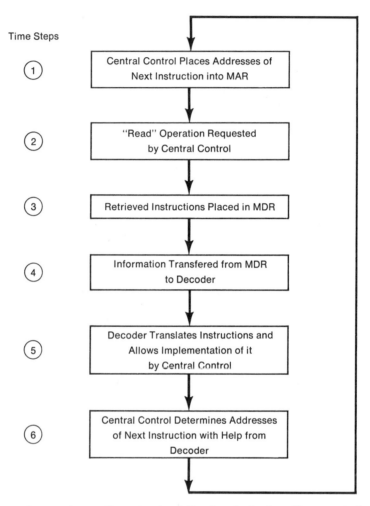

Time Steps

1 — Central Control Places Addresses of Next Instruction into MAR

2 — "Read" Operation Requested by Central Control

3 — Retrieved Instructions Placed in MDR

4 — Information Transfered from MDR to Decoder

5 — Decoder Translates Instructions and Allows Implementation of it by Central Control

6 — Central Control Determines Addresses of Next Instruction with Help from Decoder

FIGURE 7.6. A simple flowchart of the basic instruction cycle in a digital computer.

WHAT IS AN INSTRUCTION?

A computer instruction is a specific command which describes the way groups of information [bits, bytes, words] are to be processed within the computer system. To be effective an instruction must specify the particular operation to be performed, where the data are to be found, and where the result is to be placed after the operation is completed. Unlike many of the ambiguous instructions met in ordinary life, the commands given by computer instructions must involve relatively simple operations on specific sets of data.

The total collection of instructions that can be carried out by a particular computer is called the *instruction set*. This set usually includes all elementary arithmetic, logical operations, and more sophisticated commands designed to guide the transfer of information between the computer units. Typical commands found in an instruction set usually include such operations as: "fetch a number from memory;" "store a number in memory," "add two numbers;" and so forth. We note that these verbal commands in themselves fail to meet two of the three criteria for instructions named at the beginning of this section. They fail to indicate where the data are to be found and where the result is to be placed.

Computer instructions are stored in ordinary memory locations as *instruction words*. A typical instruction word composed of N bits looks like

OPERATION	ADDRESS

bit number N − 1   . . . 2 1 0

where OPERATION is a coded sequence of binary digits that, when placed in the computer decoder, will initiate a series of electrical switching operations leading to one type of operation on data stored in the memory storage locations specified by ADDRESS. (The ADDRESS field of the instruction is commonly called the operand or operands.)

In many small computers the instruction word length is chosen to be the same as that for data words. Since instructions may require fewer (or more) bits than data, such an arrangement can lead to wasted memory space. Byte oriented computers avoid this difficulty by adopting instruction words composed of fewer (or more) bytes than are used for the data words to meet the demands of a given situation.

Most of the data processing operations performed inside the central processing unit are done using two pieces of data. Examples of this include addition, subtraction, multiplication, division, the logical AND and OR, and so forth. When the operation is completed, it is necessary to specify where the result is to be stored.

Computer instruction words can be designed in many ways to satisfy the requirements of operand specification and storage of the results. The easiest way, described in detail later, provides three separate addresses in the ADDRESSES portion of the instruction word. Two addresses locate the initial data and one address indicates where the result is to be stored. Unfortunately, while three address instructions are easy to visualize, they are wasteful of memory storage space. A better method involves the use of temporary data storage sites as *implied* sources or destinations of data. These storage sites, usually called registers or accumulators, make the instructions shorter (they occupy less memory space). However, a penalty is paid for the use of shorter instruction words since extra instructions are frequently needed to move the data to or from these temporary locations.

Three Address Instructions

The format for a three address instruction is

OPERATION	X	Y	Z

in which X and Y are the symbolic memory addresses where data necessary to carry out OPERATION are stored and Z is the symbolic destination address for the result. (See Figure 7.7) As an example, suppose we wish to multiply the contents of locations corresponding to X and Y and store the result in Z. This process can be written as

$$C(Z) \leftarrow C(X) * C(Y)$$

which reads "The contents of location X and the contents of location Y are to be multiplied together and the product stored in location Z." If the OPERA-

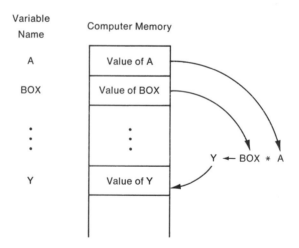

FIGURE 7.7. An arithmetic operation with two operands and a final destination.

TION code for multiplication is represented by the mnemonic MLT the instruction word format for this example could be written as

MLT	X	Y	Z

or in simpler form, MLT X, Y, Z. In this process it is implied that the computer is constructed so that the contents of locations corresponding to X and Y are correctly presented to the multiplier input and that the result is transferred into the location corresponding to Z.

The three address instructions for arithmetic operations can be summarized as:

Addition	ADD X,Y,Z
Subtraction	SUB X,Y,Z
Multiplication	MLT X,Y,Z
Division	DIV X,Y,Z

Addition and subtraction are both commutative in the sense that $C(X) + C(Y) = C(Y) + C(X)$ and $C(X) * C(Y) = C(Y) * C(X)$: The order in which data are added or multiplied does not affect the final result. This is obviously not true for subtraction and multiplication, since $C(X) - C(Y) \neq C(Y) - C(X)$ and $C(X)/C(Y) \neq C(Y)/C(X)$ ($\neq$ means "not equal to" the following quantity). Thus, SUB X,Y,Z is defined to mean

$$C(Z) \leftarrow C(X) - C(Y)$$

and DIV X,Y,Z means

$$C(Z) \leftarrow C(X)/C(Y)$$

To illustrate the use of three address instructions, consider the arithmetic replacement $A \leftarrow B + C + D * E$. The instruction set needed to carry out this replacement is

$$MLT\ D,E,A$$
$$ADD\ A,C,A$$
$$ADD\ A,B,A$$

The principal disadvantage of three address instructions is their great length and consequent excessive use of memory space. In addition, the results are always placed in the computer memory, a time consuming process involving the transferring of data from the central processing unit.

To illustrate the effects of the excessive word length, we know that storage location addresses are specified using binary numbers. For a memory having 2^n storage locations, addresses of n bits will be required to uniquely identify each storage location. Thus, a computer with 32,678 storage locations requires an address field of 15 bits. If a three address instruction were used, just the address portion of the instruction word would require 45 bits. Since the OPERATION code and other associated information usually take at least 7 bits, the result is an unacceptably large 52 bit instruction word. As we shall see, the length of instructions can be substantially reduced through the use of implied storage locations.

Two Address Instructions

Two address instructions have the form

OPERATION	ADDRESS #1	ADDRESS #2

in which OPERATION specifies the operation to be performed, using data stored in the two indicated locations. The result of OPERATION is automatically placed in ADDRESS #1 following the actual OPERATION task. (See Figure 7.8.)

The four basic arithmetic operations for two address instructions can be written as

$$ADD\ X,Y \quad \text{means} \quad C(X) \leftarrow C(X) + C(Y)$$
$$SUB\ X,Y \quad \text{means} \quad C(X) \leftarrow C(X) - C(Y)$$
$$MLT\ X,Y \quad \text{means} \quad C(X) \leftarrow C(X) * C(Y)$$
$$DIV\ X,Y \quad \text{means} \quad C(X) \leftarrow C(X) \div C(Y)$$

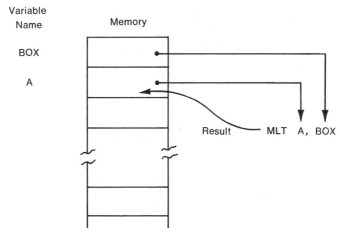

FIGURE 7.8. Two-address instructions store results in the first-referenced location.

In each operation the final result is returned to memory storage location X, destroying any previously stored information.

Using two address instructions, the arithmetic replacement A ← B + C + D ∗ E can be written as

MLT D,E $\boxed{D} \leftarrow \boxed{D} \times \boxed{E}$

TRANS A,D $\boxed{A} \leftarrow \boxed{D}$

ADD A,C $\boxed{A} \leftarrow \boxed{A} + \boxed{C}$

ADD A,B $\boxed{A} \leftarrow \boxed{A} + \boxed{B}$

Final result stored in A

In this example it has been necessary to introduce a new OPERATION, $\boxed{\text{TRANS A,D}}$, to describe the *transfer* of the contents of location D to location A. As a result, the two address instruction set is one instruction longer than the sequence of three address instructions. This extra instruction illustrates a previous statement: In reducing the storage space needed for each instruction (using an implied destination address) increasing the length of the instruction sequence is necessary. However, the removal of the redundant destination address yields far more memory storage than is taken up by the increased program length.

For many purposes the erasure of previously stored information caused by the automatic storage of the result in ADDRESS #1 is not desirable. This problem can be avoided by using a temporary storage location for the former contents of ADDRESS #1. To illustrate, consider the evaluation for the algebraic expression $A \leftarrow B + C + B/C$. If we write

TRANS A,B	$A \leftarrow B$
ADD A,C	$A \leftarrow A + C$
DIV B,C	$\boxed{B \leftarrow B/C}$ {This step destroys the previous value of B}
ADD A,B	$A \leftarrow A + B$

an error is made since the original value of B has been destroyed through DIV B,C and has been lost for subsequent computations. To overcome this difficulty, a temporary storage location (T) can be introduced and the code rewritten as

TRANS A,B	$A \leftarrow B$
TRANS T,B	$T \leftarrow B$
ADD A,C	$A \leftarrow A + C$
DIV T,C	$T \leftarrow T/C$
ADD A,T	$A \leftarrow A + T$

which preserves C(B) in its original form.

One Address Instructions

The basic steps needed to carry out a particular arithmetic or logical task (such as the comparison of two data words or multiplication of two numbers) involve: (a) the withdrawal of information from two memory storage locations and (b) the return of the result to one location. Such tasks can be specified with a single three address instruction or several two address instructions. The important feature of two address instructions lies in their use of an implied destination address with the result being automatically placed in the location specified by ADDRESS #1.

A further shortening of instruction words is possible through use of an *implied address* associated with a temporary storage location (which is just a register) in the central processing unit. This temporary storage location, often called an *accumulator*, provides the same service as *ADDRESS* #1 of the two word instruction. It stores one of the two pieces of data needed for arithmetic or logical tasks and, following the completion of OPERATION, the result is placed back in the accumulator rather than being returned directly to some location in the computer memory.

One address instructions have the form

OPERATION	ADDRESS

in which ADDRESS is the memory storage location of one of the operands. The second operand is always assumed to be present in the accumulator. Following OPERATION the result is returned to the accumulator. (See Figure 7.9.)

The four basic arithmetic operations for one address instructions are:

$$
\begin{array}{lll}
\text{ADD X} & \text{means} & C\,(\text{Acc}) \leftarrow C\,(\text{Acc}) + C(X) \\
\text{SUB X} & \text{means} & C\,(\text{Acc}) \leftarrow C\,(\text{Acc}) - C(X) \\
\text{MLT X} & \text{means} & C\,(\text{Acc}) \leftarrow C\,(\text{Acc}) * C(X) \\
\text{DIV X} & \text{means} & C\,(\text{Acc}) \leftarrow C\,(\text{Acc}) \div C(X)
\end{array}
$$

in which C(Acc) refers to the contents of the accumulator. The transfer of data between the computer memory and the accumulator requires that two new operations be defined:

$$
\begin{array}{lll}
\text{LOAD X} & \text{means} & C\,(\text{Acc}) \leftarrow C(X) \\
\text{STORE X} & \text{means} & C(X) \leftarrow C(\text{Acc})
\end{array}
$$

Using one address instructions the replacement $A \leftarrow B + C + D * E$ can be accomplished as

$$
\begin{array}{ll}
\text{LOAD E} & \text{Acc} \leftarrow E \\
\text{MLT D} & \text{Acc} \leftarrow \text{Acc} * D \\
\text{ADD C} & \text{Acc} \leftarrow \text{Acc} + C \\
\text{ADD B} & \text{Acc} \leftarrow \text{Acc} + B \\
\text{STORE A} & A \leftarrow \text{Acc}
\end{array}
$$

The one address instruction sequence is two steps longer than that obtained for three address instructions. Nevertheless, the one address sequence results in a substantial saving in overall computer memory space. To show this consider a computer with a memory storage address of 15 bits and an operation code of 7 bits. Three address instruction words would require 52 bits each or $52 \times 3 = 156$ bits of memory space to store the replacement program. With one address instructions, however, a 22 bit word is sufficient (7

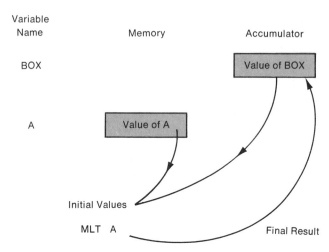

FIGURE 7.9. One-address instructions assume that one of the operands is already stored in the accumulator. The result is placed back into the accumulator.

bits + 15 bits) and a total instruction word storage space of only $22 \times 5 = 110$ bits is required in the computer memory.

Although memory storage savings play an important part in the economics of computer design, other factors relating to program operating speed and machine versatility must be considered. In particular, the versatility of a CPU is greatly increased through the presence of several general registers. CPU registers tend to be substantially faster than memory storage locations for data transfer operations and their use can decrease the time needed to make computations. Unfortunately, owing to their extensive electrical interconnections, registers are much more expensive than memory storage locations. As a result, while it is desirable to have many general registers in a CPU, only a small number† are actually present in most machines.

The introduction of multiple registers in the CPU re-introduces the need for a second address in a one address instruction word so that the different CPU data registers can be distinguished. Because there are only a few such registers, however, the register addresses are short and an address field of 3 bits or less in the instruction word is normally sufficient. With multiple registers, the modified one address instruction looks like

OPERATION	REGISTER ADDRESS	OPERAND ADDRESS

†Usually seven or less.

Most modern computers use modified one address instruction words. Frequently they are referred to as "two address" instructions even though only one address actually refers to a memory storage location.

Zero Address Instructions

Addresses can be completely removed from instruction words if the one address instruction idea of an implied data storage location is extended so that there are two implied data storage locations. In practice, such data storage locations can be created by arranging CPU registers in an ordered *stack* with each register containing one word of information. (See Figure 7.10). A two operand instruction is then assumed to refer to the contents of the two top level registers. OPERATION takes place using the data in these registers and the answer is returned to the second level. The contents of all the stack registers are then shifted upwards so that the result is now in the top level. The upwards shift is sometimes referred to as a "PULL", because it results in the loss of the previous top piece of information. (See Figure 7.11.)

To add a new data word to the stack of registers a "PUSH" operation is defined. The contents of all registers are moved downwards one level and the new information is stored in the top level. The PUSH and PULL principles of operation provide the action need to operate *push down stacks* or *last-in/first-out* [LIFO] queues. (See Figure 7.11.) Generally, organization based on the last-in/first-out principle is very unpopular particularly when buying tick-

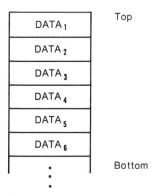

FIGURE 7.10. A data stack stored in registers.

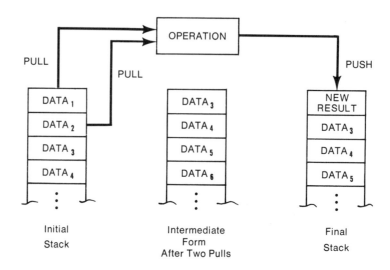

FIGURE 7.11. Effects of pulling two operands from a stack.

ets at a theatre or waiting in a doctor's office. In these cases, people tend to arrive at the "stack" in an unordered fashion and expect to minimize their waiting time. (This type of line is called a queue.) Computers, however, are unemotional organizers without such an impatient sense of time and designing efficient zero address machines using the last-in/first-out method is possible.

The basic format for a zero address instruction is

OPERATION

in which the arithmetic OPERATIONS can be listed as

$$
\begin{aligned}
\text{ADD} \quad &\text{means } C(1) \leftarrow C(2) + C(1) \\
\text{SUB} \quad &\text{means } C(1) \leftarrow C(2) - C(1) \\
\text{MLT} \quad &\text{means } C(1) \leftarrow C(2) * C(1) \\
\text{DIV} \quad &\text{means } C(1) \leftarrow C(2) \div C(1)
\end{aligned}
$$

In these definitions the numerals 1 and 2 refer to the first and second levels. As each OPERATION is executed, two PULL operations (to get the data into

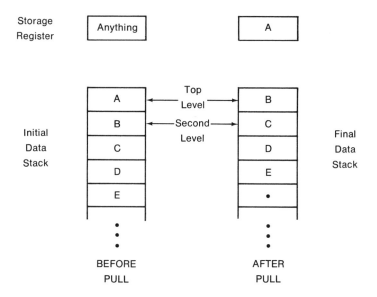

FIGURE 7.12. The stack *pull* operation.

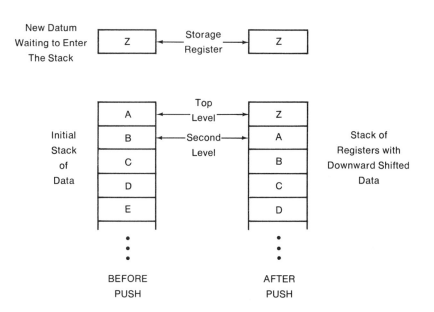

FIGURE 7.13. The stack *push* operation.

the Central Processing Unit) followed by a PUSH (to restore the result) occur automatically. (See Figures 7.12 and 7.13.)

Two additional instructions are needed to move data between memory storage locations and the stack of registers. These are similar to the one address STORE and LOAD instructions:

> LOAD X   means PUSH C(X) into the stack so C(1) ← C(X)
> STORE X   means PULL C(1) from the stack and store it in X.

Using the foregoing definitions, the zero address instruction code for the replacement $A \leftarrow B + C + D * E$ can be written as:

> LOAD B
> LOAD C
> LOAD D
> LOAD E
> MLT
> ADD
> ADD
> STORE A

These stack operations are shown schematically in Figure 7.14.

Because CPU registers are expensive and limited in number, most computers do not use CPU register stacks directly. Instead, data stacks are created within the computer memory unit using sequential storage locations. The top, or first element, of the stack is identified by a storage address which is normally contained in a special CPU register called the "POINTER". The addresses of succeeding stack elements can be found by adding their relative locations in the stack to the address stored in the "POINTER" register. (See Figure 7.15.)

As we have seen, a PUSH operation adds a new element to the top of the stack as part of the last-in/first-out policy. This can be readily done in the memory data stack through two separate operations. First, the new data word is stored in the location whose address is given by (POINTER − 1). Second, the value of the POINTER is changed to (POINTER − 1). With these actions a new stack list is established without physically moving data between the data storage locations; only the effective address of the top of the stack has been altered.†

The PULL operation in a memory stack is used to remove an element from the top of the stack (it is usually sent to a CPU register). This is done in two

---

†We have assumed here that more deeply buried items in the stack occur with progressively greater memory address locations. The situation could obviously be reversed.

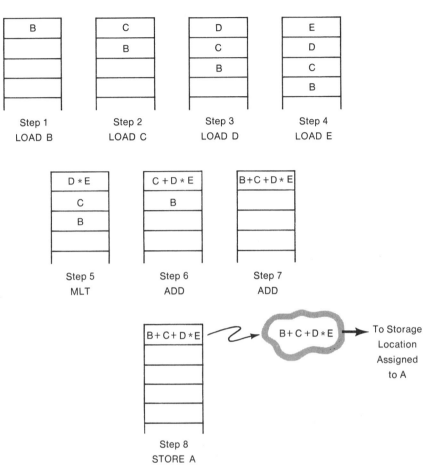

FIGURE 7.14. Stack operations in the evaluation of B + C + D * E with zero address instructions.

steps. First, the data word in the location given by POINTER is sent to some specific CPU register. Second, the address listed in POINTER is increased by one.

WHAT CAN BE DONE WITH INSTRUCTIONS?

Instructions provide specific directions for processing stored data as well as guiding the order in which new instructions are to be carried out. In operation, the functioning of a computer is based upon a two step cycle. In the first step an instruction is fetched from a storage location in memory and passed to the decoder in the CPU (see Figure 7.6 and associated discussion). In the decoder electrical connections are made which prepare the CPU, input/

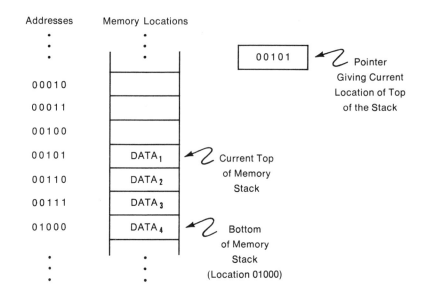

FIGURE 7.15. Sketch of the way a stack is stored in the memory.

output and other computer units for the task described in the OPERATION field of the instruction. In the second step, the instruction is actually carried out, using data provided by the connections created in the first step. The results are then entered in various registers and memory locations and preparations are made for starting the next instruction cycle.

The operations associated with computer instructions can be conveniently divided into three broad categories:

1. Data Modification Instructions
2. Data Transfer Instructions
3. Program Control Instructions

Instructions of the first category order the execution of specific arithmetic or logical operations by the CPU and result in data modification. A typical example of a Data Modification Instruction is ADD X which sums the contents of the accumulator and location X and stores the result in the accumulator.

Data Transfer Instructions guide the transfer of information within the computer, moving bits, bytes, and words between different memory storage locations, input/output buffers, CPU registers, and other storage sites. STORE X is a one address Data Transfer Instruction which moves the contents of the accumulator to memory location X. Data Transfer Instructions are of basic importance in the operation of every computer program.

Program Control Instructions cover a broad class of OPERATIONS which are generally used to choose the sequence in which program instructions are to be executed. Such instructions frequently are conditional in form:

"If the number represented by the contents of location X is less than that of the accumulator, then resume execution with the instruction stored in location L, otherwise go to the next instruction."

Program Control Instructions are essential, because they provide the computer with a branching capability which can be used to implement decision making programs.

In the following sections examples of Data Modification and Data Transfer Instructions are discussed in more detail to show the way instructions can be ordered to solve simple problems. A presentation of the Program Control Instructions is given in Chapter Eight.

Data Modification Instructions

These instructions order specific operations using CPU devices and data stored in other computer storage locations. Common arithmetic operations using modified one address instructions are

| ADD | R | Memory Address |

Add the contents of CPU register R and the reference memory address. Result is stored in register R.

| SUB | R | Memory Address |

Subtract the contents of the memory address from register R. Result is stored in register R.

| MLT | R | Memory Address |

Multiply the contents of register R by the contents of memory address. Store result in R.

| DIV | R | Memory Address |

Divide contents of register R by contents of memory address. Store result in register R.

In practice separate instructions are usually provided for integer and floating point arithmetic to accomodate the different data formats. Machines capable of bit and byte manipulation also require separate arithmetic instruction sets. Specific information regarding the instruction set for a particular computer can be found in the manufacturer's reference manual.

Arithmetic operations are carried out on numerical data using the arithmetic instructions. In a parallel fashion, logical data are processed with *logical instructions*. These instructions provide examination of logical data stored as bytes and words to perform four different operations that are similar to the arithmetic operations.

If X and Y represent logical quantities having the values TRUE or FALSE (1 or 0), we can define the following logical operations

AND

> (X AND Y). The result is TRUE (1) only if both X and Y are TRUE (1) individually.

$$
\begin{array}{c|cc}
 & \multicolumn{2}{c}{Y} \\
 & 0 & 1 \\
\hline
0 & 0 & 0 \\
1 & 0 & 1 \\
\end{array}
$$

X

OR

> (X OR Y). The result if TRUE (1) if either X or Y is true individually.

$$
\begin{array}{c|cc}
 & \multicolumn{2}{c}{Y} \\
 & 0 & 1 \\
\hline
0 & 0 & 1 \\
1 & 1 & 1 \\
\end{array}
$$

X

EXCLUSIVE OR (EOR)

> (X EOR Y). The result if TRUE (1) if X is different from Y, but is FALSE (0) if X and Y are both TRUE (1) or both FALSE (0).

$$
\begin{array}{c|cc}
 & \multicolumn{2}{c}{Y} \\
 & 0 & 1 \\
\hline
0 & 0 & 1 \\
1 & 1 & 0 \\
\end{array}
$$

X

NOT

> (NOT X). The result is TRUE (1) if X is FALSE (0) or FALSE (0) if X is TRUE (1).

$$
\begin{array}{c|cc}
 & \multicolumn{2}{c}{X} \\
 & 0 & 1 \\
\hline
 & 1 & 0 \\
\end{array}
$$

The diagrams used to illustrate the logical operations are called "truth" tables and are widely used in the analysis of problems which use logical quantities. They act as convenient tables of information listing all the possible values of the variables and the consequences of the operations. An extended treatment of logical operations and their importance to the design of computer hardware will be given in Chapters Nine and Ten.

The logical instructions corresponding to the logical operations can be written for a modified one address machine as:

Meaning

| AND | R | Memory Address |

Form logical AND, bit by bit, between contents of register R and the reference memory address. Results are stored bit by bit in register R.

| OR | R | Memory Address |

Form logical OR, bit by bit, between contents of register R and the reference memory address. Results are stored, bit by bit, in Register R.

| EOR | R | Memory Address |

Form logical EOR, bit by bit, between contents of register R and the reference memory address. Results are stored, bit by bit, in Register R.

| NOT | R | Memory Address |

Form logical NOT, bit by bit, using contents of the reference memory address. Results are stored, bit by bit, in Register R.

An example of the effect of logical operations can be given as follows. Suppose the logical variable X is assigned the value TRUE (or 1) and stored in location (X). If another variable Y is FALSE (or 0) and stored in location (Y) the operation (X EOR Y) would appear as

| Contents of (X) | 0 | 0 | 0 | 0 | 0 | 0 | 0 | 1 |

| Contents of (Y) | 0 | 0 | 0 | 0 | 0 | 0 | 0 | 0 |

| (X EOR Y) | 0 | 0 | 0 | 0 | 0 | 0 | 0 | 1 |

This example assumes a code in which only one bit of the entire word is used for the TRUE or FALSE symbol. Such a practice clearly wastes memory space.

As we pointed out in Chapter Six, the use of logical strings provides an efficient means for the storage of logical data. To illustrate, suppose that logical strings are stored bit by bit in variables X and Y. The operation (X EOR Y) using the strings in (X) and (Y) is shown below.

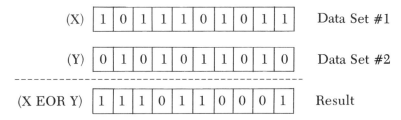

In the analysis of data stored in a computer, it is often necessary to remove the test individual bits or groups of bits from addressable bytes or words. The bits themselves do not have addresses, because they are only elements in a larger addressable entity. In many machines the identification of the desired bits can be most effectively made through the use of a *logical mask*. The function of the mask is to set to zero all bits except those bits which are to be examined. The masking process is illustrated in Figure 7.16.

In practice, the instruction AND X can be used as a masking instruction with X, the mask, having zeroes in all bit positions except those bits which are to be examined.

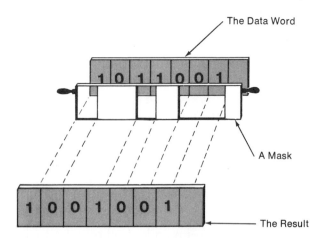

FIGURE 7.16. Schematic of the effect of a mask upon the bits of a data word.

As an example, suppose the mask X has the form

(X)

0	0	0	1	1	1	1	0	0	0

bit position
$\qquad$ 9 $\quad$ 8 $\quad$ 7 $\quad$ 6 $\quad$ 5 $\quad$ 4 $\quad$ 3 $\quad$ 2 $\quad$ 1 $\quad$ 0

If AND X is applied to the word Y, all bits of the result will be set to zero except those in bit positions 3 through 6. Thus, if we take

then

(Y)

1	0	1	0	1	0	1	0	1	1

(Y AND X)

0	0	0	0	1	0	1	0	0	0

This method can also be applied to BCD codes to extract single letters from words which have nonaddressable internal characters. An example of this is shown below where the mask Y has been designed to extract bit positions 6 to 11 from a 24 bit BCD coded data word.

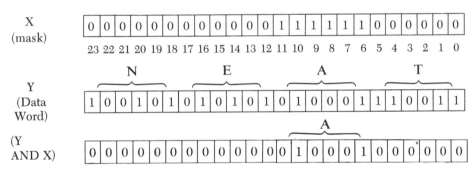

Using masks, logical strings can be analyzed bit by bit. The school class schedule needed in the example of Chapter Six, for example, could be readily found using a logical mask.

After groups of bits have been identified through masks, moving the groups to a standard location in the data word is usually necessary so that further operations can be done. The standard location most often used is the right hand side of the storage word so that the first bit of the identified group lies in bit position 0.

The instruction

SHIFT	R	T	S

will shift the bit pattern of register R, S bit positions to the left or right, depending upon the type of shifting indicated by T, with 0 and 1 indicating leftward or rightward movements, respectively.

As a register bit pattern is shifted, bits at one end will "fall off" while at the other end of the register new bits must be inserted. In a circular register shift bits which "fall off" are automatically replaced in the word at the other end. The result of a circular left shift of three bit positions on a pattern stored in register 101 would look like

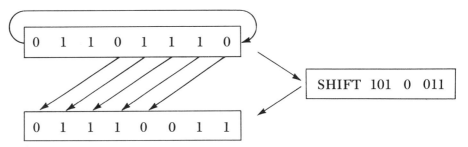

During a simple left or right shift the vacated positions must be in one state or another (0,1). For example, it is possible to fill the blanks with zeros or ones. Normally, zeros are used as fillers. A right shift of 4 bits using zeros as fillers on the pattern

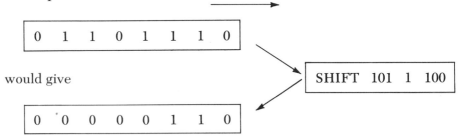

would give

As a final example, suppose we wish to examine the seventh bit of 16 bit logical data strings stored in memory. A mask, X, can be constructed as

(X)	0	0	0	0	0	0	0	0	0	1	0	0	0	0	0	0
	15	14	13	12	11	10	9	8	7	6	5	4	3	2	1	0

Thus, the instructions

```
LOAD R, Y
AND R, X
SHIFT R, 1, 6
```

will first put the contents of Y to the register R, form the logical AND between the contents of R and the contents of X, and shift the resulting bit rightward six bit positions.

Data Transfer Instructions

These instructions are needed to control the flow of data between memory storage locations and the different registers of the CPU. The basic set of data transfer instructions can be summarized as:

Meaning

| LOAD | R | Memory Address |

Load the contents of the memory address into CPU register R.

| STORE | R | Memory Address |

Store the contents of CPU register R into the given memory address.

| PUSH | R | Pointer Register |

PUSH stores the contents of register R into the LIFO stack at the address given by the value of the POINTER − 1, and decreases the pointer value by 1.

| PULL | R | Pointer Register |

PULL stores the contents of the location specified in pointer register in register R. The POINTER is then given the value (POINTER − 1).

| EXCHANGE | R | Memory Address |

The data stored in register R and the memory address are interchanged.

Most computers have a wide variety of LOAD and STORE instructions to deal with bytes, words, integer data, floating point data, and so forth. However, the list of instructions given above summarizes the basic types of instructions that are used to control the flow of data between the memory and the CPU. Other more complex instruction words are needed to move data to and from the input/output units.

Programs and Instructions

A computer's ability to process data is built upon its basic instruction set. The more varied this fundamental set of actions, the more powerful the computer becomes. In function, a single instruction is nothing more than a guide to the internal circuit settings which must be imposed to make the machine carry out a given task. Thus, the structure of the instruction set is a direct expression of the way the computer is built.

In contrast, compilers are special computer programs which translate the expressions and commands of higher level languages into machine language (i.e., the basic instruction set of a particular computer). The various standard computer languages attack problems in different ways. Nevertheless, if several compilers are used with a particular computer, the different operations of the standard languages must eventually be reduced to machine language programs written in terms of instructions contained within the basic instruction set. Because the basic instruction set varies between computers (for instance, between IBM and CDC computers), the compilers themselves must differ. FORTRAN IV on the IBM 360 computer requires a different compiler than FORTRAN IV on a CDC-3600 computer. Owing to differences in internal design, FORTRAN programs may run on these machines with different speeds and efficiencies. Thus, there is a continual competition to improve not only the internal speeds of computers, but also improvement for the internal functioning expressed by the basic instruction set.

REFERENCES TO FURTHER READINGS

GEAR, C. W.

Computer Organization and Programming. New York: McGraw Hill, 1974. An advanced text discussing many broad aspects of computer instructions and data processing.

HARRISON, M. C.

Data Structures and Programming. Glenview, Ill.: Scott, Foresman and Company, 1973.

STONE, H. S.

Introduction to Computer Organization and Data Structures. New York: McGraw Hill, 1972.

KEY WORDS AND PHRASES TO KNOW

ACCUMULATOR

ARITHMETIC OPERATIONS

BIT PATTERN

CENTRAL PROCESSING UNIT

CIRCULAR SHIFTING

CONTROL UNIT

CPU REGISTERS

IMPLICIT ADDRESS

INPUT/OUTPUT UNIT

INSTRUCTION SET

INSTRUCTION WORD

INSTRUCTIONS

LIFO QUEUE

LOAD

LOGICAL INSTRUCTIONS

LOGICAL OPERATIONS

LOGICAL STRING

LOGICAL VARIABLE

MASK

MEMORY ADDRESS

MEMORY STACK

*MODIFIED ONE ADDRESS
  INSTRUCTION*

ONE ADDRESS INSTRUCTION

POINTER

PULL

PUSH

REGISTER

REGISTER ADDRESS

SHIFT

STACK

STORAGE LOCATION

STORE

SYMBOLIC ADDRESS

*TEMPORARY STORAGE
  LOCATION*

*THREE ADDRESS
  INSTRUCTION*

TOP LEVEL

TRUTH TABLE

TWO ADDRESS INSTRUCTION

WORD LENGTH

ZERO ADDRESS INSTRUCTION

EXERCISES

1. Examine the reference manual describing your computer and list the basic instruction sets. Give several examples of the instruction word internal structure.

2. Using three address instructions, give the code needed to evaluate

   a. $Y \leftarrow (A * 2 - Y * 2)/Y$

   b. $HAT \leftarrow 5 * (HAT - 1)$

   c. $DISC \leftarrow 2 * B - 4 * A * C$

   d. $X \leftarrow X * (X - 2 * (X - 3 * (X - 4)))$

Note that constants can be stored in the memory by assigning variable names.

3. Work Problem #2 using two address instructions.

4. Work Problem #2 using modified one address instructions with two registers (001 and 002). For these examples is there any benefit in having two registers?

5. Using zero address instructions (and a register stack) write the machine language instructions needed to evaluate the expressions of Problem #2.

6. Evaluate the following logical expressions for the value of Z:

a. $X \leftarrow 1$
$Y \leftarrow 0$
$Z \leftarrow X$ AND Y

e. $Z \leftarrow 1$
$Z \leftarrow ($NOT $Z)$ OR Z

b. $X \leftarrow 1$
$Y \leftarrow X$
$Z \leftarrow X$ EOR Y

f. $X \leftarrow 0$
$Y \leftarrow 0$
$Z \leftarrow Y$ AND X

c. $X \leftarrow 0$
$Y \leftarrow 1$
$Z \leftarrow (Y$ EOR $X)$ AND Y

g. $X \leftarrow 1$
$Y \leftarrow 1$
$Z \leftarrow Y$ AND X

d. $X \leftarrow 1$
$Z \leftarrow$ NOT X

7. Given the data word shown below, write the machine language instructions necessary to extract the bit pattern stored in bit positions 4 through 8 and assign this pattern to a new variable Z. Note that the value of Z should be right shifted to the standard position.

Variable LOGIC

bit   10 9 8 7 6 5 4 3 2 1 0
position

8. Construct a logical mask, X, which extracts the bit values stored positions 16-23 in a 24 bit word. If the value of the variable Y is given by D5D6E3 (using hexadecimal representation) what is the result of X AND Y, X OR Y, NOT Y?

Putting Instructions to Work

263

BUILDING A PROGRAM

While individual instructions provide basic tools, it is the collection of instructions into an executable program that makes the computer function. In Chapter Seven, descriptions were given of the different ways information stored within instruction words can be used to modify and transfer data. This chapter presents the dynamic aspects of instructions, showing the way computers use instructions to choose the steps for different data processing tasks directed through the standard computing language.

To begin the discussion, suppose that a standard computer language program has been compiled and loaded into a computer memory for execution. In the instant before the first machine language instruction of the program be-

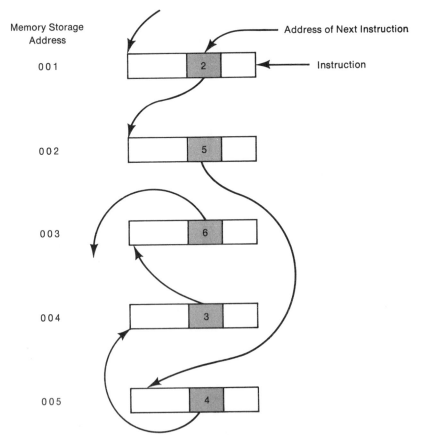

FIGURE 8.1. A linked chain of instructions where each instruction contains the address of the instruction to be executed next.

gins, let us hesitate for a moment and consider the way the computer is guided in choosing which program instructions are to be executed. Generally, the address of the first instruction of any program stored within the computer memory is provided by the computer operating system program as part of the machine language loading procedure. Thereafter, some method must be adopted so that successive instructions can be found in the computer memory and executed in proper order.

One way to find successive instructions is to provide the address of the next instruction as part of the contents of the current instruction. With this technique, instructions are linked into a chain built through explicit reference to instruction addresses. (See Figure 8.1.) However, while such a method of addressing is effective for linking data lists, the linkage address would substantially increase the number of bits required for each instruction word, and in addition, would introduce extra time into the basic instruction processing cycle.

Most modern computers avoid the need for explicit mention of instruction addresses by storing instruction words sequentially within the memory using adjacent storage locations. The transfer from one instruction to the next is governed by a special register, the *Instruction Address Counter*, found in the central control unit. This counter is constructed in such a way that it always stores the address of the next instruction to be executed. Thus, when one instruction has been completed, the address of the next instruction is automatically available in the IAC of the central control unit. (See Figure 8.2.)

As a computer steps through an instruction sequence, the address stored in the instruction address counter must be continually updated. This revision

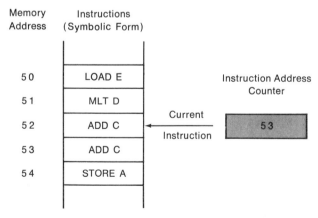

FIGURE 8.2. The Instruction Address Counter indicates the address of the next instruction to be processed during the execution of the current instruction.

can be done in one of two ways. Since successive instructions are stored in sequential memory locations, the most frequent adjustment to the counter involves increasing the current address counter address by one unit each time the execution of the new instruction is begun. After the instruction stored at address a is sent to the decoder (by way of the memory data register) the address $a + 1$ is automatically placed in the instruction address counter to indicate the location of the next instruction.

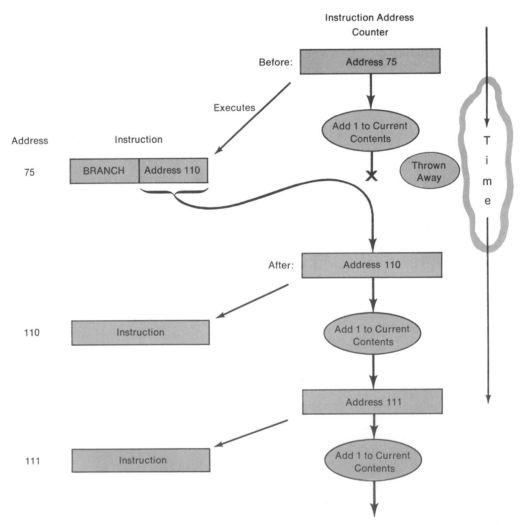

FIGURE 8.3. Modification of the normal instruction sequence and of the Instruction Address Counter when a BRANCH is executed.

The second method of choosing the proper address for the instruction address counter is more subtle. From the discussion of Chapters Three and Four we know that one of the most valuable features of the computer is its ability to analyze data with conditional branches to avoid or repeat program portions. With regard to program loops, clearly some way must be provided so that certain segments of the machine language program can be written once, then repeated upon demand. The easiest way is to introduce instructions that can change the address stored within the instruction address counter. With such *program guiding* instructions the order in which data modification and transfer instructions are executed can be changed, permitting redirection to previously executed program segments (making loops), to alternative program segments (branches), or to later instructions which bypass particular segments of the program.

The most basic instruction used to change the contents of the instruction address counter is the *unconditional branch*

$$\boxed{\text{BRANCH } a}$$

This instruction causes the address a to be placed directly in the instruction address counter, replacing whatever previous value may have been present. As a result, a indicates the address of the instruction which will be executed immediately after BRANCH a. (See Figure 8.3.)

The BRANCH instruction permits a segment of the instruction list to be repeated indefinitely (if a is smaller than the current address stored in the instruction address counter), or for other segments to be avoided (if a is larger than the current address stored in the instruction address counter). The difficulty with BRANCH lies in its unconditional nature. It says, "go to address a for the next instruction". As a result, BRANCH a provides no mechanism for escaping any loop it might create (backward branching) and a computer would find itself perpetually trapped—always returning to address a when BRANCH was again met. Forward branching, of course, does not have this particular difficulty.

To avoid the problems associated with an unconditional branch, other branching instructions have been created which become effective only if certain conditions are fulfilled. These *conditional branch* instructions can test various registers (the accumulator, for instance), or other devices to determine if a branch is required. If these tests indicate that a branch is necessary, a new address a is placed in the instruction address counter. If the conditions are not met, no action is taken since the instruction address counter already indicates the location of the instruction immediately following the conditional branch. (See Figure 8.4.)

In many computers it is convenient to generate the information needed for a conditional branch through a *comparison* instruction of the form

COMPARE R, X

This instruction compares the contents of register R and location X by subtracting the value stored in X from the value stored in R. (See Figure 8.5.) The

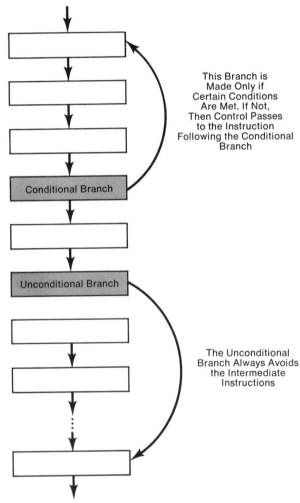

FIGURE 8.4. Examples of instruction execution pathways when conditional and unconditional branching occurs.

result, stored in a special *comparison register*, indicates a positive, negative, or zero result that can be tested by conditional branch instructions. In the comparison operation the contents of R and X remain unaltered.

Conditional branch instructions have the form:

Instruction	Meaning
BPOS *a*	Branch to *a* if the value stored in the comparison register is plus
BNEG *a*	Branch to *a* if the value stored in the comparison register is negative
BZ *a*	Branch to *a* if the value stored in the comparison register is zero
BNZ *a*	Branch to *a* if the value stored in the comparison register is not zero

and so forth. The last two, BZ and BNZ, could equivalently be called branch if equal and branch if not equal. In either case, the branch to *a* will occur only if the proper result is present in the comparison register.

To illustrate the idea of modifying the address stored in the instruction address counter, let us write a machine language instruction set for a simple loop that repeats a program segment N times before passing on to further portions of a program

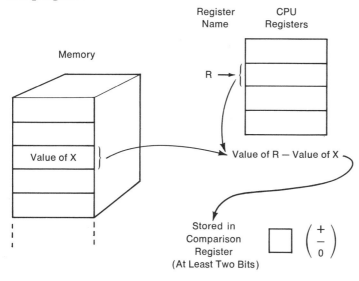

FIGURE 8.5. Schematic diagram showing the operations leading to the comparison COMPARE R,X.

Such a loop would correspond, for example, to the ALGOL-like statement

FOR J ← 1 STEP 1 UNTIL N DO [actions]

in which the actions to be accomplished are not specified.

Suppose that the instruction sequence starts by loading the value zero, corresponding to the index J, into some register, for example, register 7. Each time we pass through the loop the value stored in this register is increased by the value 1. When the value stored in register 7 is greater than N, the loop will have been repeated N times and the program should continue on to the instructions following the loop.

The program segment shown below carries out a repetition of the unspecified data modification and transfer instructions before passing on to subsequent portions of the program. Note that the initial address is arbitrarily chosen as 1000 (in binary) and that the values of the variables ZERO and ONE are 0 and 1.

Address	Instruction	Meaning
01000	LOAD 7, ZERO	Put value 0 (stored under the name ZERO) into register 7.
01001	ADD 7, ONE	Add the value 1 (stored under the variable name ONE) to register 7.
01010 01011 01100 01101		Basic list of 4 instructions which are to be repeated N times before continuing on to further parts of the program.
01110	COMPARE 7, N	Compare contents of register 7 with N.
01111	BNEG 01001	Branch to address 01001 if the contents of the comparison register are negative.
10000 . . .		Subsequent instructions

Although the instruction code given above is designed for modified one address machines, similar instructions can be designed for zero and two address use. The most important aspect lies in the use of branching instructions to revise the contents of the instruction address counter so that segments of program can be repeated or completely avoided. These *program guiding* instructions do not affect data directly, but rather are intended to examine various control registers with the goal of determining the sequence of instructions.

INDEXING AND INDEX REGISTERS

In Chapter Four we discussed how an array of data can be given a single variable name and an associated subscript. To refer to a particular element of the array we must necessarily give both the name of the array and some way of determining the integer value of the subscript. In many computer systems arrays are placed consecutively in memory so that members of the array are stored with consecutive addresses. For example, an array A might be stored as

Name	Storage Location
A_1	011011
A_2	011100
A_3	011101
A_4	011110
.	.
.	.
.	.

in which we have arbitrarily taken the address of the first element as 011011. Note that A_1 means the first (or beginning) element of the array, not that the subscript value itself is necessarily the integer 1. In many problems it is useful to have the subscript value range between quite arbitrary integer values. For instance, the subscripted variable YEAR with elements YEAR (−2000) to YEAR (2000) might prove useful to scholars classifying historical events. YEAR (−2000) could be the first element of the array, YEAR (−1999) could be the second and so forth. To make the transition from *subscript number* to *element number* of the array simple arithmetic is needed. For the above example, it follows that the Element Number = 2001 + Subscript. In the subsequent discussion we want to avoid the distinction between element numbers and susbscripts. To do this we assume that the *element number* is the same as the *subscript* of the array element. (See Figure 8.6.) This is equivalent to assuming that the subscripts start at 1 and increase in steps of 1 (i.e., A_1, A_2, A_3...). Using this convention, reference to any element of the array A stored in memory can be made once we know where A_1 is stored and the index of the particular element. For instance, the element A_J would be found in the location given by the address of $A_1 + (J - 1)$.

Symbolic Name of Location	True Physical Location	Contents
A_1	011011	"one"
A_2	011100	"right"
A_3	011101	"after"
A_4	011110	"the"
A_5	011111	"other"

FIGURE 8.6. Relationship between the symbolic name of an alphanumeric array and the actual memory location.

The use of subscripts on variables presents some difficulty to our previous methods of defining the ADDRESS field of instructions. This problem arises because the actual value of the index for an array element is computed rather than being a fixed value. Thus, the true address needed for the ADDRESS field of an instruction word must permit changes in the subscript values, particularly in loops repeating the same set of instructions using different values of the subscripts. Since it is not possible to specify in advance which particular memory address will be needed for a subscripted variable, a method is needed to allow the operand addresses of instructions to be rapidly computed.

The computation of addresses for subscripted variables is most frequently done through the use of a register which holds the value of the index of a particular element of the array. The *effective address* to be used in the AD-

DRESS portion of the instruction word is then the sum of the address of A_1 minus 1 and the contents of the index register.

To illustrate, consider a modified one address instruction of the form

OPERATION	R	Memory Address

where R refers to the address of register R. To accomodate the demands of subscripted variables, we realize that "Memory Address" must refer to the *effective address* of the variable element.

the effective address

OPERATION	R	I	Memory Address

Here I represents the address of a register which holds the value of the index, while "Memory Address" contains the address of A_1 minus one. By summing this address with the contents of the register I, the address of the particular element of the subscripted variable can be readily found.

Because there are only a small number of registers in the central processing unit, the field for I uses only a few bits. Furthermore, a zero address in the I field means that no indexing is to be done. The variable is not subscripted and the address indicated in the address field of the instruction word is the actual address of the variable.

The introduction of indexing means that new program guiding instructions are needed to manipulate the addresses. To treat the different elements of a given array, the values of the index must be able to be changed easily and rapidly. To show simple index manipulations, let us introduce the extended instructions LOAD R,I,A and ADD R,I,A as two-address instructions meaning: Add the contents of general register I(the index value) to the address of A to find the effective location address (that is, location [A + C (I)]). This address is then used to obtain data which will be loaded into register R or added to the contents of register R, depending upon the operator involved.

As an example, consider the code necessary to evaluate the replacement statement $A_I \leftarrow B_I/C_I$ for I = 1, 2, 3, . . ., 100.

Location	Instruction	Meaning
110	LOAD I, ZERO	Put the value 0 (stored in a variable called ZERO) in to general register I.

	111	ADD I, ONE	Add 1 to I (the value 1 is stored in variable ONE)
	112	LOAD J, I, B	Put the value of B_I into register J.
a loop	113	DIV J, I, C	Perform B_I/C_I. This result is stored in register J.
	114	STORE J, I, A	Store the result in A_I.
	115	COMPARE I, K100	COMPARE I to value 100 (the value 100 is stored in variable K100).
	116	BNEG 111	Go back to location 111 if the number stored in I is less than 100.
	117	Rest of program	

In summary, the use of index registers is a way of increasing the efficiency of a computer by providing an effective, rather than absolute, address for use in instructions. These addresses are dynamic in the sense that the actual addresses are unknown before actual computations begin. The computer can alter its instruction code to meet the conditions imposed by the standard computing language program.

IMMEDIATE TYPE INSTRUCTIONS

The basic data modification and data transfer instructions introduced in the last chapter obtain their operand addresses from information provided in the address field of the instruction word. As we have seen in the last section, however, situations arise in which small integer numbers are needed in a program for various purposes such as: executing simple counting operations; giving initial values to variables; and so forth. In the examples of the last section, we stored these numbers in memory locations using suggestive variable names like ZERO, ONE, and K100. Through the usual data transfer instructions these numbers could then be retrieved from memory and made available for use in the central processing unit.

To avoid the extra effort involved in storing and retrieving small integer numbers, special *Immediate Type* instructions are usually included in the machine language instruction set. These instructions use the address field of the instruction word to store integer numbers directly. Thus, the immediate type instruction address field does not redirect the computer to some memory location, but instead gives a number to be used as part of the instruction. As a result, when these instructions are used in a machine language program there is a considerable saving in operation time and a reduction in the required memory storage space.

To introduce immediate type instructions, recall that the previously used instruction LOAD R, ZERO fetches the value of the variable ZERO from memory and stores it in register R. In this particular case, the value 0 was stored under the name ZERO and two memory locations were required; one for ZERO (0) and one for the instruction itself. A more efficient approach is the load immediate instruction of the form LOADI, R, 0. This instruction causes the integer number zero, stored in proper form in the address field, to be loaded directly into register R, erasing any previous contents. Arithmetic instructions such as ADD, SUB, MLT, DIV and COMPARE can be expressed as the immediate type counterparts ADDI, SUBI, DIVI, COMPAREI with appropriate register information, as shown below.

Instruction	Meaning
ADDI R, N	Add the integer N to the contents of register R.
SUBI R, N	Subtract the integer N from the contents of register R.
MLTI R, N	Multiply the contents of register R by the integer N.
DIVI R, N	Divide the contents of register R by the integer N.
COMPAREI R, N	Compare the integer N with the contents of register R and store the sign of the result in the comparison register.

To illustrate the usefulness of immediate type instructions, we have rewritten the simple loop given in the last section where a program segment is repeated N times (using arbitrary decimal addresses):

Address	Instructions	Meaning
75	LOADI I, 0	Put the value zero into register I.
76	ADDI I, 1	Increment I by one.
77	⎧ Other	
·	⎪ Repeated	
·	⎨ Instructions	
110	⎩	
111	COMPARE I,N	Compare contents of register I with N.
112	BNEG 76	Branch to address 76 if comparison register is negative.
113	⎧ Subsequent	
·	⎨ Instructions	
·	⎩	

Although this program has the same number of instructions as used before, it represents a more effective instruction set. Not only are two memory storage locations (needed to store the values 0 and 1) now available for other uses, but also there is a saving in the time required to fetch the two values from memory.

Another application of the immediate type instruction involves manipulation of the addresses of variables. Situations frequently occur in which it is useful to treat a memory address as if it were a piece of data so that it can be stored or transfered between parts of a program. Such a procedure can be done through the immediate type instruction

$$\boxed{\text{LOADI R, A}}$$

in which A is the symbolic address of a variable. The bits representing the *address* of A are loaded by this instruction into the register R. The contents of that address, namely the value of the variable A, are not affected in this procedure.

The actions of regular and immediate load instructions are shown in Figure 8.7.

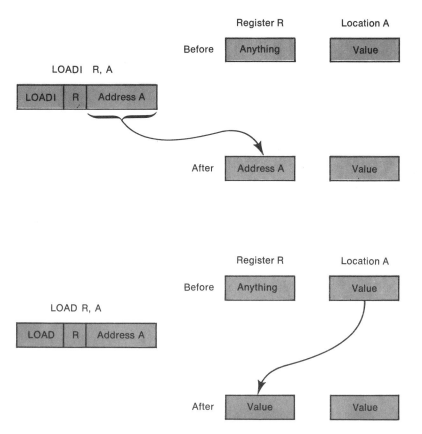

FIGURE 8.7. The different operating characteristics of an immediate (top) and normal (bottom) loading instruction.

INDIRECT ADDRESSES

Immediate type instructions give us a way to use integer numbers placed directly in the address field of an instruction word. With regular instructions the information of the address field is interpreted simply as an effective address for the location of the actual data in the computer memory. Thus, with the *direct addressing* of the regular instructions data stored in a computer memory is referenced by the address field of the instruction. Direct addressing is written symbolically with the name of the variable representing the true binary memory address. For example, the instruction

$$\boxed{\text{ADD R, BOX}}$$

means that the contents of register R and the value stored in the location called BOX are to be added with the final result placed in R.

For many applications an extension of direct addressing is necessary to provide greater flexibility in computer programs. *Indirect addressing* involves a simple re-interpretation of the meaning of the address field of an instruction. Using direct addressing, contents of the address field tell us where to find a piece of data. With indirect addressing, however, we interpret the information stored in the indicated location as an intermediate or *indirect address* showing us where the actual address we need is stored. Thus, we regard the address given in an *indirect instruction* only as a *pointer* telling us where to go to find the actual data address. The final address is indicated to us in an indirect manner.

Most instructions, with the exception of immediate type, can use indirect addresses. Usually, one bit of the instruction operation code field is devoted to indicating direct or indirect addressing. However, to avoid further complicating the symbolic notation of various instructions we will indicate indirect addressing by showing an asterisk (*) just before the quantity stored in the address field. Thus, as shown in Figure 8.8.

$$\boxed{\text{LOAD R, *A}}$$

means that the contents of register R will be replaced with data taken from a location whose address is stored in A.

The greatest advantage of indirect addressing is that it permits sets of instructions to be written in a general form without specifying the exact addresses of the variables to be manipulated. By so doing we can specify any sequence of data modification and data transfer instructions, leaving the actual data addresses anonymous and using only some temporary locations (such as *A) in which we promise to insert, at some future time, the true data addresses. Similarly, the symbolic notations used here to represent machine instructions assumes implicitly that the proper binary form, address and all, will be stored in the machine during execution of the program. Indirect addressing allows the "symbolic" or promisory" technique to be carried on during execution. In another context, we could call payments by credit card or check indirect payments, because the information on the card or check really tells the recipient where to go for the cash.

The process of avoiding reference to a specific variable opens the way for the development of computer *subprograms*. (Remember the term *subalgorithm* of Chapter Four; i.e., specialized segments of instructions which

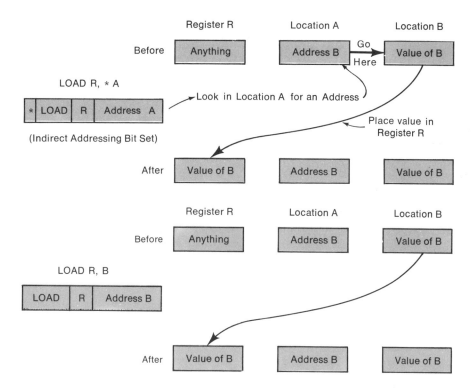

FIGURE 8.8. An illustration contrasting an indirect loading (top) with a normal loading operation (bottom). Broken line indicates the indirect path.

accomplish specific manipulations such as: comparison; finding square roots; solving equations; and so forth). These subprograms are written using indirect addresses so that we can enter any data into the subprograms at a future time simply by changing the addresses stored in our indirect pointer location.

SUBPROGRAMS AND THE BRANCH AND LINK INSTRUCTION

Normally, instructions of a program are stored one after the other in memory in the same sequence in which they are to be executed. A special register, the Instruction Address Counter (IAC), holds the address of the current instruction and it is incremented by unity near the end of the instruction execution cycle to obtain the address of what is usually the next instruction. Branches, as we have seen, modify this procedure by replacing the contents of the IAC with the new address held in the branch instruction address field. In this way control can be transferred forward or backward in the main stream of code or to an entirely different stream. In all cases, the branching instructions do not preserve the address of the current instruction; the program always looks ahead to the next instruction.

In this section we will introduce a different type of branch instruction called *branch and link* (BAL), which not only branches the program to a new address, but also retains the address where the branch occurred. Using this instruction it is possible to transfer to an isolated segment of the code (a subprogram), carry out a sequence of instructions, then return to the original branch point and continue with the original instruction set.

A simple branch and link instruction in a modified one address computer has the form

Operation Code	Register	Memory Address
BAL	R	SUB

or, in mnemonic form, BAL R, SUB where SUB is our symbolic address for a particular memory location. This instruction causes the address of the instruction subsequent to BAL R, SUB to be placed in register R and an unconditional branch to be made to the instruction located in location SUB.

Suppose the BAL R, SUB instruction were stored in location a. During the execution of this instruction the Instruction Address Counter (IAC) would have been incremented to the value $a + 1$, as usual. Instead of throwing away this value, as happens with a normal branch, it is stored in register R. The address SUB is then inserted into the IAC and the appropriate instruction (the one in location SUB) is executed. Consequently, register R holds the address, $a + 1$, of the instruction immediately following the BAL instruction. If the separate section of code which started in location SUB were, at its conclusion, to branch to the address being held in register R, we would then have effectively inserted the section of code into the mainstream of the program. Furthermore, at a later point in the program, say at location b, another branch and link instruction to location SUB could cause execution of the same section of code followed by a return to location $b + 1$. It follows that the "and link" part of the instruction name refers to remembering, via register R, where to link back and resume the original stream of the program. (See Figure 8.9.)

The section of code starting in location SUB and ending with a return linkage is called a *subprogram*. It is invoked, or *called*, by a branch and link operation to location SUB, and it returns to the calling program at the instruction following the BAL command. Subprograms are commonly used to execute a given set of operations at different points in a program, but without

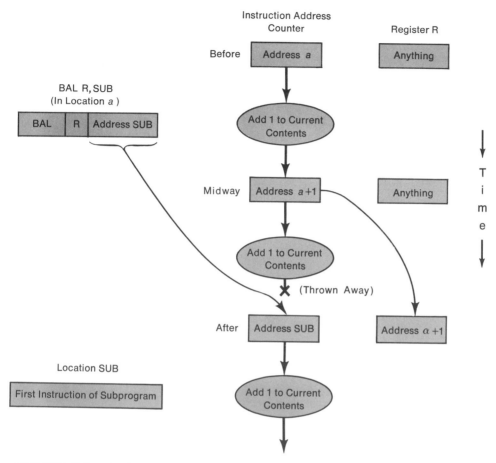

FIGURE 8.9. Actions caused by a Branch and Link instruction. Compare this with a normal branch as in Figure 8.3. where register R plays no role.

actually inserting the full subprogram instruction set each time. *In effect, subprograms become one large special machine instruction as far as the user is concerned.* They can be written separately from the main computer program. For example, common functions such as square root, logarithms, read, and write are subprograms supplied by the computer manufacturer and stored within the computer system. A program written to solve a given task can easily be converted into a subprogram of a larger program. Thus, the effort of computer programming can pay extra dividends if older programs are used as building blocks for larger, more general programs. (See Figure 8.10.)

Thus far we have discussed one of three important points regarding the use of subprograms namely, how do we transfer *control* to the subprograms. Two points remain:

a.   How to return to the calling program?

b.   How to communicate data between the subprogram and its calling program?

All the tools are at hand for solving these programs. Let us consider first the problem of returning to the calling program.

If an instruction BAL R, SUB were executed in location *a* then register R would be loaded with the location *a* + 1 that is, not the value held *in* location *a* + 1, but rather the address itself. At the end of the subprogram, which

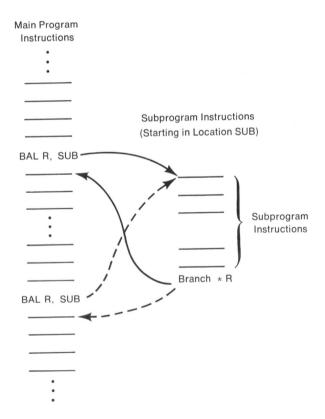

FIGURE 8.10.   The use of Branch and Link instructions to effectively insert the subprogram instructions into two places in the main program.

started at location SUB, we want to branch or return to location $a + 1$. Thus, an unconditional branch instruction done indirectly through register R will do nicely.

$$\boxed{\text{BRANCH } *\text{R}}$$

This will obtain the content of register R (the address $a + 1$), insert it in the instruction address counter, and finally branch to the address represented by those bits. This kind of indirect branch is usually the last instruction in a subprogram.

The third aspect of subprograms involves the transfer of data between the subprogram and the calling program. Since a subprogram executes a particular task and may be used at several places within a program, it is not practical to write a subprogram that uses the same variable names as the calling program, because the data sent to or received from a subprogram usually corresponds to different variables at each point it is used. Consequently, the subprogram needs to be told, each time it is called, which data to use and where to place the results.

As a general example of this technique, consider a text editing program that sets type for a newspaper. This program requires a subprogram to examine characters and determine if they are letters, numbers, punctuation marks, spaces, or other special symbols. In operation, this subprogram is first given the character. It then returns a value which reflects the type of character (letter, etc.) found. For this subprogram, two pieces of data are exchanged between the main and the subprogram. Other subprograms could involve more or fewer transferred values. For historical and mathematical reasons the data exchanged between the main and the subprograms are called the *arguments* of the subprogram. The arguments may appear to be in the form of constants (numbers or alphanumeric data) or variables.

One easy method of transferring arguments between programs is to make a list of the argument addresses and store it in the computer memory. This list can then be given to the subprogram so that it knows where to find the data values needed for the subprogram calculations and can return the results to the proper places.

Although the list of argument addresses could be stored anywhere in the computer memory, it is most convenient to place it in the storage locations immediately after the branch and link instruction, BAL R, SUB. The first item of the list, however, is not an address, but a number describing how many arguments are in the list. Thus, if BAL R, SUB is stored in location a, the number n of arguments is stored in location $a + 1$ and the rest of the main program continues at $a + n + 2$.

An example of a branch and link instruction, together with a list of two arguments is shown (with arbitrary addresses):

	Location	Contents	Meaning
	33	BAL R, SUB	Go to the subprogram starting in location SUB
	34	2	The number of arguments.
Argument list	35	X	address of the first argument
	36	Y	address of the second argument
	37	next instruction of the main program	

In operation, the first task of the subprogram is to obtain the addresses of the arguments from the argument list and substitute them for the addresses of quantities used in the subprogram instruction set (remember indirect addressing). Next, the return address to the main program must be computed; that is, where the subprogram should link back to the calling program after the subprogram calculations are finished.

To illustrate in more detail, suppose that the arguments of the example were called X and Y in the calling program. In the subprogram they could be named I and J. Each time a value for I is needed in the subprogram the address X must be used and similarly for J and Y. This correspondence is easily accomplished if the subprogram is written so that instead of looking into location I to obtain a *value*, it looks into location I to obtain the *address* of X where the required value is actually stored. In short, the subroutine must *indirectly address* I and J so that these variables correspond to X and Y.

Using the two argument subprogram of the previous example, let us write an outline of the subprogram instruction set. To begin with, we recall that the calling instruction BAL R, SUB located in the storage location given by the address a did two things. It stored the address $a + 1$ in register R and it placed the address location corresponding to SUB in the instruction address counter so that the next instruction to be executed will correspond to the subprogram instruction set.

The following instruction list, which begins at the address SUB, is designed to properly address all subprogram arguments as well as prepare for the eventual return of control to the main program instruction sequence.

A Two Argument Subprogram Instruction List

Location	Contents	Meaning
SUB	LOAD S, *R	Obtain the number of arguments via register R (holds address $a + 1$) and put it into register S.
SUB + 1	COMPAREI S, 2	Compare the contents of register S with the value 2.
SUB + 2	BNZ ERROROUT	Go to an error handling section if there are not two arguments.
SUB + 3	ADDI R, 1	Add 1 to the contents of register R. R now holds address $a + 2$.
SUB + 4	LOAD S, *R	Put address of X into register S by looking into R for the address $a + 2$ then putting the contents of location $a + 2$ into register S.
SUB + 5	STORE S, I	Store the address of X in location I.
SUB + 6	ADDI R, 1	Increment R to hold $a + 3$.
SUB + 7	LOAD S, *R	Put the address of Y into register S.
SUB + 8	STORE S, J	Store the address of Y in location J.
SUB + 9	ADDI R, 1	Increment R to hold $a + 4$. This is the return address.
SUB + 10	rest of subprogram	
.		
.		
.		
SUB + n	BRANCH *R	Return to the calling program at location $a + 4$.

Using this subprogram, each time the value of I or J is required, an indirect addressing instruction is used. For example,

$$\boxed{\text{MLT S, *J}}$$

multiplies the contents of register S by the current value of the variable J (in reality the variableY). In effect, the variables I and J act as *pointers* to the actual quantities X and Y which remain stored in the calling program.

As shown, at the end of the subprogram the return linkage to the calling program is

BRANCH *R

since register R now holds the proper address, $a + 4$, of the next instruction of the calling program. The instruction sequence then continues until, at some later point, a new transfer to the subprogram is made with the BAL R, SUB instruction and the list of argument addresses.

Finally, it is not necessary for subprograms to be called into action exclusively by the main program. The branch and link instruction could also be placed within the instruction list of a subprogram so that one subprogram can call upon another. In fact, by taking special care, subprograms can be arranged which can call themselves into action with what is called a *recursive call*. Such an arrangement can save time when certain repetitive actions are needed in the program, but special methods are needed to allow the subprogram to unwind gracefully.

COMPILING, LOADING, AND EXECUTION

Every computer has a basic set of instructions that include operations similar to those described in the foregoing sections. This instruction set is intimately linked to the internal structure of the computer and reflects many of the engineering and economic factors associated with the particular computer design. Small computers, for instance, may have a somewhat restricted instruction set limiting the range and efficiency of their operations for certain tasks and even restricting their use to a particular standard computing language. Large computers, in contrast, can be given a wide variety of instructions that can be used to implement many different languages.

With our new knowledge of computer instructions, let us return once more to the compilation and execution of a computer program. As before, the compilation process is a translation of statements given in a standard computing language into machine language instructions. The compiling program examines each statement of the computer program, identifying variables, constants, and operations in terms of the basic instruction set. During this translation process the entire structure of the machine language program is created in all respects except one: The absolute addresses of the program are not yet established.

When compilation is complete, the machine language program is ready for loading into the computer. The computer operating system then decides where in the computer memory the instructions are to be placed (i.e., the addresses are given for all quantities and operations). In addition, subprograms are gathered and assigned to specific memory locations. When the loading is complete and execution of the program is at hand, the address of the first program instruction is placed in the instruction address register and control passes to the program. In some computers internal control remains with this one program until the execution is completed. Newer, timesharing computers, however, store several programs simultaneously in the computer memory and related storage areas. Optimal use of the computer system is then made by passing control between the different programs as time saving opportunities arise. To accomplish this sophisticated sharing process, special attention must be given to the computer guidance programs of the central control unit.

A Synopsis of Modified One Address Instructions

Instruction	Meaning
ADD R, X SUB, R, X MLT R, X DIV R, X	Arithmetic operations in direct address form. X may represent an effective address for subscripted variables. R represents a register address.
LOAD R, X STORE R, X	Data transfer instructions, direct address form. X may represent an effective address for subscripted variables. R represents a register address.

ADDI R, number
SUBI R, number
MLTI R, number
DIVI R, number
LOAD R, number
	Arithmetic and data transfer operations for type immediate instructions. Small binary integers stored as a number in the address field of the instruction are used in connection with register R.

LOADI R, A	Loads the address of A into register R.

ADD R, *A
SUB R, *A
MLT R, *A
DIV R, *A
LOAD R, *A
	Arithmetic and data transfer operation for indirectly addressed quantities. In execution the address of the operand is sought in A.

Instruction (continued)	Meaning (continued)
AND R, X OR R, X EOR R, X NOT R	Logical instructions specifying bit by bit operations between data stored in R and X. X may be an effective address for subscripted variables. The bit by bit results are stored in R.
SHIFT R, n	Shifts the contents of register R by n positions to the right with a circular shift.
BRANCH *a*	Branch to the instruction at address *a*.
BRANCH *R	Branch to the instruction whose address is contained in R.
BAL R, A	Branch to the instruction associated with A. The address of the next instruction after BAL R,A is stored in Register R.
COMPARE R, X	Compare the contents of R and location X (this is an effective address for subscripted variables). Store the result $(+, 0, -)$ in the comparison register.
COMPAREI R, number	Compare the contents of register R and number. Store the result $(+, 0, -)$ in the comparison register.
BPOS *a* BNEG *a* BEZ *a* BNZ *a*	If the comparison register is positive, negative, zero or nonzero, branch to *a*.

REFERENCES TO FURTHER READINGS

DONOVAN, J. J.
  Systems Programming. New York: McGraw Hill, 1972.
GEAR, C. W.
  Computer Organization and Programming. New York: McGraw Hill, 1974.
WEGNER, P.
  Programming Languages, Information Structures and Machine Organization. New York: McGraw Hill, 1968. An advanced text.

KEY WORDS AND PHRASES TO KNOW

ADDRESS FIELD

ARGUMENT OF A
SUBPROGRAM

BRANCH AND LINK

CONDITIONAL BRANCH

COMPARISON INSTRUCTION

COMPARISON REGISTER

DIRECT ADDRESSING

EFFECTIVE ADDRESS

ELEMENT NUMBER

INDEX REGISTER

INDIRECT ADDRESSES

INDIRECT INSTRUCTION

INSTRUCTION ADDRESS
COUNTER

INSTRUCTION ADDRESSES

IMMEDIATE TYPE
INSTRUCTIONS

MACHINE LANGUAGE
PROGRAM

POINTER

PROGRAM GUIDING
INSTRUCTIONS

SUBPROGRAMS

SUBSCRIPT NUMBER

UNCONDITIONAL BRANCH

EXERCISES

1. Write a machine language program that will carry out the operations specified in the flowchart segment shown below. Adopt appropriate arbitrary memory addresses for instructions and data.

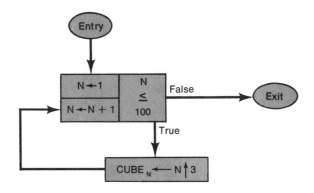

2. Explain the difference between directly and indirectly addressed instructions. Why are indirectly addressed instructions useful?

3. Explain the meaning of the instruction LOADI R, A. How does it differ from LOAD R, *A?

4. Write a machine language program which accomplishes the tasks shown in the flowchart given. The array A is assumed to have five elements.

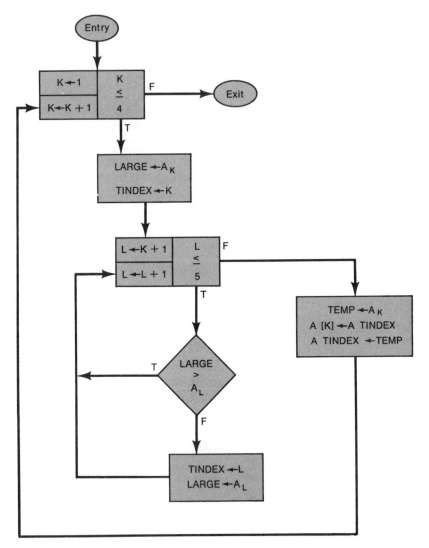

5. If the instruction set of a small computer is composed of 80 separate instructions, what is the smallest number of bits needed for the operation code field of the instruction words?

6. If subprograms were not permitted in a small computer, would it be necessary to include instructions using indirect addressing?

7. Write the portion of machine language code necessary to evaluate the expression

$$\text{TABLE}_K \leftarrow A * (A + B_K * (A + 2))$$

for values of K between 5 and 20 in unit steps. Assume A and B_K are stored in the computer memory. Seven CPU registers are available for temporary data storage, if needed.

8. Suppose that an array A_K is stored in the computer. K is supposed to range from -100 to $+100$ in unit steps. If A_{-100} is stored in location 10110111, where will A_{50} be found? Assume that the array is stored in sequential locations with more positive indices having larger addresses.

PROBLEMS

1. Write the main program and subprogram machine language code which takes three initial data values X, Y, Z and returns the value LARGEST as a fourth variable A. The call for this subprogram in the main program should be written in terms of the variables A, B, C and D, respectively.

2. Write a machine language program solving the equation

$$x = y(y - 3)(y + 4)$$

for values of y ranging in unit steps from 1 to 20. For data input and output, use the instructions READ A and WRITE A where A is a memory storage location.

3. Write a machine language program which compares values of A, B and C (stored in locations 01110, 01111, and 10000) and stores the larger in location 11111. The program should start at location 00000.

4. Write the machine language program which accomplishes the operations specified in the square root algorithm of Chapter four. Use the same variable names and assume that data input and output can be done through READ A and WRITE A instruction words which place and remove values directly from the indicated computer memory location.

5. The subprogram SQRT computing square roots has one argument, X. In operation, we want to specify a number for X and have the value of the square root substituted for the name SQRT(X). This usage is illustrated below.

$$Y \leftarrow [B + \text{SQRT}(B * B - 4 * A * C)]/2A$$

in which the quantity within the parentheses is first evaluated to give a number, the square root is then found, and finally, this value is used in the complete expression.

Using the BAL R, SQRT instruction, write the subprogram and portion of the main program code which actually evaluates the replacement statement given above. Note that the algorithm for determining the square root is given in Chapter Four. Rather than reading in an error limit, take $e = 10^{-8}$. You will need to consider how the result of the square root will be given to the main program. One popular method is to always replace the value in a specified general register; then the main program would expect to find the value there and finish evaluating the whole expression.

nine

Binary Arithmetic for Computers

THE NEED FOR BINARY ARITHMETIC

In previous chapters we have seen how computers are able to store external numerical data through the use of codes. Although many interesting applications of computers exist in areas removed from direct numerical analysis, it turns out that the basic arithmetic operations of binary addition, subtraction, multiplication, and division are still of substantial importance. To some extent these operations are done using the methods of decimal arithmetic. Because of the smaller character set of the binary system, however, some simplifications are possible which greatly reduce the labor involved in making binary computations.

There are two approaches to storing numerical quantities in a digital computer. (See Figure 9.1.) The first is to treat numbers and alphabetic characters in the same way by creating a character code of binary digits to represent both types of symbols. With this approach, arithmetic computations can be made by writing special programs to interpret each character of a number and to generate a result (using the character code) according to the rules of arithmetic. While such a method works, it is somewhat cumbersome and time consuming.

The second, most widely used method of number storage represents num-

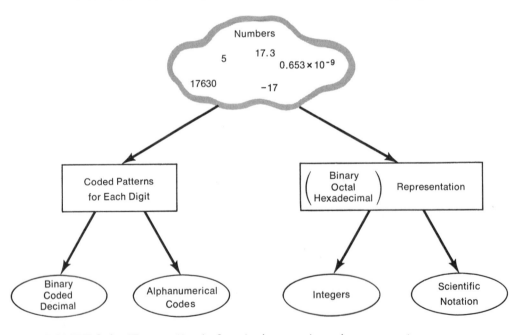

FIGURE 9.1. Two methods for storing numbers in a computer.

bers as sets of individual bits using a positional notation within a computer word. This allows arithmetic computations in computers to be made in almost the same way as we do with pencil and paper allowing, of course, for the differences between binary and decimal numbers. Since the speed of computation is far more rapid when numbers are represented directly, almost all general purpose computers perform computations using this method.

In the following paragraphs the basic elements of binary arithmetic are described. Application of these results to actual digital computation devices is made in the next chapter following a discussion of Boolean algebra and the methods of computer logic.

BINARY ADDITION

The basic features of binary addition can be found in the binary addition table shown below.

Value of Augend

	0	1
0	0	1
1	1	10

Value of Addend

sums

augend
+ addend
carry and sum

There are only four combinations of binary digits. Three are direct, while the fourth, involving a carry-out digit of 1, is only slightly more complicated. The carry out digit is similar to the carry of decimal arithmetic of adding two numbers. We must frequently carry a digit to the next left column. This carry also occurs in binary addition.

$$
\begin{array}{ccccc}
1 & 1 & & & \\
& 1 & 1 & 1 & 1 \\
+ & 0 & 1 & 0 & 0 \\
\hline
1 & 0 & 0 & 1 & 1 \\
\end{array}
\qquad
\begin{array}{cccccc}
1 & 1 & 1 & 1 & 1 & \\
& 1 & 0 & 1 & 0 & 1 \\
+ & 0 & 1 & 1 & 1 & 1 \\
\hline
1 & 0 & 0 & 1 & 0 & 0 \\
\end{array}
$$

$$
\begin{array}{cccccccccc}
1 & 1 & 1 & 1 & 1 & 1 & 1 & 1 & 1 & \\
& 1 & 1 & 0 & 1 & 1 & 0 & 1 & 1 & 1 \\
+ & 1 & 0 & 1 & 1 & 0 & 1 & 1 & 0 & 1 \\
\hline
1 & 1 & 0 & 0 & 1 & 0 & 0 & 1 & 0 & 0 \\
\end{array}
$$

These examples show that it is necessary to add three digits: The augend (top), addend (bottom), and the carry. This addition of three digits gives both a sum digit and a possible unit carry out digit. Consequently, as shown in the next chapter, a digital device performing binary addition should have elementary components which can add three binary digits (bits) and give both a sum bit and a carry out bit to the next digit (bit) position to the left. Using these ideas, we can enlarge the addition formula as follows:

Bits to be added			Result	
Carry in	Augend	Addend	Carry out	Sum bit
0	0	0	0	0
0	0	1	0	1
0	1	0	0	1
0	1	1	1	0
1	0	0	0	1
1	0	1	1	0
1	1	0	1	0
1	1	1	1	1

or, starting from the far right,

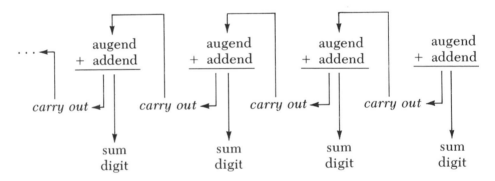

When one or both numbers to be added are negative then special consideration must be given to the signs of the numbers. This is discussed in the next section.

BINARY SUBTRACTION

Before going on to subtraction in the binary number system, consider the rules developed for subtracting decimal numbers. Assume that the two numbers are written with decimal points in proper alignment and that the number of largest magnitude is in the upper (minuend) position. The algorithm for subtraction then reads (starting from the right):

a. If the subtrahend digit (the digit being subtracted) is smaller than the minuend digit, then the resulting digit is (minuend digit − subtrahend digit).

b. If the subtrahend digit is larger than the minuend digit, then "10" additional units are borrowed from the next left position and the subtraction is carried out as before (minuend digit + "10" − subtrahend digit).

As shown below, subtraction of binary digits follows the same procedural rules:

	Value of Minuend	
	0	1
Value of Subtrahend 0	0	1
Subtrahend 1	$1 + b$	0

Difference

        Minuend
    + Subtrahend
        Difference

The character b in this table means that a digit must be borrowed from the next left minuend digit. The art of borrowing a digit from the next left position is important in both binary and decimal subtraction. Frequently, borrowing from one digit can lead to borrowing from even higher ranks (further left). Try, for example, $(1,000 - 3)_{10}$.

In a computer, each small operation consumes time and the possible cascading of borrowing each time one digit (a bit) is subtracted from another can be very wasteful. In addition, borrowing leads to digital design problems which are difficult to overcome with inexpensive devices. If we disregard for a moment the question of computation time, we can ask two related questions associated with the subtraction of binary numbers: Namely, is it possible to subtract two binary digits while avoiding the necessity for borrowing digits, and, if so, is it possible to automate such an operation? As shown below, both questions can be answered affirmatively through the use of a number representation called *complements* whereby binary addition can be used to accomplish subtraction.

Binary Integers and Complements

Suppose that we use a computer word of N bits to represent binary integers. From the last section we know that a direct form of subtraction can be done as shown below with continual borrowing from further left digits:

0 1 0 1 1 0 1 1	Minuend
− 0 0 1 0 1 1 0 1	Subtrahend
0 0 1 0 1 1 1 0	Difference

We now ask if there is any possible way to change the subtrahend so that the old minuend and the subtrahend, as expressed in a new form, can be *added together* to find the correct difference?

To answer this question and develop the method of *complements*, let us consider first the simple subtraction corresponding to $3 - 3 = 0$. In binary notation with an eight bit word this subtraction looks like

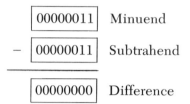

	00000011	Minuend
−	00000011	Subtrahend
	00000000	Difference

Now, is it possible to rewrite the subtrahend so that the same result is obtained through addition? That is,

	00000011	Minuend
+	????????	New Subtrahend
	00000000	Difference

In a previous section we have found that the addition of two binary numbers gives a result equal to or greater than the two integers themselves. This would make it seem unlikely that we can find a way to find the correct *difference* through addition. However, as shown above, suppose that we look for the result of the summation only in the first N bits of the difference, ignoring any carry bits going to the (N + 1) position. If we agree to drop the (N + 1) binary digit the bit values shown previously as question marks can be written as

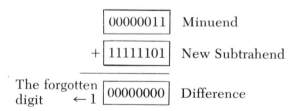

	00000011	Minuend
+	11111101	New Subtrahend
	00000000	Difference

The forgotten digit ← 1

and the carry into the ninth bit position "falls off" the left hand side of the word and is ignored. The tricks of this method are clearly 1) finding the new form for the subtrahend and 2) ignoring digits carried into the (N + 1) digit position. Further, although we have used a simple example $(3 + (-3)) = 0$ to illustrate how subtraction can be done through addition, the discussion of the next paragraphs will show the method is completely general and that it is possible to represent any subtrahend as a new number which, when added to the minuend, gives the correct difference.

Let us consider the method for obtaining the bit pattern of the new subtrahend. First, we make a *complementary image* of the old subtrahend by writing zeros to replace ones and vice versa:

| 1 | 1 | ... | 1 | 0 | 1 | 1 | 0 | 1 | 0 | $\rightarrow$ | 0 | 0 | ... | 0 | 1 | 0 | 0 | 1 | 0 | 1 |

bit
number   N N−1 ... 7 6 5 4 3 2 1   N N−1 ... 7 6 5 4 3 2 1

old subtrahend   complementary image

At this point, if we try to add the old subtrahend, I, and the new complementary image, $\bar{I}$, the result is a string of N ones:

| 1 | 1 | ... | 1 | 1 | 1 | 1 | 1 | 1 | 1 |

N N−1 ... 7 6 5 4 3 2 1

$$I + \bar{I}$$

The complementary image $\bar{I}$ is called the *one's complement* of I. As shown above, when a number I and its one's complement are added, the result is a string of ones. Thus, we can deduce that

$$I + \bar{I} = 2^N - 1$$

where 2^N, when represented in our computer word, is the bit occuring in the $N + 1$ bit position. This is just the bit we "forget" or allow to "fall off".

Now to get the final, negative form of any integer I we can put the equation

$$I + \bar{I} = 2^N - 1$$

in the form

$$-I = \bar{I} + 1 - 2^N.$$

Thus, to represent a negative integer we first make a one's complement $(\bar{I})$, add 1 to it, then drop the bit corresponding the the term 2^N since it "falls off" our N bit data word. When formed in this manner, $-I$ is called the *two's complement* of I and is written as $\tilde{I}$.

From the previous definitions it follows that

$$\tilde{I} + I = \bar{I} + 1 + I = 2^N - 1 + 1 = 2^N + 0$$

which is just what we looked for in our original subtraction $(3 - 3 = 0)$: A number, when added to its "negative form", should give zeros for those bits used to represent the number.

Examples of this conversion between negative numbers and the one's and two's complement form are given below for four bit data words

Number	I	$\bar{I}$	$\tilde{I}$	$I + \tilde{I}$
3	0 0 1 1	1 1 0 0	1 1 0 1	0 0 0 0
6	0 1 1 0	1 0 0 1	1 0 1 0	0 0 0 0
7	0 1 1 1	1 0 0 0	1 0 0 1	0 0 0 0

Looking at the bit patterns used to represent both the positive integer (I) and the negative integers $(\tilde{I})$, we see that a four bit word could be used to represent not only the positive integers 1 to 15, but also -1 to -15. Previously, the bit pattern 1001 would have represented $+9$, but now it can also be -7. Likewise, the bit pattern 1100 can represent either $+12$ or -4. Thus the two's complement form of number representation introduces some confusion into the process of deciding what number is stored in a given bit pattern. To overcome this difficulty we need a definite rule: If the leftmost bit is a 1, the number is represented in two's complement form and is negative. If the leftmost bit is a zero, the number is positive and in its normal form. Using this convention, a four bit word using two's complement notation can represent the numbers $-8, -7, -6, \ldots -1, 0, 1, 2, \ldots 7$. An N-bit computer word can be used to represent numbers from $-(2^{N-1})$ through 0 to $+(2^{N-1}-)$. Negative binary numbers in two's complement notation are always recognizable by having a 1 in the leftmost bit position; positive numbers have a zero there.

ON TO BINARY SUBTRACTION

The subtraction of two numbers X and Y can be represented as $X - Y$ where $-$ is the subtraction operator. Using parentheses we can re-express $X - Y$ as $X + (-Y)$. In making this rearrangement, the minus sign has changed its meaning: In the first case the minus sign indicates an operation between two numbers, while in the second, it is a *unary* operation acting on one number alone. In effect, X + (−Y) requires us to change the sign of Y (the unary operation) and add the result to X.

Now, from our previous discussion we know how to represent (−Y) using two's complements. Assuming that Y is a binary integer number (either positive or negative) −Y = $\hat{Y}$ is formed by adding 1 to the one's complement image $\overline{Y}$ obtained from Y. Afterwards, X and $\hat{Y}$ are added to obtain the answer (X − Y). Examples follow.

Examples of Binary Subtraction with Complements

X and Y are positive, X is larger than Y:

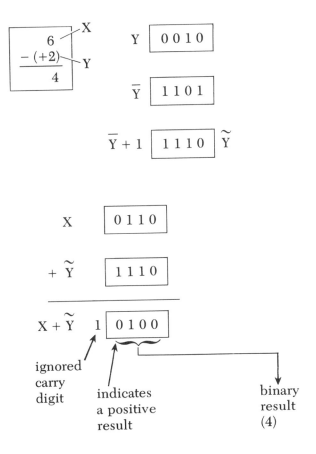

X and Y are positive, X is smaller than Y:

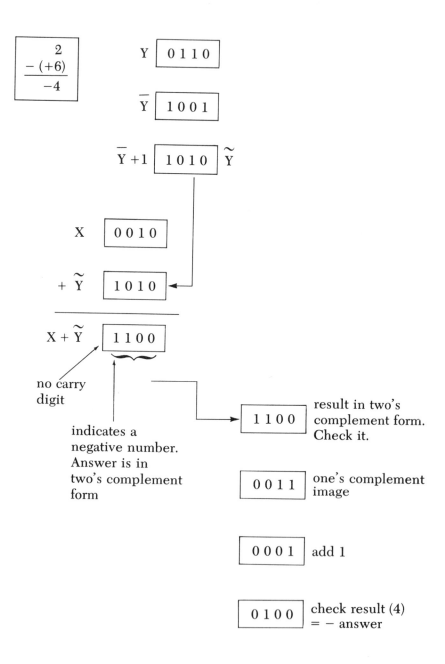

$$\begin{array}{r} 2 \\ - (+6) \\ \hline -4 \end{array}$$

Y $\boxed{0\ 1\ 1\ 0}$

$\overline{Y}$ $\boxed{1\ 0\ 0\ 1}$

$\overline{Y} + 1$ $\boxed{1\ 0\ 1\ 0}$ $\tilde{Y}$

X $\boxed{0\ 0\ 1\ 0}$

$+\ \tilde{Y}$ $\boxed{1\ 0\ 1\ 0}$

$X + \tilde{Y}$ $\boxed{1\ 1\ 0\ 0}$

no carry
digit

indicates a
negative number.
Answer is in
two's complement
form

$\boxed{1\ 1\ 0\ 0}$ result in two's
complement form.
Check it.

$\boxed{0\ 0\ 1\ 1}$ one's complement
image

$\boxed{0\ 0\ 0\ 1}$ add 1

$\boxed{0\ 1\ 0\ 0}$ check result (4)
= − answer

X is negative and Y is positive:

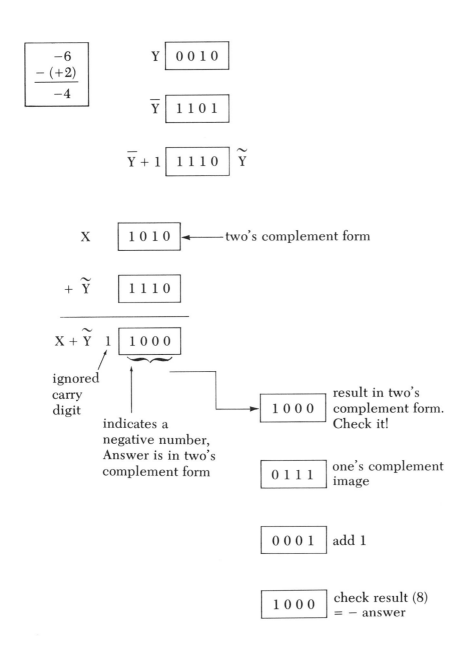

$$\begin{array}{r} -6 \\ -(+2) \\ \hline -4 \end{array}$$

Y | 0 0 1 0

$\overline{Y}$ | 1 1 0 1

$\overline{Y} + 1$ | 1 1 1 0 | $\widetilde{Y}$

X | 1 0 1 0 ←———— two's complement form

$+ \widetilde{Y}$ | 1 1 1 0

$X + \widetilde{Y}$ 1 | 1 0 0 0

ignored carry digit

indicates a negative number, Answer is in two's complement form

1 0 0 0 | result in two's complement form. Check it!

0 1 1 1 | one's complement image

0 0 0 1 | add 1

1 0 0 0 | check result (8) = − answer

X and Y are both negative:

$$\begin{array}{r} -3 \\ -(-2) \\ \hline -1 \end{array}$$

Y $\boxed{1\ 1\ 1\ 0}$ ←——two's complement form

$\overline{Y}$ $\boxed{0\ 0\ 0\ 1}$

$\overline{Y}$ +1 $\boxed{0\ 0\ 1\ 0}$ $\widetilde{Y}$

X $\boxed{1\ 1\ 0\ 1}$ ←——two's complement form

+ $\widetilde{Y}$ $\boxed{0\ 0\ 1\ 0}$

_____

X + $\widetilde{Y}$ $\boxed{1\ 1\ 1\ 1}$

indicates a
negative number
in two's
complement form

$\boxed{1\ 1\ 1\ 1}$ result in two's complement form
Check it.

$\boxed{0\ 0\ 0\ 1}$ one's complement image

$\boxed{0\ 0\ 0\ 1}$ add 1

$\boxed{0\ 0\ 0\ 1}$ check result (1)
= − answer

BINARY MULTIPLICATION

The details of binary multiplication are summarized in the next table:

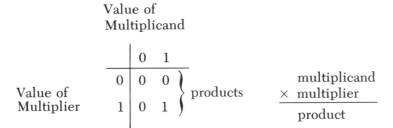

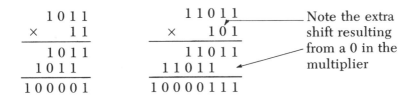

Examples of Multiplication with Positive Numbers

```
      1 0 1 1              1 1 0 1 1 _____ Note the extra
    ×     1 1            ×       1 0 1       shift resulting
    ─────────           ─────────────── ┐ from a 0 in the
      1 0 1 1              1 1 0 1 1     ┘ multiplier
    1 0 1 1             1 1 0 1 1  ◄
    ─────────          ───────────────
    1 0 0 0 0 1         1 0 0 0 0 1 1 1
```

In computers, binary multiplication can be accomplished by means of repeated sums and shifts. To show this, consider the three data registers shown in Figure 9.2. The top, or multiplicand register, holds the value of the multiplicand. The second register holds the value of the multiplier, while the final product is developed in the product register. Before the multiplication begins, the initial data values are stored in the respective registers while the bits of the product register are set to zero.

In operation, the first (right hand) bit of the multiplier register is examined. If it is a 1, the number stored the multiplicand register is added to the right side of the product register. If the first bit is a zero, nothing happens. In the next step, the bit patterns of the product and multiplier registers are shifted one bit position to the right. An examination of the first bit of the multiplier register is again made with an addition between the multiplicand and product register being made if the digit is a 1.

The basic cycle of addition and right shifting is continued until all m bits of the multiplier register have been examined. (The actual number of bits placed in the multiplier is n, where n ≤ m). At this point the multiplication is completed and the final result is stored in the product register. To accomodate the full result without a possibility of overflow,the product register must be able to contain 2m bits.

Negative numbers in binary multiplication require special attention. If the sign magnitude notation were used then the multiplication would procede as discussed before. The sign bits would not be multiplied, of course. Afterward, the sign bit of the product would be set appropriately. However, two's complement notatation is sufficiently different so that it is sometimes quicker to put the numbers in sign magnitude notation, carryout the multiplication, and then to convert back to two's complement form. There is a somewhat complicated way of doing the multiplication directly using numbers in two's complement form. The explanation of the method is given in more advanced texts.

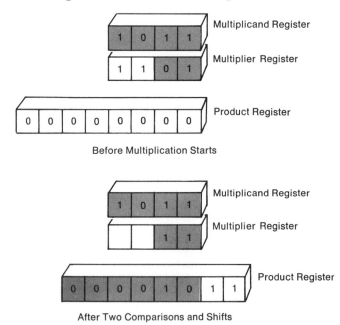

FIGURE 9.2. Schematic operation of a multiplication device.

BINARY DIVISION

Division in binary is similar to division in any other radix system. Essentially, we seek to find the number of times (the quotient) the denominator is contained in the numerator and how much of the numerator remains (the remainder) after this is done. The principles of binary division are illustrated here for positive integers only, because the extension to negative numbers and to fractional numbers is not difficult of accomplish once the basic operations have been defined.

$$\begin{array}{r}\text{quotient + remainder}\\ \text{denominator } \overline{)\ \text{numerator}}\end{array}$$

		Numerator N	
		0	1
Denominator	0	0	undefined
D	1	0	1

The most straightforward division method of computing N/D is to repeatedly subtract D from N until the resulting N would become smaller than D. Counting the number of subtractions gives the quotient, and the remaining part of the numerator N is the remainder. This is not the quickest way to do division (it might well be the longest), and it certainly is not the way we are accustomed to doing decimal division. (The division of 1,000,000 by 10 using this method would involve 100,000 subtractions.)

To accomplish division we have all been taught to divide 6784321 by 12 by writing $12\ \overline{)\ 7654321}$ rather than $\overline{7654321}\ (\ 12$. This implies that we start the subtraction process using the *leftmost* part of the numerator and then continue by working slowly to the right. Although it might not be immediately obvious, place value notation is being exploited here to shorten the work.

A typical binary division conducted by the familiar method of working from left to right would appear as follows:

$$\begin{array}{r}00011101\\ 101\ \overline{)\ 10010101}\\ -\ 101\\ \hline 1000101\\ -\ 101\\ \hline 011101\\ -\ 101\\ \hline 01001\\ -\ \ \ 101\\ \hline 0100\quad \text{remainder}\end{array}$$

$$\begin{array}{r}29\quad +4\\ 5\ \overline{)\ 149}\end{array}$$

$$\text{quotient} = [11101]_2 = 29$$
$$\text{remainder} = [100]_2 = 4$$

To be generally useful, the rules for this method need to be written in a detailed manner.

Our thinking goes something like this: Let N be the numerator and D be the denominator, both of which are positive whole (integer) numbers. If the denominator D is zero we abandon the division, because no answer exists in such a case. This is called a "divide fault" in computer usage. If D is non-zero,

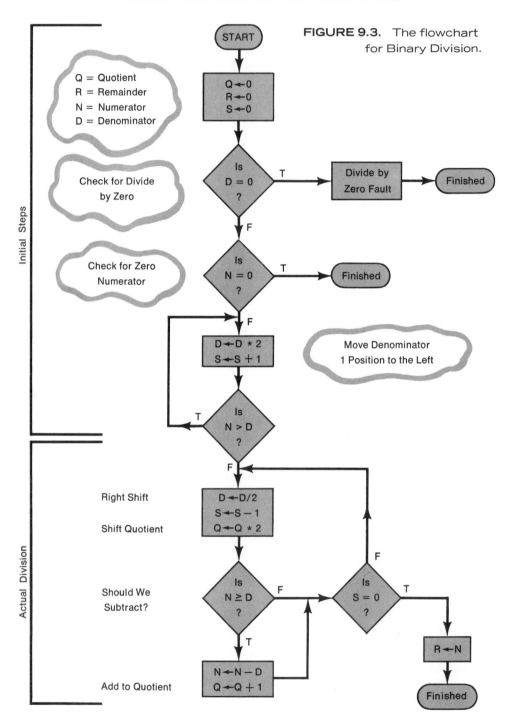

FIGURE 9.3. The flowchart for Binary Division.

then we check to see if the numerator N is zero, in which case we would, of course, obtain a zero result. One more preliminary check is made to see if the numerator is smaller than the denominator, in which case the quotient Q is clearly zero and the remainder R is just the numerator. The usual case is, however, that the numerator is larger than the denominator and we are expected to compute both the quotient and the remainder.

The division process then proceeds as follows: Move the denominator to the left as many bit positions as possible until one more move to the left would make it larger than the numerator. Effectively, the denominator D has been multiplied by 2^s where s represents the number of left shifts needed to achieve the arrangement above. In the example of dividing 10010101 by 101, the denominator 101 would be shifted left s = four bit positions. Five shifts would make D larger than N.

$$
\begin{array}{ll}
10010101 & \text{Numerator} \\
1010000 & \text{Denominator shifted left four places.}
\end{array}
$$

By our construction, the new D (1010000 in the example) is equal to or slightly smaller than the numerator N. Subtract D from N and enter a 1 in the 2^s bit position of the quotient.

$$
\begin{array}{ll}
10010101 & \text{Old numerator} \\
- \underline{1010000} & \text{$-$New denominator} \qquad (s = 4) \\
01000101 & \text{New numerator} \\
\\
1000 & \text{Quotient}
\end{array}
$$

The original denominator was thus contained in the numerator at least 2^s times. This clearly saves about 2^s continuous subtractions, so naturally we started by making s as large as possible. Repetition of the algorithm gives us the rest of the quotient and the remainder. The new numerator is, of course, now smaller than the (shifted) denominator due to the subtraction so we shift the denominator one place to the right and deduct 1 from s.

$$
\begin{array}{ll}
1000101 & \text{New numerator} \\
- \underline{101000} & \text{$-$New denominator} \ (s = 3) \\
01101 & \text{Still newer numerator} \\
\\
11000 & \text{Quotient}
\end{array}
$$

If N is still less than D, enter a 0 in the 2^s bit position of the quotient. Otherwise, subtract D from N and enter a 1 in the 2^s bit position of the quotient. This right shifting and possible subtracting continues until the final cycle is finished with s = 0. Whatever remains of the numerator is called the remainder R.

$$
\begin{array}{ll}
11101 & \text{Numerator} \\
-10100 & -\text{Denominator} \quad (s = 2) \\
\hline
01001 & \text{New numerator} \\
\end{array}
$$

$$11100 \leftarrow \text{Quotient}$$

$$
\begin{array}{ll}
1001 & \text{Numerator} \\
1010 & \text{Denominator} \quad (s = 1) \\
\hline
\end{array}
$$

No subtraction

$$11100 \leftarrow \text{Quotient}$$

$$
\begin{array}{ll}
1001 & \text{Numerator} \\
-0101 & -\text{Denominator} \quad (s = 0) \\
\hline
0100 & \text{Remainder} \\
\end{array}
$$

$$11101 \leftarrow \text{Quotient}$$

In effect, the process finds how many times $D * 2^s$ is contained in the numerator for each value of s, with s = 4. 3, 2, 1, 0, starting with the largest s. If the numerator consists of n bits and the denominator of d bits, with higher order bits all being zeroes, then there would be n − d cycles of shift and possible subtraction. This is much shorter than the brute force technique of successive subtractions. In the example, there would be a maximum of five shift/subtraction cycles (only four were needed) as compared to 29 or 30 subtractions of the simpler method. The quick method is summarized in the form of a flow chart in Figure 9.3. It might be noticed that if we were to allow s to assume negative values, then the integer remainder could be converted into a binary fraction. (In the example, the fraction 4/5 is the repeating pattern .11001100. . . .)

References to Further Readings

BARTEE, T. C.
 Digital Computer Fundamentals. New York: McGraw Hill, 1972.

NASHELSKY, L.,
 Digital Computer Theory. New York: John Wiley & Sons, 1966.

WOOLONS, D. J.
 Introduction to Digital Computer Design. London: McGraw Hill, 1972.

KEY WORDS AND PHRASES TO KNOW

ADDEND

AUGEND

BINARY ADDITION

BINARY INTEGERS

BINARY SUBTRACTION

CARRY OUT BIT

COMPLEMENTARY IMAGE

DENOMINATOR

DIFFERENCE

MINUEND

MULTIPLICAND

MULTIPLIER

ONE'S COMPLEMENT

PRODUCT

QUOTIENT

SUBTRAHEND

SUM

TWO'S COMPLEMENT

UNARY SUBTRACTION
  SYMBOL

EXERCISES

1. Perform the following binary additions:

   a. 10110
        100

   b. 101101
        11011

   c. 110110
       11101
         101

   d. 1111
       111
        11
         1

2. Perform the following binary subtractions without the method of complements:

   a. 10011
      −100

   b. 110110
      −101101

   c. 110110
      −1001

   d. 100011
      −11100

3. Using the method of complements, perform the following operations showing all steps, including one's and two's complement images and the interpretation of the final result:

   a. 110110 − (011010)
   b. 10110 − (110111)
   c. 1010 − (10001)
   d. −1011011 − (1010)

   e. −1111 − (10001)
   f. −1100110 − (−101)
   g. −1110 − (−110111)

4. Perform the indicated binary multiplications:

   a. 1011
      × 11

   b. 110011
      × 111

   c. 101
      × 10

   d. 100.01
      × 1110.

   e. 10.
      ×10.

   f. 101.1011
      × 11.10

5. Perform the binary divisions given below:

    a. $10110 \div 111$ d. $1.0 \div 11$
    b. $11011 \div 1001$ e. $1010. \div 100.$
    c. $101.1 \div 1.1$ f. $1101101 \div 1110$

6. Explain why addition and subtraction are easier with a number value system such as Roman numerals than with a place-value system such as decimal or binary.

PROBLEMS

1. In Problem 5 of Chapter Three a discussion was given of a method of multiplication used by Russian peasants. In essence, the method worked by forming two columns headed by the multiplicand and multiplier. One column is then divided successively by 2 until the number 1 is reached. The remaining column is multiplied by the factor of 2 the same number of times, row by row. Even numbers in the first column are then cancelled out; the corresponding number in the second column is also cancelled. The list of numbers of the second column, when added together, give the correct product.

    This method of multiplication can be readily accomplished using binary numbers. After practicing with several multiplications, explain why this is so. Express the method using the machine language instructions of the last chapter assuming that numbers are stored as binary integers in the computer memory.

2. The division process shown in Figure 9.3 can be written as a machine language code using the instruction set of the last chapter. Write the necessary program including sample READ, WRITE, and STOP instructions. This approach, using the instruction set to accomplish a data processing task, is a "software" or programming method. A "hardware" technique, actually used in most computers, accomplishes the same result by a digital device constructed along the principles described in the next chapter. In this case, although the task of division can be done in two ways, the "hardware" method is much faster and more economical. The price? An expensive specialized unit having only one function—division.

3. Along the direction given in Problem 2, suppose that a computer lacks a multiplier in its central processing unit. Even without such hardware it is possible to multiply two integer numbers, A and B, (stored in 24 bit words with bit 23 corresponding to sign) if a series of shifts and additions can be accomplished. Assuming the presence of a 48 bit product register and two additional 24 bit operand registers, write the machine code describing the steps needed to multiply the variables A and B. The presence of an overflow condition (the number bits of the integer result being greater than 23) should be noted with an appropriate PRINT instruction.

ten

Boolean Algebra

313

ALGEBRAS AND REALITY

The Islamic civilization transferred two extraordinary ideas to the Western World: The notion of place-value numbers and the mathematical foundations of modern algebra. As we have seen in previous chapters, place-value notation plays an important part in the functioning of computers, permitting numbers to be represented in several ways (as integers, as portions of numbers expressed in scientific notation) and providing the basic means of value identification (addresses) within the computer system. Now, we must turn to the more active reality of the computer in which data and instructions are continually examined and altered using various kinds of processing and guidance units. It is in this environment that algebra becomes important by providing a simple logical basis for the design of all digital units used within computer systems.

The electrical circuits of the digital units which function as adders, multipliers, comparators, instruction decoders or any of the other numerous specialized units contained with a computer system are rather complex. Quite appropriately, the details of the designs for these devices belong to the world of computer engineers in which electrical connections, voltages, currents and timing must all be given special attention. Underlying the practical complexity of these devices, however, is an internal structure which is based upon the rules of mathematical logic. Using these rules, it is possible to derive explicit equations describing the behavior of any digital device. Once these equations have been obtained, the general scheme of the internal circuitry necessary to implement the mathematical model can be devised using modern solid-state electronic devices. Thus, it is possible to specify the required functional nature of a digital unit. In addition, one can determine the basic internal structure using smaller structural units combined according to the logical structure of the problem.

The fundamental ideas behind the design of digital processing devices are not based upon bytes, words, or other bit groupings, but are derived from the

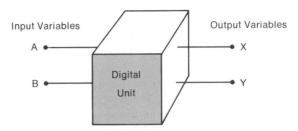

FIGURE 10.1. A view of a general digital unit which translates the initial values of A and B, into output values for X and Y.

two value character of binary variables (i.e., variables which can only have the values 0 or 1). In the design of digital devices, the values of one or more binary variables are given to a digital circuit which, through the action of certain internal operations, results in values being assigned to output binary variables. Clearly there is a direct link between the input values and the output results. The problem of digital design is to create the necessary internal circuits which will permit us to specify the output variable values for each combination of input values. (See Figure 10.1.)

To be more specific, suppose that we need to create a digital device which has the following properties:

a.   There are to be two independent variables, A and B
b.   There is to be one output variable, f
c.   When A = 0 and B = 0, then f = 0
         A = 0 and B = 1, then f = 1
         A = 1 and B = 0, then f = 1
         A = 1 and B = 1, then f = 0

A sketch of this device is shown in Figure 10.2 in schematic form. To judge the importance of a device having an output as specified by f one might consider the possible results occuring in the addition of two binary one digit numbers, here represented by the variables A and B. Clearly, the logic given by f is the first step of the complete description of a device needed for binary addition.

Using the functional statements given by property c listed above, it is necessary to ask how can one obtain an adequate mathematical description of the

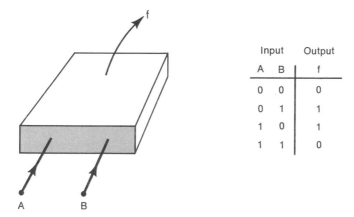

| Input | | Output |
A	B	f
0	0	0
0	1	1
1	0	1
1	1	0

FIGURE 10.2.   A simple digital device which reproduces the result of two bit addition without carries.

internal circuits which will give the desired values to f as A and B take on different values?

The answer to this question can be found in the way we use mathematics to describe relationships between objects in terms of symbols and systematic operations. The algebra taught in high schools, for example, permits quantitative reasoning through the use of certain rules governing the values which can be given to variables. In ordinary algebra these values include all real numbers while the rules correspond to the basic arithmetic operations and exponentiation. As a consequence, the variables of ordinary algebra can be given any value in the realm of real numbers irrespective of a particular number system. To illustrate this last point, a problem of algebra using the octal number system is given.

Example: Algebra with Octal Numbers

Two mathematicians, A and B, recently caught $(36)_8$ trout while fishing at Lake Octal. Fisherman A caught $(4)_8$ times as many fish as B. What were the respective catches?

To solve this problem, let the variables x and y represent the respective catches of A and B. Then, from the given relations we have

Total fish:	$x + y = (36)_8$
Ratio of fish:	$x = (4)_8 y$
giving	$(5)_8 y = (36)_8$
or	$y = (6)_8$ and $x = (30)_8$

Ordinary algebra is useful to us, because its variables and operations reflect the nature of our world. Within a world of two value variables, however, a new algebra must be used to describe the various possible relationships and operations between different quantities. At first glance it might appear that we could use our ordinary algebra with binary numbers to represent operations with two value variables. Further consideration, however, leads to the conclusion that the use of binary numbers with ordinary algebra will not help reproduce the discreteness needed for two value variables. The proper description of such quantities must be sought in a new algebra based upon two value variables and constants and a new set of basic operations. As described in the rest of this chapter, Boolean algebra meets these requirements and has proven to be of extraordinary value in describing the way that practical digital devices can be designed to transform any set of initial variable values into a desired set of output values.

THE IDEAS OF BOOLEAN ALGEBRA

Boolean algebra was developed in the middle of the nineteenth century by George Boole, an English mathematician who sought to provide a means for the rigorous analysis of problems of deductive logic (in which the values of variables and constants are taken as either TRUE and FALSE). This algebra, while mildly interesting to many mathematicians, remained essentially a curiosity until the late 1930s when Claude Shannon realized that it provided a description of the passage of electrical signals through networks of electrical switches, each of which could be opened or closed. Using the ideas of Boolean algebra, Shannon soon found that by arranging these switches in the proper way, groups of signals having binary values could be processed to simulate any digital transformation such as the operations of ordinary arithmetic or the routing of telephone calls through complicated circuits. As a consequence of these discoveries, Boolean algebra and its application to the logic of gates and switches provides an important tool for the design of digital devices and gives the basis for the design of internal digital processing networks of all modern computers.

To give a simple illustration of the way that practical problems can be transformed into an operating digital device consider the question. "Shall we go swimming?" The ultimate response to this question is either Yes or No, but the decision must depend upon the condition of certain variables. A few of these might be expressed as

"Yes, we will go swimming if:
   (a) the sun is shining and it is not too windy; or if
   (b) the sun is shining and the water is warm but, even if both
      (a) and (b) are true;
   (c) the car must have enough gas; or
   (d) there must be enough money to pay for gas."

As shown in the diagram of Figure 10.3, there are five independent variables in this problem (sun, wind, water temperature, gas, and money) which can have independent Yes or No values. The final digital device, shown in Figure 10.4, is built to give a single Yes or No answer when the values of the Boolean variables are given to it, (i.e., its internal structure correctly represents the logic of the verbal Boolean expression given above so that a single value—Yes or No—is assigned to the expression when values are given to the variables.) (See Figure 10.4.)

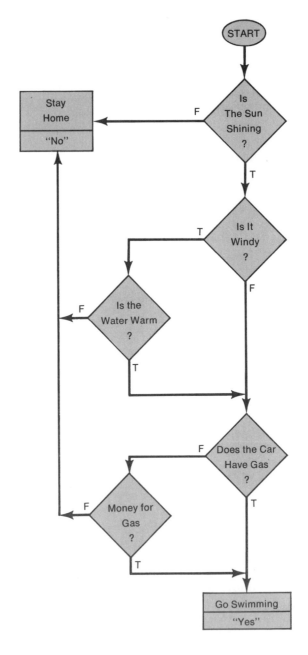

FIGURE 10.3. The internal logic of the digital decision maker shown as a YES/NO decision network.

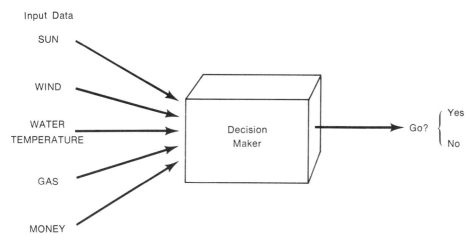

FIGURE 10.4. The function of the digital decision maker involves interpreting the initial values of five binary variables in terms of a final action variable, GO.

The ideas expressed in this simple example closely parallel those needed for the design of computer data processing devices. The values of different quantities can be used within a device (designed according to the rules of Boolean algebra) to give results which depend upon a series of logical statements. In the following sections the properties of Boolean algebra are discussed, then applied to the design of simple digital devices similar to the complex units actually used in computers.

THE FORMALITIES OF BOOLEAN ALGEBRA

The constants and variables of Boolean algebra are limited to the two discrete values, 1 and 0, which we identify as True and False, respectively. As in ordinary algebra, we are interested in using certain basic operations to define functional relationships between different variables and constants. The three fundamental tools of Boolean algebra are OR (+), AND (•), and NOT (−), operations we presented earlier in the discussion of logical variables. The definitions of these operations, given in figure 10.5, show the different results found when these operators are applied to the two possible values of Boolean variables and constants. Both the OR and AND operations are binary operators (meaning that the result depends on two quantities), while NOT is unary. NOT operates only on a single quantity.

The names for the Boolean operators follow directly from statements of the operational results: A AND B is TRUE only if A *and* B are individually TRUE.

while A OR B is TRUE when either A *or* B is TRUE. Finally, NOT A is TRUE only if A is FALSE.

In some ways OR and AND are somewhat similar to binary addition and multiplication. Comparison of the binary arithmetic tables of last chapter with the Boolean operations of Figure 10.5 shows that AND and multiplication are identical in form while the digit pattern of OR differs from the addition table only through the lack of a carry digit. As a consequence of these similarities, OR and AND operations are occasionally referred to as logical addition and multiplication.

<u>Boolean Operations</u>

<u>AND</u>

	B	
A · B	0	1
A 0	0	0
1	0	1

The result is true (1) only if *both* A *and* B are true individually.

<u>OR</u>

	B	
A + B	0	1
A 0	0	1
1	1	1

The result is true (1) if *either* A *or* B is true individually.

<u>NOT</u>

	$\overline{A}$
A 0	1
1	0

The result is true (1) if A is 0 and vice versa.

FIGURE 10.5.

The basic operations of Boolean algebra can be used to specify some important relationships. For Boolean constants, the definitions of Figure 10.5 can be used to give:

OR	AND
$0 + 0 = 0$	$0 \cdot 0 = 0$
$0 + 1 = 1$	$0 \cdot 1 = 0$
$1 + 0 = 1$	$1 \cdot 0 = 0$
$1 + 1 = 1$	$1 \cdot 1 = 1$

For combinations of single variables and constants the following relations can be derived:

$$A + 0 = A \tag{1a}$$
$$A \cdot 0 = 0 \tag{1b}$$

$$A + 1 = 1 \tag{2a}$$
$$A \cdot 1 = A \tag{2b}$$

$$A + A = A \tag{3a}$$
$$A \cdot A = A \tag{3b}$$

$$A + \overline{A} = 1 \tag{4a}$$
$$A \cdot \overline{A} = 0 \tag{4b}$$

$$\overline{(\overline{A})} = A \tag{5}$$

Finally, for variables taken together the following combinational relationships can be found

Commutative:

$$A + B = B + A \tag{6a}$$
$$A \cdot B = B \cdot A \tag{6b}$$

Associative:

$$(A + B) + C = A + (B + C) \tag{7a}$$
$$(A \cdot B) \cdot C = A \cdot (B \cdot C) \tag{7b}$$

Distributive:

$$(A + B) \cdot C = A \cdot C + B \cdot C \tag{8a}$$
$$(A + B) \cdot (A + C) = A + B \cdot C \tag{8b}$$

These last expressions emphasize the parallels existing between ordinary algebra and Boolean algebra. In the more complicated expressions we note the convention of precedence is such that AND operations must be done before OR operations, taking into account any intervening parentheses. Thus, the Boolean function $A + B \cdot C$ means $A + (B \cdot C)$ rather than $(A + B) \cdot C$.

The functional relationships (1) through (8) have been given without proof of their validity. While the simple relations between constants and constants and variables can be ascertained through inspection of the operation tables of Figure 10.5, the situation for the multivariable expressions (6) through (8) requires a greater sophistication with more formal proofs since their equality is not readily apparent.

The rigorous proof of the equality of Boolean functional expressions requires that we verify the equality of the left and right hand sides for *all* possible values of the variables. Since each variable can have only two values, it is possible and practicable to prove (or disprove) a particular relation by considering all combinations of values for the variable concerned.

To illustrate this method, consider the distributive relation

$$(A + B) \cdot (A + C) = A + B \cdot C \quad (8b)$$

In the table, the first column lists the eight possible combinations of values ($2^3 = 8$) for the variables A, B, and C. In succeeding columns the values of $(A + B)$, $(A + C)$, and $(A + B) \cdot (A + C)$ are computed using the definitions of the basic operations and the variable values. Next, the values of $B \cdot C$ and $(A + B \cdot C)$ are determined for all values of A, B, and C. In the final step, we must compare the row by row result for $(A + B) \cdot (A + C)$ and $(A + B \cdot C)$. If we find identical values for *all* rows (all values of A, B and C) we have proved the validity of the basic relationship. A single discrepancy, however, is sufficient to disprove the equality.

Example: Truth Table for $(A + B) \cdot (A + C) = A + B \cdot C$

All possible combinations of variable values			Left hand side of relation			Right hand side of relation	
A	B	C	$(A + B)$	$(A + C)$	$(A + B) \cdot (A + C)$	$(B \cdot C)$	$(A + B \cdot C)$
0	0	0	0	0	0	0	0
0	0	1	0	1	0	0	0
0	1	0	1	0	0	0	0
0	1	1	1	1	1	1	1
1	0	0	1	1	1	0	1
1	0	1	1	1	1	0	1
1	1	0	1	1	1	0	1
1	1	1	1	1	1	1	1

Left and right sides of equation give same values for all combinations of possible values for A, B, C.

This tabular method of proof is essentially one of exhaustive examination of all possible variable values. The table used to construct the different values of the variables is usually referred to as a *truth table* and the process itself is called the truth table method of proof. Another example of this technique is given here.

Example: Truth Table for $\overline{A + B} = \overline{A} \cdot \overline{B}$

A	B	A + B	$\overline{A + B}$	$\overline{A}$	$\overline{B}$	$\overline{A} \cdot \overline{B}$
0	0	0	1	1	1	1
0	1	1	0	1	0	0
1	0	1	0	0	1	0
1	1	1	0	0	0	0

Identical results show the expression is valid for all values of A and B.

A second method of the proof of equality between Boolean functions involves algebraic manipulation using the basic rules and theorems to reduce one side of the equation to equality with the other. For example, to prove again that

$$A + B \cdot C = (A + B) \cdot (A + C) \quad (8b)$$

we can carry out the steps shown, listing the justification (reference to prior proof) for each step in an extra column.

Example:

Show that: $A + B \cdot C = (A + B) \cdot (A + C)$

Step 1	$= (A + B) \cdot A + (A + B) \cdot C$	(8a)
2	$= A \cdot A + B \cdot A + A \cdot C + B \cdot C$	(8a)
3	$= A \quad + B \cdot A + A \cdot C + B \cdot C$	(3a)
4	$= A \cdot (1 + B) + A \cdot C + B \cdot C$	(8a)
5	$= A + A \cdot C + B \cdot C$	(2 a,b)
6	$= A \cdot (1 + C) + B \cdot C$	(8a)
7	$= A + B \cdot C$	(2 a,b)
	Q.E.D.	

As we shall see in the next section, the algebraic manipulations needed to prove basic theorems are also useful for the simplification of Boolean expressions.

A list of the most important elementary relationships of Boolean algebra is given below.

$$A + 0 = A \tag{1a}$$
$$A \cdot 0 = 0 \tag{1b}$$
$$A + 1 = 1 \tag{2a}$$
$$A \cdot 1 = A \tag{2b}$$
$$A + A = A \tag{3a}$$
$$A \cdot A = A \tag{3b}$$
$$A + \overline{A} = 1 \tag{4a}$$
$$A \cdot \overline{A} = 0 \tag{4b}$$
$$\overline{(\overline{A})} = A \tag{5}$$

Commutative
$$A + B = B + A \tag{6a}$$
$$A \cdot B = B \cdot A \tag{6b}$$

Associative
$$(A + B) + C = A + (B + C) \tag{7a}$$
$$(A \cdot B) \cdot C = A \cdot (B \cdot C) \tag{7b}$$

Distributive
$$A \cdot (B + C) = A \cdot B + A \cdot C \tag{8a}$$
$$(A + B) \cdot (A + C) = A + B \cdot C \tag{8b}$$

DeMorgan's laws $\Big\{$
$$\overline{A + B} = \overline{A} \cdot \overline{B} \tag{9a}$$
$$\overline{A \cdot B} = \overline{A} + \overline{B} \tag{9b}$$

$$A + A \cdot B = A \tag{10a}$$
$$A \cdot (A + B) = A \tag{10b}$$
$$A + \overline{A} \cdot B = A + B \tag{11}$$
$$A \cdot (\overline{A} + B) = A \cdot B \tag{12}$$
$$(A + B) \cdot (\overline{A} + C) = A \cdot C + \overline{A} \cdot B \tag{13}$$

The pair of relations (9a) and (9b) are know as DeMorgan's laws and give useful results for negation of Boolean functions involving AND and OR operators. In essence, they state: To negate any simple function of two quantities joined by an AND or by an OR operation we replace the AND with an OR (and vice versa) and negate each of the two quantities. If either quantity is composed of several terms then the negation can be carried out afterward on these as well by the same rule.

Example: Negate $A + \overline{B} \cdot C$

$$\overline{(A + \overline{B} \cdot C)} = \overline{A} \cdot \overline{(\overline{B} \cdot C)}$$
$$= \overline{A} \cdot (B + \overline{C})$$

Example: Negate $A \cdot B + \overline{C} \cdot \overline{D}$

$$\overline{A \cdot B + \overline{C} \cdot \overline{D}} = \overline{(A \cdot B)} \cdot \overline{(\overline{C} \cdot \overline{D})}$$
$$= (\overline{A} + \overline{B}) \cdot (C + D)$$
$$= \overline{A} \cdot C + \overline{B} \cdot C + \overline{A} \cdot D + \overline{B} \cdot D$$

Although the development of Boolean algebra can be continued past the level of Equations (1) through (13), these relations provide a satisfactory elementary basis for the description of the processing and control circuits used within computers. Thus, we will now proceed into the discussion of the way abstract Boolean algebra is used to create practical digital devices.

THE ALGEBRA OF GATES AND SWITCHES

Boolean algebra is concerned with two valued variables and the three basic operations $(+, \cdot, -)$ which can be performed on them. While this algebra was created for solving problems of mathematical logic, it applies equally well to the description of the behavior of electrical networks composed of active switching devices. In practical terms this means it is possible to convert any abstract Boolean expression composed of constants and variables from its mathematical form into a real electrical network which, in its operation, will faithfully reproduce the values of the Boolean expression for all values of the variables involved.

In modern computers transistors, diodes and more sophisticated solid-state components are used to perform the basic operations of Boolean algebra. The three basic functional units needed for Boolean expressions are: OR gates, AND gates, and an inverter (NOT). The functions of these units are normally represented as

Inputs   Output

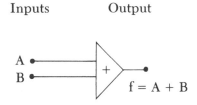

$f = A + B$

Inputs		Output
A	B	f
0	0	0
0	1	1
1	0	1
1	1	1

OR GATE

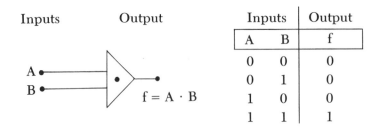

| Inputs | | Output |
A	B	f
0	0	0
0	1	0
1	0	0
1	1	1

AND GATE

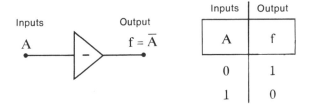

| Inputs | Output |
A	f
0	1
1	0

Invert (NOT)

Each device, or gate, is built so that when values (0s and 1s) are given to A and B (as electrical pulses) the resulting output value of the unit (0 or 1) corresponds to the particular logical operation. Using combinations of these three devices, we can construct logical circuits which reproduce the complexities of any Boolean function.

For a practical example, consider a Boolean function such as $f = A + B \cdot C$. The value of f will be 0 or 1, depending upon the values chosen for A, B, and C (only 0s or 1s, of course). The logical circuit corresponding to this function looks like

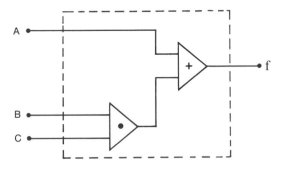

Following the rule of precedence (AND before OR) the value B • C is first obtained in an AND gate. This result is then combined with A in the OR gate to give the final Boolean expression, f. Now, when values are given to A, B, and C, the values for f will be exactly those given by the original Boolean function.

Using the three basic gates and obeying the precedence rule, we can readily devise circuits to match any Boolean function. Several examples of the method are shown below

Example: $f = A \cdot B + \overline{A} \cdot \overline{B}$

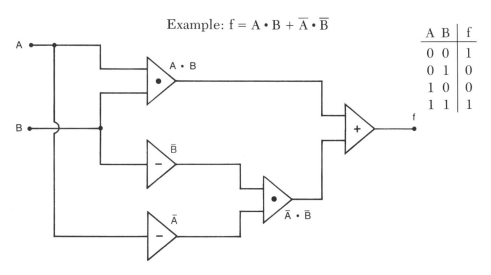

A B	f
0 0	1
0 1	0
1 0	0
1 1	1

Example: $f = A \cdot \overline{B} + \overline{A} \cdot B$ (This is called an *Exclusive OR*)

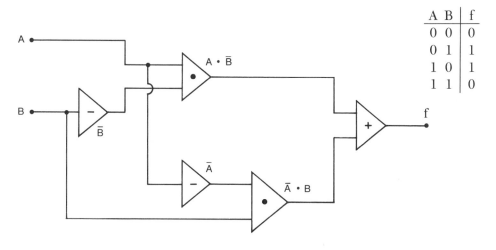

A B	f
0 0	0
0 1	1
1 0	1
1 1	0

Although the logic gates used by computers involve very specialized devices, it is possible to think about these units in terms of simple electrical switches. To show this, suppose we have two switches, which are named A and B, a source of power (12 volts), and a light bulb. Using the parallel switch arrangement shown below, we can reproduce the Boolean OR operation as A + B = state of lightbulb.

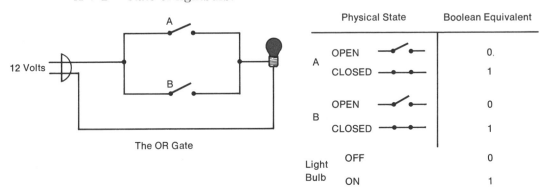

The OR Gate

When *either* A *or* B is CLOSED (state 1) current will flow through the circuit causing the light bulb to go ON (state 1). When both A and B are OPEN (state 0), no current flows and the light bulb is OFF (state 0). If we let the Boolean variable f represent the state of the light bulb, then the simple OR circuit above describes A + B = f.

A second arrangment of the switches can be used to describe the Boolean AND function. In the series connection shown below, when both A and B are CLOSED (state 1), the light bulb is ON (state 1) while if *either* A *or* B is OPEN (state 0), no current can flow and the light bulb is OFF. This circuit is a physical representation of the expression f = A • B, where f is again the state of the light bulb. (If you find the electrical circuits confusing then imagine the wires as water pipes and the switches as valves. The true result in this analogy is then the flow of water through the piping system.)

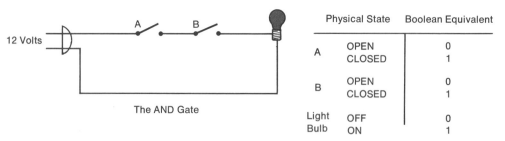

The AND Gate

The third fundamental operation of Boolean algebra, negation, unfortunately cannot be done using switches alone, but requires the presence of an active circuit element, such as an electromagnet, that can invert values (i.e., change yes to no and vice versa).

Some examples of simple Boolean functions and their equivalent switching circuits are shown in Figure 10.6. The presence of OR implies the use of a parallel arrangement, while AND is made with a series connection. It is possible to decompose any Boolean expression into a real circuit composed of properly connected switches and NOT units.

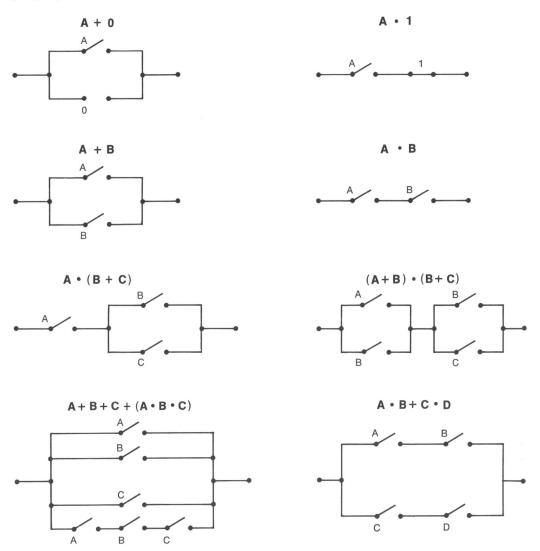

FIGURE 10.6. The switch states of some Boolean functions.

LOGICAL DESIGN

From the results of the last section we have found it possible to construct electrical circuits which behave according to the rules of Boolean algebra. We now wish to consider the next step of logical design whereby the operations of processes such as addition, subtraction, comparison, and so forth are expressed in terms of Boolean functions. Once these functions are obtained an electric circuit using electronic gates (or switches) can be readily constructed to convert the initial values of specified Boolean variables into the desired set of output values.

To show how logical design can be done, let us consider the simple household problem of designing a two switch lighting system for a hallway. At either end of the hall we have a switch; we can identify the two switches as A and B. When both A and B are off, the hall light should be off; If either A or B is on, the light bulb should be lit. Finally, when A and B are both on, the light should be off.

To formalize the logic of the situation, the table below shows all possible combinations of states for A and B and the desired output of the light bulb. The characters 0 and 1 correspond, of course, to the states OFF and ON for both the switches and the hall light.

A	B	Lightbulb
0	0	0
0	1	1
1	0	1
1	1	0

To proceed further, we need to be able to express f, the state of the light bulb, in terms of A and B. (i.e. we must construct a logical expression involving A, B and the three operations AND, OR, NOT in a way which reproduces the values for f for the variable values given in the function table.) One easy way to do this is to make a series of logical statements about the function f. If, for consistency, we let $0 \rightarrow$ FALSE and $1 \rightarrow$ TRUE, we can examine the function table and express the value of the function f as:

$$\text{when f is TRUE, then } \overline{A} \text{ and B are TRUE}$$
$$\text{or A and } \overline{B} \text{ are TRUE}$$

We see that each of the rows of the function table gives both the value of f and the conditions for A and B. Direct conversion of the logical expression to its Boolean functional form can be made by substituting an equal sign (=) for then, an AND sign ($\cdot$) for and, and an OR sign (+) for or.

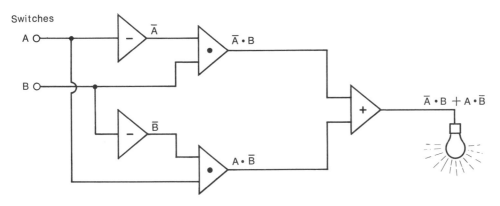

$$A \quad ON \rightarrow 1 \qquad B \quad ON \rightarrow 1$$
$$A \quad OFF \rightarrow 0 \qquad B \quad OFF \rightarrow 0$$

FIGURE 10.7. Logic circuit for a Two-way hall light.

Thus,
$$f = \overline{A} \cdot B + A \cdot \overline{B}$$

is the correct Boolean functional form which gives the proper values to f for different combinations of A and B. The same results could be achieved by considering the cases for which f is FALSE.

Using electronic logic gates, a circuit can now be constructed to implement the function f (see Figure 10.7).

While the circuit shown above is perfectly adequate for computer usage, our problem of a simple hallway lighting system requires one more step. Thus, we need to rearrange the conncections of Figure 10.7 using series and parallel switches to carry out logical AND and OR functions. The result is shown in Figure 10.8. We note that a two way light switch is actually two switches in one. By throwing the external switch lever to ON or OFF we open and close *two* internal switches to produce A and $\overline{A}$ so that if A is ON (closed circuit), $\overline{A}$ if OFF (open circuit) and vice versa.

To give further insight in the derivation of Boolean expressions and equivalent circuits, consider the arbitrary function table shown below:

A	B	f
0	0	0
0	1	1
1	0	1
1	1	1

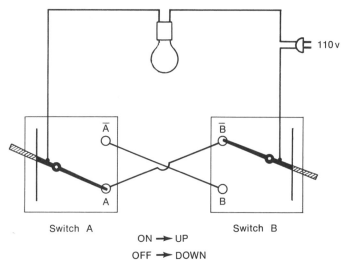

Switch A　　　　　　　　Switch B

ON → UP
OFF → DOWN

When A is ON and B is OFF, light is ON
When A is OFF and B is ON, light is ON

When A and B are OFF or A and B are ON,
light is OFF

FIGURE 10.8. A schematic diagram of the way a two-way lighting system works. Note the construction of the switches which expresses the logic of Figure 10.7.

Using our previous method, the logical statement for f can be written as

> When f is TRUE, then $\overline{A}$ and B are TRUE
> or A and $\overline{B}$ are TRUE
> or A and B are TRUE

Thus,

$$f = \overline{A} \cdot B + A \cdot \overline{B} + A \cdot B$$

Before proceeding with the actual circuit for f, we see in advance that seven separate gates will be required (two inverters, two ORs, three ANDs). At this point it is legitimate to ask whether the circuit based on this function will be as economical as possible (i.e., will it use a minimum number of electronic components?)

Let us consider the function again:

$$f = \overline{A} \cdot B + A \cdot \overline{B} + A \cdot B$$

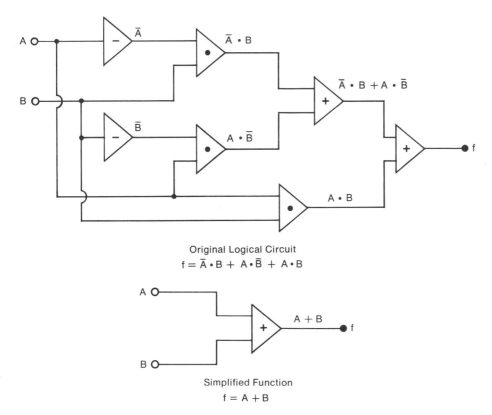

Original Logical Circuit

$$f = \overline{A} \cdot B + A \cdot \overline{B} + A \cdot B$$

Simplified Function

$$f = A + B$$

FIGURE 10.9. Illustrating the simplification of a Boolean expression using the rules of Boolean algebra.

If we regroup terms as

$$f = \overline{A} \cdot B + A \cdot \overline{B} + A \cdot B = (\overline{A} + A) \cdot B + A \cdot \overline{B}$$

we can use several basic relations given in the first part of this chapter to obtain

$$f = B + A \cdot \overline{B} = B + A$$

This simplified function still represents the desired states, but instead of the previous seven gates it now requires only one device, an OR gate, as shown in Figure 10.9.

The simplification of Boolean expressions is an important task of computer designers who are concerned not only with logical function, but the economic factors associated with circuits. Advanced techniques and even computer programs have been developed to ensure that functions are expressed in their simplest possible form. The advantages gained from simplification are shown in the next example.

Example: Given the arbitrary three variable function table shown below, find an expression for f which involves a minimum number of electronic gates.

A	B	C	f
0	0	0	0
0	0	1	1
0	1	0	0
0	1	1	1
1	0	0	0
1	0	1	1
1	1	0	0
1	1	1	1

When f is TRUE, then $\overline{A}$ and $\overline{B}$ and C are TRUE
or $\overline{A}$ and B and C are TRUE
or A and $\overline{B}$ and C are TRUE
or A and B and C are TRUE

Thus,

$$
\begin{aligned}
f &= \overline{A} \cdot \overline{B} \cdot C + \overline{A} \cdot B \cdot C + A \cdot \overline{B} \cdot C + A \cdot B \cdot C \quad \text{(13 gates)} \\
&= \overline{A} \cdot C \cdot (\overline{B} + B) + A \cdot C \cdot (\overline{B} + B) \quad\quad\quad \text{(9 gates)} \\
&= \overline{A} \cdot C + A \cdot C \quad\quad\quad\quad\quad\quad\quad\quad\quad\quad \text{(4 gates)} \\
&= (\overline{A} + A) \cdot C \quad\quad\quad\quad\quad\quad\quad\quad\quad\quad\quad \text{(3 gates)} \\
f &= C \quad\quad\quad\quad\quad\quad\quad\quad\quad\quad\quad\quad\quad\quad \text{(0 gates)}
\end{aligned}
$$

The output function f is the same as the Boolean variable C and does not depend upon the values of either A or B. This result could also have been found from an inspection of the function table.

As a final problem we can return to our original illustrative example of the digital decision maker needed to decide whether or not to go swimming. If we name the variables as shown below, a five variable decision table can be constructed.

Variable	Name
sun	SUN
wind speed	WIND
water temperature	TEMP
gas for car	GAS
money for gas	MONEY

Digital Decision Maker
"Shall we go swimming?"

SUN	WIND	TEMP	GAS	MONEY	f
1	0	1	1	0	1
1	0	0	1	0	1
1	0	1	0	1	1
1	0	0	0	1	1
1	1	1	1	0	1
1	1	1	0	1	1
1	1	1	1	1	1

All other cases (25) lead to a zero value for f

It is apparent that this decision table is slightly different than those made previously since only combinations of variables which lead to a Yes (1) value are listed. However, it is just these terms which are sufficient to allow us to derive the form of the logical expression f.

As before,

when f is TRUE, the SUN and $\overline{\text{WIND}}$ and TEMP and GAS and $\overline{\text{MONEY}}$ are TRUE
  or SUN and $\overline{\text{WIND}}$ and $\overline{\text{TEMP}}$ and GAS and $\overline{\text{MONEY}}$ are TRUE
  or SUN and $\overline{\text{WIND}}$ and TEMP and $\overline{\text{GAS}}$ and MONEY are TRUE
  or SUN and $\overline{\text{WIND}}$ and $\overline{\text{TEMP}}$ and $\overline{\text{GAS}}$ and MONEY are TRUE
  or SUN and WIND and TEMP and GAS and $\overline{\text{MONEY}}$ are TRUE
  or SUN and WIND and TEMP and $\overline{\text{GAS}}$ and MONEY are TRUE
  or SUN and WIND and TEMP and GAS and MONEY are TRUE

Conversion to the Boolean functional form gives

$$f = SUN \cdot \overline{WIND} \cdot TEMP \cdot GAS \cdot \overline{MONEY} +$$
$$SUN \cdot \overline{WIND} \cdot TEMP \cdot GAS \cdot \overline{MONEY} +$$
$$SUN \cdot \overline{WIND} \cdot TEMP \cdot \overline{GAS} \cdot MONEY +$$
$$SUN \cdot \overline{WIND} \cdot TEMP \cdot GAS \cdot MONEY +$$
$$SUN \cdot WIND \cdot TEMP \cdot GAS \cdot \overline{MONEY} +$$
$$SUN \cdot WIND \cdot TEMP \cdot \overline{GAS} \cdot MONEY +$$
$$SUN \cdot WIND \cdot TEMP \cdot GAS \cdot MONEY$$

involving many gates in this unreduced form. Successive simplifications using the basic relations of Boolean algebra lead to the final form

$$f = SUN \cdot (\overline{WIND} + TEMP) \cdot (GAS + MONEY)$$

which is composed of 5 electronic gates in the arrangement shown in Figure 10.10. This circuit, if provided with appropriate real connections, power, etc., would provide the logical decision making capability essential to the device of Figure 10.4.

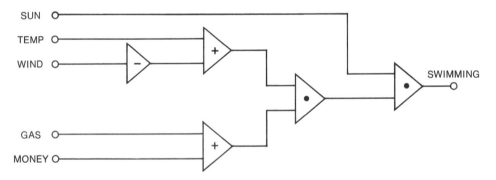

FIGURE 10.10. The final form of the Swimming Decisions maker implemented by AND, OR, and NOT logic gates.

A PRACTICAL APPLICATION OF LOGICAL DESIGN

Let us now consider a more practical problem. Suppose we wish to design a device (called an adder) which will add two binary numbers together to obtain a binary sum. An addition of two typical numbers is shown below

$$\begin{array}{lccccc}
 & \textcircled{1} & \longleftarrow & \text{a carry digit} & & \\
\text{number A} & 1 & 0 & 1 & 1 & 0 \\
\text{number B} & 0 & 0 & 0 & 1 & 1 \\
\hline
\text{sum} & 1 & 1 & 0 & 0 & 1
\end{array}$$

The addition begins with the right most bits and continues to the left with the addition including both the bits of the two numbers and the possible carry in bit from the next right, or previous, addition. For the first addition no carry in digit will be present, but each succeeding sum of digits must involve three bits. To show the carry digits explicitly, the above example can be rewritten as

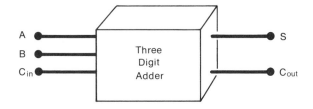

	carry out			carry in
carry digit	0 1	1	0	0
number A	1	0	1	1 0
number B	0	0	0	1 1
sum	0 1	1	0	0 1

The digital device we wish to design looks like Figure 10.11.

A
B
C_{in}

Three
Digit
Adder

S
C_{out}

FIGURE 10.11. The outside view of a three digit machine to be used as a part of a computer adder.

We will feed succeeding bits of A, B and the carry in digit (C_{in}) into our device. The sum digit will represent the sum of the three digits with a new carry out digit being generated and returned to the input in time to be added with the next group of bits taken from the two numbers being added.

The function table for our adding device follows the usual rules of three number addition with the extra novelty of *two* output functions:

A	B	Carry In Digit C_{in}	Sum S	New Carry Out Digit C_{out}
0	0	0	0	0
0	0	1	1	0
0	1	0	1	0
0	1	1	0	1
1	0	0	1	0
1	0	1	0	1
1	1	0	0	1
1	1	1	1	1

The logical statements for the two output functions S and C_{out} are:

$$\text{when S is TRUE then } \overline{A} \text{ and } \overline{B} \text{ and } C_{in} \text{ is TRUE}$$
$$\text{or } \overline{A} \text{ and } B \text{ and } \overline{C}_{in} \text{ is TRUE}$$
$$\text{or } A \text{ and } \overline{B} \text{ and } \overline{C}_{in} \text{ is TRUE}$$
$$\text{or } A \text{ and } B \text{ and } C_{in} \text{ is TRUE}$$

and

$$\text{when } C_{out} \text{ is TRUE then } \overline{A} \text{ and } B \text{ and } C_{in} \text{ is TRUE}$$
$$\text{or } A \text{ and } \overline{B} \text{ and } C_{in} \text{ is TRUE}$$
$$\text{or } A \text{ and } B \text{ and } \overline{C}_{in} \text{ is TRUE}$$
$$\text{or } A \text{ and } B \text{ and } C_{in} \text{ is TRUE}$$

Thus,

$$S = \overline{A} \cdot \overline{B} \cdot C_{in} + \overline{A} \cdot B \cdot \overline{C}_{in} + A \cdot \overline{B} \cdot \overline{C}_{in} + A \cdot B \cdot C_{in}$$

and

$$C_{out} = \overline{A} \cdot B \cdot C_{in} + A \cdot \overline{B} \cdot C_{in} + A \cdot B \cdot \overline{C}_{in} + A \cdot B \cdot C_{in}$$

Although these functions seem amenable to simplification, the best that can be done is

$$S = \overline{C}_{in} \cdot (A \cdot \overline{B} + \overline{A} \cdot B) + C_{in} \cdot \overline{(A \cdot \overline{B} + \overline{A} \cdot B)}$$

$$C_{out} = C_{in} \cdot (A + B) + A \cdot B$$

Using these functions, the digit by digit adder unit looks like Figure 10.12 when Exclusive-OR gates are not available.

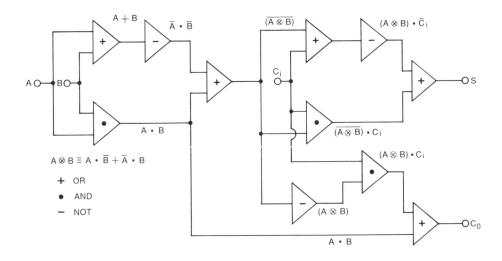

FIGURE 10.12. The logic circuit of a full adder using only AND, OR, and NOT gates.

Addition units in a computer processing unit can be built in two ways. *Serial* addition, shown below, involves two initial data registers, an adder, and a sum register. The two numbers to be added are stored in the two registers and the initial carry in bit (C_{in}) is set to zero. The right most bits of the two registers are then fed into the adder and a sum digit and a carry digit are generated. The sum digit is then placed in the left most bit position of the sum register, the carry out digit, C_{out}, is placed in the carry in input on the adder, the digits in the two number registers and the sum register are shifted one bit position to the right, and the entire summing process is repeated.

One difficulty with serial addition is in its slowness, because n bit addition will take n separate time steps. A better scheme avoids this difficulty to a large extent by providing in separate adders as shown in Figure 10.14. Each adder transmits its carry bit to the next left adder so that the entire addition can be done for all bits in the two data registers in just slightly more time than it takes for the carries to "ripple through" the string of adders. The time previously needed for shifting registers has been saved. The disadvantage with this scheme, of course, is its expense. An even faster method for addition has been

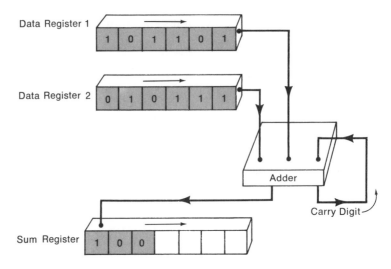

FIGURE 10.13.   A simple serial adder (one digit at a time).

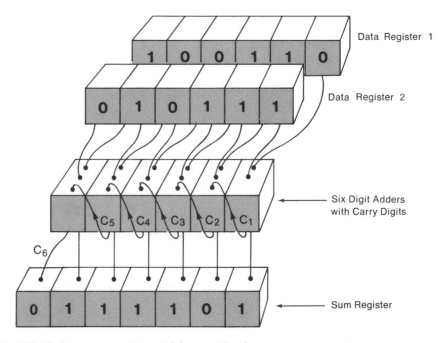

FIGURE 10.14.   A parallel addition method.

devised which does the bit by bit adding nearly simultaneously for all bit positions using adders and some preceding logic which precompute the carry-in bit for each adder. This parallel addition technique is called carry-look-ahead addition and it is used on almost all modern machines even though much more expensive than pure serial or parallel addition.

Although we have emphasized the design of a unit to perform binary addition, the technique of logical design using Boolean algebra and electronic gates is completely general. It is possible to create enormously complex structures which, when given the values of a set of bits will produce answers according to a particular logical network. The trick in making such networks useful, of course, lies in the logical analysis connecting the desired operations with the rules of Boolean algebra.

REFERENCES TO FURTHER READINGS

NASHELSKY, L.
Digital Computer Theory. New York: John Wiley & Sons, 1966.

PEATMAN, J. B.
The Design of Digital Systems. New York: McGraw Hill, 1972.

KEY WORDS AND PHRASES TO KNOW

ADDER

ALGEBRA

AND

BINARY OPERATOR

*BOOLEAN FUNCTIONAL
   EXPRESSIONS*

DE MORGAN'S LAW

EXCLUSIVE-OR

LOGIC GATE

LOGICAL DESIGN

NOT

OR

PARALLEL ADDITION

PROOF OF EQUALITY

SERIAL ADDITION

*SIMPLIFICATION OF
   BOOLEAN EXPRESSIONS*

TRUTH TABLE

UNARY

EXERCISES

1. Using truth tables, prove the following laws of Boolean algebra:

   a. $A \cdot (B + C) = A \cdot B + A \cdot C$ c. $\overline{A \cdot B} = \overline{A} + \overline{B}$

   b. $\overline{A + B} = \overline{A} \cdot \overline{B}$ d. $\overline{A} \cdot B + A \cdot \overline{B} = (A + B) \cdot (\overline{A} + \overline{B})$

2. Simplify the following Boolean expressions:

   a. $(A \cdot B + C) \cdot A$ d. $\overline{B \cdot C + A \cdot B}$

   b. $\overline{A} \cdot B + A$ e. $\overline{A \cdot B \cdot C + D \cdot \overline{A}}$

   c. $\overline{A} \cdot B + A \cdot B + \overline{A} \cdot \overline{B}$

3. Using the algebraic method of proof, prove the following relations:

   a. $M + \overline{M} \cdot N = M + N$

   b. $(A + B) \cdot \overline{(A \cdot B)} = A \cdot \overline{B} + \overline{A} \cdot B$

   c. $(X + \overline{Y}) \cdot (\overline{X} + Y) = X \cdot Y + \overline{X} \cdot \overline{Y}$

   d. $A \cdot (1 + \overline{C}) + B \cdot C + \overline{A} \cdot B = A + B$

4. Construct logical circuits composed of AND, OR and NOT gates for each of the following Boolean functions:

   a. $f = (A + B) \cdot (\overline{A} + B)$

   b. $f = A \cdot B + \overline{A} \cdot \overline{B}$

   c. $f = X \cdot (Y + Z) + \overline{X} + \overline{(Y \cdot Z)}$

   d. $f = A \cdot B \cdot C + \overline{A} \cdot \overline{B} + C$

   e. $f = (U + V) \cdot (W + X) + \overline{(\overline{U} + V) \cdot (W + \overline{X})}$

5. Find the Boolean expressions appropriate to describe the operation of each of the logical circuits shown below:

   a)

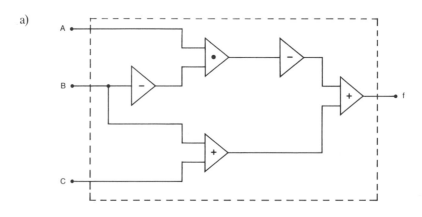

b)

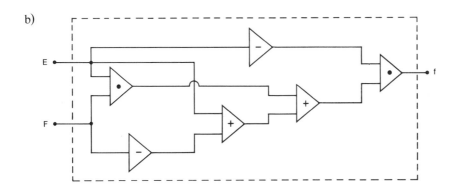

c)

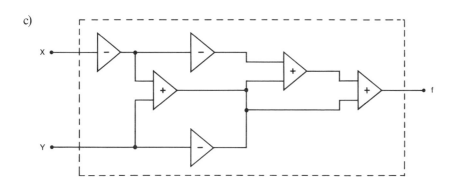

d)

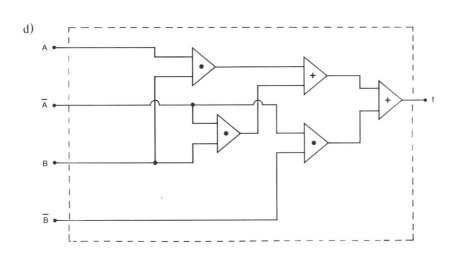

6. Write out the Boolean functional expressions corresponding to the following statements. Simplify where possible.

   a. Skiing is fun: if the sun is shining, the snow is not too deep, and I have a companion (independent of the wind or my type of skis); or if the sun is not shining, there must be deep snow, no wind, and I must have my fast skis; or, if it is snowing, I must have a companion, my fast skis, and no wind.

   b. We can study together, if the library is open and there are two adjacent seats. Even if this is so, you must have homework to do and I must have already completed my math assignment and be in the proper mood to work with you.

   c. A fire can burn only when oxygen, heat, and fuel are present.

PROBLEMS

1. Suppose that you wish to build a two bit adder which takes two bits and forms their sum according to the following table:

A	B	S	C_{out}
0	0	0	0
0	1	1	0
1	0	1	0
1	1	0	1

   Write the functional expressions for the sum digit, S, and the carry out digit, C_{out}, then construct a logical circuit having the two outputs S and C_{out}.

   Using the two bit adder, which is also called a half-adder, simplify the design of the full three bit adder described in the text.

2. Design a device that will subtract two binary digits and indicate the need for a borrow operation from the next left position. (Note that complements are not to be used here.) The function table is shown below:

X	Y	D	B_{out}
0	0	0	0
0	1	1	1
1	0	1	0
1	1	0	0

   Simplify the resulting expressions for the difference bit D and the borrow bit B_{out}.

3. A full subtractor is a device which operates using two input bits (the two being subtracted) and the borrow generated from the next lower order subtraction. The function table for full subtraction is shown below.

X	Y	B_{in}	D	B_{out}
0	0	0	0	0
0	0	1	1	1
0	1	0	1	1
0	1	1	0	1
1	0	0	1	0
1	0	1	0	0
1	1	0	0	0
1	1	1	1	1

Using the values given in the function table derive expressions for the difference D and borrow bit B_{out} and design the necessary logical circuits. Simplify where possible.

4. Design a circuit for two bit multiplication.

5. We wish to design a digital unit capable of computing the two's complement of any positive four bit binary number. If the digits of the initial number are represented as $d_3 d_2 d_1 d_0$ and the final number appears as $c_3 c_2 c_1 c_0$, the function table can be written as shown below:

d_3	d_2	d_1	d_0	c_3	c_2	c_1	c_0
0	0	0	0	0	0	0	0
0	0	0	1	1	1	1	1
0	0	1	0	1	1	1	0
0	0	1	1	1	1	0	1
0	1	0	0	1	1	0	0
0	1	0	1	1	0	1	1
0	1	1	0	1	0	1	0
0	1	1	1	1	0	0	1
1	0	0	0	1	0	0	0
1	0	0	1	0	1	1	1
1	0	1	0	0	1	1	0
1	0	1	1	0	1	0	1
1	1	0	0	0	1	0	0
1	1	0	1	0	0	1	1
1	1	1	0	0	0	1	0
1	1	1	1	0	0	0	1

d_3 d_2 d_1 d_0

two's complementer

c_3 c_2 c_1 c_0

Find the necessary expressions for c_3, c_2, c_1, c_0 and construct the corresponding logical circuits. Simplify where possible.

6. Design a circuit that compares two bits, A and B, to give an output 1 when A and B are the same and a 0 when A and B are different.

7. Design a "majority rule" network that takes three binary inputs and yields an output which agrees with at least two of the three input values.

8. Design a "three-out-of-four" majority rule network that yields an output which indicates a 1 when three or four of the inputs are 1, but gives 0 otherwise.

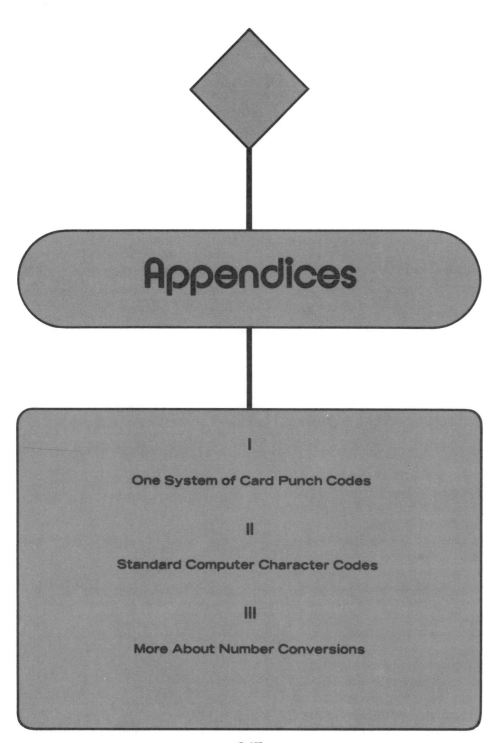

Appendices

APPENDIX I

One System of Card Punch Codes

External Symbol	Card Punch Code	External Symbol	Card Punch Code
A	12-1	0	0
B	12-2	1	1
C	12-3	2	2
D	12-4	3	3
E	12-5	4	4
F	12-6	5	5
G	12-7	6	6
H	12-8	7	7
I	12-9	8	8
J	11-1	9	9
K	11-2	[	12-8-2
L	11-3	.	12-8-3
M	11-4	<	12-8-4
N	11-5	(	12-8-5
O	11-6	+	12-8-6
P	11-7	|	12-8-7
Q	11-8	&	12
R	11-9	]	11-8-2
S	0-2	$	11-8-3
T	0-3	*	11-8-4
U	0-4	)	11-8-5
V	0-5	;	11-8-6
W	0-6	¬	11-8-7
X	0-7	− (minus)	11
Y	0-8	/	0-1
Z	0-9	\	0-8-2
		,	0-8-3
		%	0-8-4
		—	0-8-5
		>	0-8-6
		?	0-8-7
		:	8-2
		#	8-3
		@	8-4
		'	8-5
		=	8-6
		"	8-7

Standard Computer Character Codes

Character	EBCDIC	Hexadecimal Equivalent	SBCD	Octal Equivalent
A	1100 0001	C1	010 001	21
B	1100 0010	C2	010 010	22
C	1100 0011	C3	010 011	23
D	1100 0100	C4	010 100	24
E	1100 0101	C5	010 101	25
F	1100 0110	C6	010 110	26
G	1100 0111	C7	010 111	27
H	1100 1000	G8	011 000	30
I	1100 1001	C9	011 001	31
J	1101 0001	D1	100 001	41
K	1101 0010	D2	100 010	42
L	1100 0011	D3	100 011	43
M	1101 0100	D4	100 100	44
N	1101 0101	D5	100 101	45
O	1101 0110	D6	100 110	46
P	1101 0111	D7	100 111	47
Q	1101 1000	D8	101 000	50
R	1101 1001	D9	101 001	51
S	1110 0010	E2	110 010	62
T	1110 0011	E3	110 011	63
U	1110 0100	E4	110 100	64
V	1110 0101	E5	110 101	65
W	1110 0110	E6	110 110	66
X	1110 0111	E7	110 111	67
Y	1110 1000	E8	111 000	70
Z	1110 1001	E9	111 001	71
0	1111 0000	F0	000 000	00
1	1111 0001	F1	000 001	01
2	1111 0010	F2	000 010	02
3	1111 0011	F3	000 011	03
4	1111 0100	F4	000 100	04
5	1111 0101	F5	000 101	05
6	1111 0110	F6	000 110	06
7	1111 0111	FF7	000 111	07
8	1111 1000	F8	001 000	10
9	1111 1001	9	001 001	11

Character	EBCDIC	Hexadecimal Equivalent	SBCD	Octal Equivalent
blank	0100 0000	40	110 000	60
.	0100 1011	4B	110 010	32
+	0100 1100	4E	010 000	20
−	0110 0000	60	100 000	40
*	0101 1100	5C	101 100	54
/	0110 0001	61	110 001	61
[	0100 1010	4A	001 111	17
]	0101 1010	5A	111 010	72
$	0101 1011	5B	101 011	53
>	0110 1110	6E	101 111	57
=	0111 1110	7E	001 011	13
<	0100 1100	4C	011 010	32
,	0110 1011	6B	111 011	73
:	0111 1010	7A	001 010	12
@	0111 1100	7C	none	none
(	0100 1101	4D	111 100	74
)	0101 1101	5D	011 100	34

APPENDIX III

More About Number Conversion

Suppose that we wish to convert a number $[N]_r$ in the radix r system into its equivalent $[\mathcal{N}]_t$ in the radix t system. Using radix point notation, the number $[N]_r$ is written as

$$[N]_r = [M \bullet W]_r$$

— radix integer
— radix fraction
— radix point

Through the division and multiplication operations described below, it is possible to rapidly find the *separate* conversions $[M]_r = [\mathcal{M}]_t$ and $[W]_r = [\mathcal{W}]_t$ so that

$$[\mathcal{N}]_t = [\mathcal{M} \bullet \mathcal{W}]_t$$

Algorithm to convert $[M]_r$ to $[\mathscr{M}]_t$

a.   Divide $[M]_r$ by the radix t (t is expressed as a number in the radix r system) using the rules of arithmetic valid for the r system. This gives a quotient plus a remainder.

b.   Keep the remainder in a separate column.

c.   Divide the quotient obtained in a) by radix t as before.

d.   Repeat b) through c) until the quotient is equal to zero, being sure to list the remainders in the order in which they were obtained.

e.   Reverse the order of the remainder list (last becomes first).

f.   Convert the individual digits (radix r) of the new list to their radix t representation. This is the final answer for $[\mathscr{M}]_t$.

Example: Convert $[735.]_8$ to its decimal equivalent

$$M_r = [735]_8$$
$$r = [10]_8$$
$$t = [10]_{10} = [12]_8$$

Remainder
List

$$
\begin{array}{r|l}
12 & 735 \\
12 & 57 \ldots\ldots 7 \\
12 & 4 \ldots\ldots 7 \\
& 0 \ldots\ldots 4 \\
\end{array}
$$

[Division is done in the octal system]

$$[\mathscr{M}]_{10} = 477$$

$$[735.]_8 = [477.]_{10}$$

Note that a literal expansion is more rapid in this example:

$$[735.]_8 = [7 \times 10^2 + 3 \times 10^1 + 5 \times 10^0]_8$$
$$= [7 \times 8^2 + 3 \times 8^1 + 5 \times 8^0]_{10}$$
$$= [477.]_{10}$$

The second set of operations needed to determine equivalent numbers deal with the $[W]_r$ to $[\mathscr{W}]_t$ conversion.

Algorithm to convert $[W]_r$ to $[\mathscr{W}]_t$

a.   Multiply $[W]_r$ by the radix t (t is expressed as a number in the radix r system) using the rules of arithmetic valid for the r system. This gives a product which may have a fractional part.

b.   Keep the integral part of the product in a separate column.

c.   Multiply the radix fraction (the portion to the right of the radix point) of the result by radix t as before.

d.   Continue a) through c) until the desired precision of the resulting fraction is reached.

e.   Convert the individual digits (radix r) of the ordered column to their radix t representation. This is the final answer for $[\mathscr{W}]_t$.

Example: Convert $[0.432]_{10}$ to its octal equivalent

$$[W]_r = [.432]_{10}$$
$$r = [10]_{10}$$
$$t = [10]_8 = [8]_{10}$$

$8 \times$ | .432 | $= 3$ | .456

$8 \times$ | .456 | $= 3$ | .648

$8 \times$ | .648 | $= 5$ | .184

$$[\mathscr{W}]_8 = [.33513]_8$$

$8 \times$ | .184 | $= 1$ | .472

$8 \times$ | .472 | $= 3$ | .776

etc.

$$[0.432]_{10} = [0.33513\ldots]_8$$

In this example the radix fraction (octal fraction) has been truncated at five significant figures. By direct attack the method of literal expansion is shown to be not very useful in calculating radix fractions. As a general guide, the multiplication method is always most rapid in determining the radix fraction. For the radix integral, literal expansion is best for radix r to decimal conversion and the division method is best for decimal to r conversion.

The rationale guiding these conversion methods is derived from the ideas of positional notation. In converting a radix integer expressed in the r system to the t system, we are extracting the appropriate number of ts (i.e. 2s, 8s, 10s, 16s, etc.) which are contained in the r system number. Suppose the original number is written as

$$[\ldots d_3 \times 10^3 + d_2 \times 10^2 + d_1 \times 10^1 + d_0 \times 10^0]_r = [M]_r$$

and that we express the number in the t system as

$$[\ldots D_3 \times 10^3 + D_2 \times 10^2 + D_1 \times 10^1 + D_0 \times 10^0]_t = [M]_t$$

where the Ds represent the as yet unknown digits in the t system number. We now define T to be the new radix, t, expressed in the old r system. In the t system, $t = 10$, but in the r system T is some other number such that $[T]_r = [10]_t$.

Now suppose we divide both $[M]_r$ and $[M]_t$ by the radix t. In the t system we get (with $t = [10]_t$)

$$[\ldots D_3 \times 10^2 + D_2 \times 10^1 + D_1 \times 10^0 + (D_0/10)]_t = [M]_t/[10]_t$$

Notice that $[D_0/10]_t$ is a fraction while the rest of the number is an integer. It should be remembered that the largest digits, d or D, are always less than the radix; that is, each d lies between 0 and $r - 1$ and each D between 0 and $t - 1$. In the octal system for example, the allowed digits are 0, 1, 2, 3, 4, 5, 6, 7. To do the division of $[M]_r$ by t we first convert to to the r system. $[T]_r = [10]_t$, then divide and get

$$\left[\ldots \frac{d_3 \times 10^3}{T} + \frac{d_2 \times 10^2}{T} + \frac{d_1 \times 10^1}{T} + \frac{d_0}{T}\right]_r$$

This last division will give some integer, $[I]_r$, and generally

a fractional part $\left[\dfrac{J}{T}\right]_r$

Equating fractional parts of the t and r system equations we have

$$\left[\frac{D_0}{10}\right]_t = \left[\frac{J}{T}\right]_r$$

Multiplying both sides by t, in their own systems, we obtain the result

$$[D_0]_t = [J]_r$$

This shows that the remainder $[J]_r$ of the division $[M_r/T]_r$ is just the lowest order digit $[D_0]_t$ of the new equivalent number.
We can now repeat the process on the integer result.

$$\left[\frac{M}{T}\right]_r = \left[I + \frac{J}{T}\right]_r = \left[\ldots D_3 \times 10^1 + D_2 + \frac{D_1}{10}\right]_t$$

and identify each successive remainder with the successive unknown digits $D_2, D_3, D_4 \ldots$. At some point $[M]_r$ will equal zero and the final digit of the equivalent number will have been determined.

For conversion of radix fractions a similar set of actions is needed. Suppose we are given a radix fraction W_r written as

$$[d_{-1} \times 10^{-1} + d_{-2} \times 10^{-2} + d_{-3} \times 10^{-3} + \ldots]_r = W_r$$

and that we express the unknown number in the t system as

$$[D_{-1} \times 10^{-1} + D_{-2} \times 10_{-2} \times 10^{-3} t \ldots]_t$$

with Ds again representing the individual digits of the equivalent number. As before we take $[T]_r = [10]_t$, and instead of dividing, we will multiply both sides by t, in the appropriate systems.

$$T \times [d_{-1} \times 10^{-1} + d_{-2} \times 10^{-2} + d_{-3} \times 10^{-3} + \ldots]_r$$
$$= [D_{-1} + D_{-2} \times 10^{-1} + D_{-3} \times 10^{-2} + \ldots]_t$$

or

$$T \times [d_{-1} d_{-2} d_{-3} \ldots]_r = [W]_r + [s]_r$$

The left side will generally have the form of an integer $[W]_r$ plus a remaining fraction $[s]_r$ with, similarly, $[D_{-1}]_t$ as the integer and $[D_{-2} \times 10^{-1} + \ldots]_t$ as the fractions on the right side. Equating the integer parts tells us that

$$[W]_r = [D_{-1}]_t$$

and

$$[s]_r = [D_{-2} \times 10^{-1} + D_{-3} \times 10^{-2} + \ldots]_t$$

By multiplying both sides by t ($[T]_r$ or $[10]_t$) we can repeat the same arguments given above: The whole number result of each multiplication by t is just one of the sequence of digits $D_{-1}, D_{-2}, D_{-3}, \ldots$. As noted previously, the sequence for equivalent radix fractions may not terminate, requiring a truncation of the fraction without an exact representation between the radix r and t numbers.

Index

Page numbers in italics indicate primary references.